PAUL GASCOIGNE

PAUL GASCOIGNE

FourFourTwo | GREAT FOOTBALLERS

Paul Simpson

This edition published in 2004 by
Virgin Books Ltd
Thames Wharf Studios
Rainville Road
London W6 9HA

First published in 2001 by Virgin Books Ltd

Copyright © Paul Simpson 2001, 2004

The right of Paul Simpson to be identified as the author of this work
has been asserted by him in accordance with the Copyright, Designs
and Patents Act 1988.

A catalogue record for the book is available from the British Library.

ISBN 0 7535 0897 4

Typeset by TW Typesetting, Plymouth, Devon

Printed and bound in Great Britain by
Clays Ltd, St Ives plc

CONTENTS

ACKNOWLEDGEMENTS

There are, as usual, some people to be thanked. These include Olivia Blair, Alex Fynn, Patrick Barclay, Henry Winter, Steve Curry, George Sik, Don Howe, Alan Smith, Craig Hignett, Terry Butcher, Paul Parker, Kevin Buckley, Maurizio Concita, Roddy Forsyth, Uli Hesse Lichtenberger, Andy Porter, Jean Claude Pagal, Hunter Davies, Cormac Bourne and Ray Spiller. Damian Hall has been an immense help with research. I'd also like to thank the two people to whom this book is jointly dedicated: my son Jack, for not destroying all my Word files, and my wife Lesley, for proofreading the text at scandalously short notice.

I'd also like to thank Gazza, without whom, obviously, this book would have even less reason to exist.

Paul Simpson
Shepperton
December 2000

INTRODUCTION

This is very definitely an unauthorised biography of Paul John Gascoigne. His long time legal representative, Mel Stein, chose not to comment on any matters of fact raised in this book. And many of Gascoigne's team-mates were actively encouraged not to help with this book. There are also plenty of people in football (Glenn Hoddle, Graham Taylor and David Platt, to name but three) who would rather have teeth extracted than to talk about the man whose nickname, Gazza, became a registered trademark.

This book was originally written from the point of view of an informed spectator, someone who launched the 'adult' football magazine *FourFourTwo* as editor in 1994. I have seen Gazza just twice off the pitch. The first sighting was after an England friendly against the USA. After a dull game, at the reception for assorted blazers, hacks, hangers-on and dignitaries, Gascoigne strolled through the crowd in a translucent Versace suit, with the press pack in frenzied pursuit. On that occasion, the player showed an impressive turn of speed, of the kind we hadn't seen from him on the pitch for a while (he was then in the middle of a second long-term injury at Lazio) and treated them to a repetition of his celebrated televised address to the Norwegian people.

With the second word – 'off' – still resounding, he gave the crowd a wave before Chris Waddle, one of many mentors during Gazza's footballing career, escorted him to a roped-off, VIP area, where security guards kept anyone who didn't have the appropriately coloured plastic badge on their lapels at a safe distance.

That was in the autumn of 1994 and this little vignette seemed to contain all the essential themes of what, since the tears in Turin in 1990, had been Gascoigne's way of life: the love/hate relationship with the press, the football friends looking out for him, the flashy suits, the public behaviour which, depending on your sympathies, could be deemed cheeky or boorish. The pressure was never quite understood by a general public which was constantly invited, by the tabloids, to let their minds boggle at the size of his salary. The oh-so-subtle sub-text was that, as Stan Collymore later discovered, no pity or sympathy could be extended to someone who was earning thousands a week; a point invariably made by some cab driver, real or metaphorical.

The rock critic Nik Cohn famously wrote that the difference between British and American rock'n'roll was that 'Tommy Steele made it to the London Palladium and Elvis Presley made it to god'. And, by the mid-1990s, Gazza's celebrity had become so immense that it completely outshone the merely ordinary fame enjoyed even by an England team-mate like Alan Shearer. The rest of the team seemed to be able to exchange the usual banter with the press but Gazza's relationship with the media machine that publicised and criticised him was of a different, unsettling, variety.

Four years later, his friend, mentor and (briefly) manager Bryan Robson compared Gazza to another great 20th century icon: 'Since Diana died, the papers have decided that Gazza's the next best thing.' It was while waiting to interview Robson at Middlesbrough's plush football academy-cum-training-ground at Rockliffe that I caught my second glimpse of Gazza off the pitch. He'd put on some weight since the last sighting but nowhere near as much as I had. He strolled over to reception, joked with the receptionist, smiled as she talked to the kids, and then breezed out with a slightly quizzical glance in my direction.

As we now know, things didn't work out at Middlesbrough and his next move, to Everton, saw him reunited with another mentor Walter Smith, his old boss at Rangers. The move was greeted with understandable cynicism by the media. But one of the mysterious features of Gazza's fame is that, even after the kebabs, the dentist's chair, the spousal abuse, the belching into the microphone, the alcoholism (denied and later acknowledged), the days when he played football as if he couldn't be arsed or was simply ridiculously unfit, the fake plastic breasts, the photo-session in a clown's outfit, the fans (myself included) still felt some emotional investment in his future.

Like many other thirty-something men, I had read enough stories as a kid of heroic comebacks against all the odds, to feel that it was time to see something like that happen in real life. And, for a few weeks, the comeback seemed a real possibility – he played well enough to prompt semi-serious talk of him playing for England. And then another injury, an innocuous looking strain, put paid to that. Everton soon became Burnley and Burnley became America, When America – or DC United to be specific – didn't work out, the oddest twist of all saw him join Gansu Tianma, in the northern Chinese city of Lanzhou. Remotest China seemed to suit him but that ended messily. He has since been linked with a plethora of clubs (Wolverhampton Wanderers, Total Network Solutions, Buckley Town [in the Cymru Alliance league], Darlington, Hartlepool United, Al Jazira in Abu Dhabi, Queen of the South, Dundee, Exeter City) but, as this book went to press, his footballing career seemed headed for just the kind of undignified, pointless, end that the naysayers (with, sadly, George Best among them) had long predicted.

It's easy to forget, as his career as his star wanes, just how talented he was. Each lost year, every missed opportunity, every 'this time I'm serious' comeback bid, almost undermines the precious memories of his talent we still share. Did he really boss Lothar Matthaus in 1990? Was that free-kick against Arsenal really that good?

Gazzamania is a thing of the past now – the very term sounds more dated than Beatlemania, even though Gazza's media frenzy occurred less than 15 years ago. But Paul Gascoigne was one of the most gifted English footballers of the last half century. As a midfield genius, he has done the business at the highest level – the semi-final of a World Cup. Only Bobby Charlton can match that. Becks, for all the hype, can't yet say the same.

This is a footballing biography, not a tabloid tell-all, so it only looks into the parallel universe that is Gazza's existence off the pitch for clues to his success, or failure, as a player. But with Gazza, more than any footballer since – to pluck a name out of the air utterly at random – George Best, it's hard to divide the footballer and the private individual. The crassest, apparently inexplicable, escapades in his up and down career have, often, coincided with private crises. He did beat his wife, as he tearfully confessed, but the story of Paul and Sheryl, seems more, now, like a strange love story, albeit one that baffles the world at large. That apart, in an age where seldom a Sunday passes without more tales of football orgies and rape charges, his private life seems more sad than scandalous.

He is still only in his late thirties so it would be presumptuous to pretend this is a definitive biography.

The retirement he evidently so dreads may loosen tongues and there are plenty of episodes in his life which are still contentious, controversial and only partly explicable – even, perhaps, to the man himself. But this is an attempt to cast an unprejudiced eye over the life and times of a player who, at his best, could make a Saturday afternoon magical.

1. THERE'S ONLY ONE PAUL GASCOIGNE

Who is Gazza?

Justice Harman

The question was raised, in September 1990, in a court of law, by a judge who was later found guilty of playing to the gallery. Lawyers acting on behalf of Paul Gascoigne Ltd were trying to stop publication of a biography, by Robin McGibbon, of the footballer called, simply enough, Gazza.

There then followed the kind of exchange which lawyers and judges seem to stage, mainly, to convince the rest of the world that the English, especially the upper classes, are as eccentric as they would love to think.

'Do you think Mr Gascoigne is more famous than the Duke of Wellington was in 1815?' Justice Harman asked the lawyer.

'I have to say I think it's possible,' said the lawyer, Silverleaf, a surname straight out of Charles Dickens. It was, as far as Mr Silverleaf's client was concerned, the wrong answer because it meant that he – and Paul Gascoigne Ltd – lost the case.

Justice Harman's question may sound stupid but it's still valid. Who is Gazza? It is now twenty years since an oddly shaped (for a footballer) boy, with a frankly unwise haircut and thighs like tree trunks made his first-team debut for Newcastle United. Since that time we have wept with him, jeered him, cheered him, thrown Mars bars at him (that's you, Middlesbrough and Everton fans) and, now and then, just got fed up or

7

bored with him. Much like his team-mates really. There was always Naff Off Time, the point at which Gascoigne was advised, for his safety and his peers' sanity, to pick up his angling gear and go and annoy some fish instead.

We have been remote spectators at a wedding, listened to medical bulletins about the state of his knees and shins, bought records and books (somebody must have, 'Fog On The Tyne' got to No. 2 in the charts), watched him apologise for beating his wife, reserved judgement as he promised yet another comeback, and, too rarely, been able to watch him play football. He was the most famous English footballer since George Best and before David Beckham. And the first immensely gifted English footballer to have emerged as football started to become part of the entertainment industry: Robbie Williams' signature tune, 'Let Me Entertain You', played (in hope as much as expectation) at countless football grounds, could have been Gazza's theme. He is, and this is merely one of his minor achievements, one of the few winners of the BBC Sports Personality of the Year award to actually have a personality.

His life has been portrayed, in the media, as an intermittent soap opera although, as with the dear departed Merseyside soap Brookside, the later episodes have not captivated us in quite the same way as the first. But we have seen and heard enough about Gazza to feel we know him.

The odd thing, though, is that friends, family and even occasional acquaintances in the football-writing fraternity say that the Gazza they know differs drastically from the cartoonish caricature portrayed by the media. Henry Winter, of the *Daily Telegraph*, observed: 'He was painted as a thick Geordie but I remember, in about 1995, he came out to a press conference – there were only a few of us there – and talked about the state of

English football. He was saying how the kids needed educating on the technical side of the game and he knew what he was talking about. It was the sort of stuff people started saying five years later. He's got an impressive knowledge of football.' So maybe, after all these years, we are just as in the dark about who Paul Gascoigne is as Justice Harman.

Everyone has a Paul Gascoigne story or anecdote. Here's one which has nothing to do with football but sheds some light on his twilight existence at Rangers. In a hotel by Loch Lomond one night, he was having a quiet drink with a sports psychologist called George Sik. An American youth hosteller came up to Gascoigne and said: 'Don't I know you from somewhere?'

'No I don't think so, I'm a golfing instructor,' said Gazza.

'Oh, is there so much work around here for a golfing instructor?'

Gascoigne, replied, completely deadpan: 'Yes, there is in the summer, but in the winter there aren't many people around so I have to teach golf to the rabbits.'

The American accused him of taking the mickey.

'No, I'm serious', Gascoigne insisted.

It says something for Gazza's persuasive powers that the American left the bar half-believing that he had met someone who made a living in the winter months teaching rabbits to play golf.

His conversation isn't always that imaginative. Quizzed at a press conference once, he stared at the journalist and said: 'Have you ever played football?'

'No not really,' the journalist replied.

'Well f***ing shut up then,' Gazza shot back.

Brutal, uncalled for, rude . . . this was all of that but Gascoigne was really just letting the cat out of the bag. Most people in football think like that – as Howard

Wilkinson showed when, in a brief stint as England manager, he challenged the hack pack: 'How many caps have you got?' Only for Jimmy Armfield to shoot back: 'Forty-three.'

Gazza might, though, have reflected that at least, on that occasion, he was being asked about football, the thing he actually did for a living. The media often overlooked his day job to bring us exciting bulletins about models who may or may not have travelled 300 miles to have sex with him, the number of pints he may or may not have consumed on his latest binge, and to use him as a moral lesson, like George Best, warning errant young stars – and prodigious geniuses like Wayne Rooney – that the primrose path led, ultimately, to drying out clinics and nightmarish days wondering what might have been. The moral was made explicit when the 15-year-old Rooney, watching a haggard Gazza run around the Bellevue training ground, was told: 'Take care of yourself son or you could end up like that.'

He deserves better than this – and so do we. When he signed for Lazio, and told the cheering *tifosi*, 'One day I will become as big a star Ruud Gullit or Maradona', it wasn't a ridiculous boast. Arrogant, yes, but not, it seemed then, unachievable. In the 1990 World Cup, against Holland and Gullit, he had outshone Ruud – and he did the same in 1992 until one of Gullit's team-mates smacked him. He didn't turn out to be Maradona, though he did score against him in a friendly. And if he didn't become the next Maradona, neither did he become the next Tony Currie.

If you remember Gascoigne in his prime, all this goes without saying. Gazza played football like nobody else has done since. But the memories are a fragile resource – if you didn't have them and assessed his career by poring over the statistics you would probably wonder what all the fuss was about. He earned 57 England caps, a respectable tally but less than say Gary Neville or Dave Watson, and should have had a hundred. When he played his last game for Burnley, his all-time career record showed that he had played 410 games and scored 108 goals in all competitions – in England, Italy and Scotland. Hardly the kind of figures you would expect from the most creative English midfielder since Bobby Charlton.

The record might be more impressive if it weren't for the lifestyle, the injuries and the punishment he took. The famous broken legs are only part of the story. As far back as November 1986, he missed a month for Newcastle with a groin strain. His comeback strained the muscles again and he couldn't train until February 1987. He then needed stitches in a leg wound and, preparing for an FA Cup tie, twisted his knee and didn't return to the first team till March. The pattern of that particular annus horribilis has become depressingly familiar. He has, at different times: been plagued by tendinitis; suffered from injuries to his knee, calf, hamstring, thigh and ankle; ruptured his cruciate ligament; had surgery for another groin injury and for a depressed fracture of the cheek bone; had his arm broken (in a forearm smash against George Boateng) and wounded his ruptured knee on, if reports are to be believed, the floor of a nightclub.

Gazza endured 27 operations in his career and enough medical crises to fill several episodes of *Casualty* partly because he was too keen for his own good. John Pickering, his coach at Newcastle, told Robin McGibbon: 'He wanted to play so badly that two or three times he tried to get back before he was fit because he thought he could get away with it, only to aggravate the injuries further.' The same syndrome led him to keep a knee injury secret so he would be selected for an Under-21 international against West Germany.

Later in his career, in an interview with BBC's *Football Focus*, he had the realism to acknowledge just how much of the damage was self-inflicted. 'I would tell kids not to do what I did. I'd tell them how drinking can affect your muscles and how not having enough blood supply to your muscles can cause injuries. At least four of my operations were down to drink.'

If he wasn't stretchered off, there was always the risk he might be sent off or suspended. His acts of indiscipline are so notorious that they need to be put in perspective. He was only once sent off twice in the same English league season – in 1987/88 for Newcastle against Derby and QPR. Apart from an occasional habit of leading with the elbow, he has thrown punches, been charged for head-butting and often been booked for dissent. In his 'red-card hell' at Rangers, his volcanic rages, sprung out of frustration or self-doubt or self-loathing or indignation, invited punishment from officials – as did, to be fair, some of the treatment meted out to him. In the Aberdeen game which led to the head-butting charge, he noted: 'I was spat on, I was punched, and I had the doctor to see my ribs.' Yet he was also honest enough to admit, as he said: 'I don't know why I do it, I just don't count up to ten.'

In October 1996, he famously failed to count at all when he kicked Ajax's Winston Bogarde and got himself sent off as Rangers lost 4–1 in the UEFA Champions League. That wasn't intelligent play from a footballer who knew that Rangers had paid £4.5m for him mainly in the hope that he'd help them progress in the cash cow that was the Champions League.

And then there was boredom. He has never played more than 100 League games for a club because, as

Walter Smith, who managed him twice, says, he couldn't settle down to the kind of continuity and routine that ordinary mortals crave. He has often instigated his own departures, telling his then agent Alistair Garvie to get him a move to Wimbledon or Sheffield Wednesday long before Newcastle sold him to Tottenham. He was equally keen to leave White Hart Lane, although the club desperately needed to cash him in. At Rangers, with Smith moving on, he mused in public about leaving for America – four months before he joined Middlesbrough.

The matter shouldn't be over-stated. He is no one-club man like Tony Adams but neither was he a serial changer of clubs like Andre Kanchelskis. Most of his moves made sense, of a kind, for him and for the selling club. But this did mean that he spent a disproportionate amount of his career settling in to a new club, new team-mates, a new culture and new accommodation. Transfer speculation is now so intense, hysterical and continuous that we accept the fact that a great player might move on every season or so yet, if you look at the career trajectories of most of the truly great players, even today, continuity and stability has been the key.

Gong Hai, the coach who gambled on his fitness and form by signing Gazza for his second division Chinese league side Gansu Tianma, probably summed it up best when he said: 'He has lived so many football lives. Maybe it's hard for us to understand everything that he has gone through.' And at each new club, Gascoigne increasingly seemed – even to his own team-mates – less like a valuable new recruit and more like a circus freak, a bearded lady hired to arouse the crowd's curiosity and sell a few tickets.

Timing can be everything. Gazza's timing as an international was impeccable. He became a star of one of the three best England sides of the last 50 years and it was six or seven years before another player emerged who could offer something like his creativity in midfield. But his timing as a club footballer was not so good. Only once in his career, at Rangers, was he a regular fixture in a settled, successful, club side. Archie Knox, Walter Smith's deputy at Ibrox and Goodison, said: 'The best way to get the best out of him is to keep him playing on a regular basis in a decent team and give him a bit of freedom to do what he does best. He was afforded that opportunity at Rangers along with Brian Laudrup. Maybe other players had to compensate a bit for his freedom but they were happy to do that in view of what Gascoigne produced as an individual.' The figures – 30 goals in 70 appearances at Ibrox – back Knox up.

At Newcastle, Spurs, Lazio, Middlesbrough and Everton, he played in teams which weren't at the top of their game – and for clubs that weren't the best in the business. Newcastle were a selling club when he played for them. Spurs were about to enter a financial and footballing recession from which they have still not emerged. Lazio were hardly the finished article – much less capable than the side with which Sven-Göran Eriksson won the *scudetto*.

This partly explains why his record as a club footballer seems so paltry when compared to the obvious reference point, George Best's. Best was voted European Footballer of the Year and English Footballer of the Year in 1968, won two League Championship medals (1965 and 1967), and bagged a European Cup winners' medal in 1968. Gascoigne, by comparison, was never voted European Footballer of the Year, or even English Footballer of the Year, and his club honours amount to one FA Cup winners' medal, two Scottish

League titles, one Scottish Cup medal, and one Scottish League Cup medal. Apart from Rangers, he has never played in a European club side which finished higher than third in the league (as Tottenham did in 1989/90).

But the comparison is slightly unfair. Between 1964 and 1968, the Manchester United team Best played in was – and there's no way of giving this pun the swerve – simply the best. His team-mates included Denis Law, Bobby Charlton, Nobby Stiles and Brian Kidd. Gascoigne never played in a club side of comparative quality – which makes the thought he could have joined Manchester United in 1988 one of the most tantalising roads not taken in a career – and life – littered with them. He might too have left Newcastle for Liverpool. Mel Stein claimed that Kenny Dalglish was a 'great admirer' and Gascoigne had originally declared that he really wanted to go to Anfield. But there was no serious bid for him though, when Tottenham came in for him, he tried to persuade his new chairman Irving Scholar to put a clause in his contract which would have released him if Liverpool ever bid for him. Scholar, understandably, wasn't keen and Gazza had to back down.

Ultimately though, David Seaman may offer the best explanation for his friend's disappointing record as a club footballer. He felt that, as Gazza's career wore on, the player judged his career mainly on the basis of how he was doing for England or whether a move would help his cause in trying to return to international football. He finally gave up this hope, after the 2002 World Cup, the first such finals in his career he spent entirely as a 'TV personality'. He made his biggest impact at ITV racking up a bar bill for £9,869.92. Yet, if he still fantasises about scoring a great goal, as you suspect he must, he probably scores that goal wearing an England shirt.

2. NORTH AND SOUTH

NEWCASTLE UNITED

If you don't start treating the senior pros around here with a little respect, you're out the frigging door.

Jack Charlton

It took Paul Gascoigne three years to become an overnight success at St James' Park. The first six months of his life as an apprentice there support the contention, later made by John Cartwright, now the Crystal Palace youth coach, that talents like Gazza flourished despite the system, not because of it. Football is full of great talent-spotting goofs to go alongside the record label Decca's decision to turn down the Beatles because 'groups with guitars are on their way out'. Kevin Keegan and Kevin Phillips were turned down because they were too small, but the problem with the sixteen-year-old Paul Gascoigne was even more obvious. He was too fat. And lazy. And cheeky with it.

His shape was the main reason that Ipswich, managed by a certain Bobby Robson, had turned him down as a fourteen-year-old prospect. As Robson said, 'He was the original Milky Bar kid. He was a real Billy Bunter, as broad as he was tall, and so roly-poly that the natural talent rippled through rolls of fat. There was no way you could gamble on a player of his stature on our budget.'

Newcastle's youth development policy was not that different to most other clubs' at the time. Fundamentally, the sixteen-year-olds were told, 'You fit the system, we can't change the system to suit you.' So when Gascoigne signed for Newcastle, when he wasn't cleaning senior pros' boots or the toilets he was being told to track back, to mark an opponent, to lay off the ball quickly. Gazza wanted to run past players, take them on with the ball at his feet, but when he tried to show off his repertoire he was told that such tricks belonged in a circus. After a few months he came into the club one morning, in tears, and said he wanted to chuck it all in. The confidence was, if you like, almost being drilled out of him.

He was persuaded to stay by the scout who had signed him, Peter Kirkley, and Joe Harvey, the former Newcastle skipper and manager. And then Jack Charlton took over as manager. In his review of the playing staff he was told, by youth coach Colin Suggett, that the young Gascoigne was a disruptive influence. Maybe, it was suggested, the club ought to let him go. Kirkley and Harvey went out to bat for the young player. Eventually Charlton agreed to see the boy. Gazza had been in his office just seven minutes when the manager came out, close to tears, asking for two cups of coffee and shaking his head sadly, saying, 'What a life he's had.'

Gascoigne had obviously told Charlton a sob story. (He wouldn't have had to make much up: his dad had left home by that stage and he was around a friend's house so often that the boy's parents had given Gazza a spare key to the house.) The manager bought it, but laid down the law too. The player had three weeks to get his act together, or be fired. The threat shocked Gazza into action. He ran himself slimmer, shot up a few inches, and could now run by players almost at will. So Gazza didn't entirely triumph on his own terms. Suggett, his enemy turned ally, had been more than half right. The extra effort had improved his game, although Charlton hadn't been as worried as Robson and others by the boy's physique. 'In the case of most fit players, you can pick out every stomach muscle when they strip. But there are others, people like Alan Foggon, who can train six hours a day and still look podgy. When they make it through to the top these players are normally very strong, however, and Gazza is a classic case in point.'

The budding genius didn't mend all his ways. Glenn Roeder threatened to chin him after one prank. This prompted Charlton to give the player a final frigging ultimatum. Not, he suspects, that it did any good. 'I don't think it changed him one iota. He didn't get caught after that, but that was just because he became a little cuter.'

When Roeder wasn't threatening to chin Gascoigne, he was starting to look out for him.

I met Paul on my first day at Newcastle. I was left to my own devices at the training ground and it wasn't long before I noticed him organising jobs for all the others, but not for himself. That was Paul. I ended up going back to the hotel on the bus with him and the other apprentices and that was the start of our friendship. We were opposites really. He was an extrovert, while I was more content with my own company. But we gelled. One weekend, after we had played in London, he stayed with me and I remember we ended up parked outside Trevor Brooking's house. I told him he could have a house like that if only he realised what he could do and grabbed the opportunities. He told me, 'I'll never have a house like that.' By now, he could have bought the whole road.

Charlton's other clear memory of Gascoigne was the 1985 FA Youth Cup final against Watford. He described the incident in his memoirs:

He went for a throw-in on the right and as he ran for the ball, he chucked and ducked and the ball went over the player who was marking him. Then he started running diagonally towards the centre flag on the other side of the pitch, before suddenly stopping at the angle of the penalty area. His chaser slid past him and now the ball was between his feet. Your ordinary player would at that point have shifted it to one or other foot and tried the shot. But Paul spotted the keeper off his line, and with the ball still lodged between his feet, swung his leg and with the outside of his right boot, got it up, over the keeper and down just beneath the crossbar.

The ball was struck while he was totally off balance. To do it, he had to produce the kind of intuitive skill that you see perhaps once in a lifetime. I remember turning to Maurice Setters and saying, 'If you live to be a hundred, Maurice, you'll never see a better goal than that.'

Charlton left Newcastle after just one year in charge and never saw the boy-genius's promise fulfilled at first hand. But he has remained eternally grateful to Kirkley and Harvey for changing his mind. 'I've made some mistakes,' he said once, 'but letting Gazza go, that would have been the worst of my life.'

That Youth Cup run forced new manager Willie McFaul to consider Gascoigne for the first team. He and Joe Allon had scored nineteen goals between them in that campaign; the official club history states that 'he was on such a different level that he looked like a Brazilian World Cup star in a Sunday pub game'.

So Paul Gascoigne made his full debut against Southampton in August 1985. If it had been a Hollywood film, at that point the director would have cut to a highlights sequence demonstrating the rookie's immediate and infinite mastery of his chosen sport. But this wasn't a movie, and after an impressive performance he was taken off because McFaul felt he was beginning to show off and, with the score at 1–1, he didn't want to throw away a vital away point. Roeder remembered Gascoigne's debut very well.

> He picked up the ball fifteen yards outside his own box and facing his own goal. Jimmy Case was marking him and we were all screaming at him to clear the ball but, no, he controlled it and started dribbling towards his own penalty box with Jimmy Case up his backside. Suddenly he dropped his shoulder and went the opposite way, turned, and then dribbled the ball out of the penalty box to the halfway line. You just did not do those sort of things when you were eighteen, unless you were Paul Gascoigne.

While he was dipping in and out of the first team, he was adopted, almost as if he were a stray, by three women in the commercial office. All of them were old enough to be his mum and he would confide in them, stuff, perhaps, that he couldn't tell his own mum, like which girl he'd been with the night before and how it had gone.

It wasn't long before Roeder, by this stage firmly ensconced as Gazza's mentor, introduced him to an agent, Alistair Garvie, who wasn't impressed by his hyperactive, daft new client but trusted Roeder's judgement. Almost as soon as Garvie took over, Gascoigne began pressing him to arrange a move. He was fed up of having no money to spend and fed up because the crowd were getting on his back.

Gascoigne was not an easy player to watch then. Displays of artistry alternated with defensive howlers which had the crowd baying for his blood. It's possible he may have taken the shouts too much to heart. The fans still voted him the most promising player of the season and he had scored nine League goals in 31 appearances. Not bad from midfield and in a below-par side. But it was not an easy time to be a Newcastle fan. They yearned, as another of Gascoigne's biographers, Ian Hamilton, said, for a Jackie Milburn to lead them to glory, but every time a star was unearthed (Chris Waddle, Peter Beardsley) he was sold. To many, getting too attached to Gascoigne seemed pointless. Even then the harsh laws of football economics dictated that he would be simply passing through.

Patrick Barclay of the *Sunday Telegraph* still remembers the first time he saw Gascoigne play. 'Newcastle had a poor, poor team at the time. I remember he was running everywhere, chasing everything, all over the pitch, trying to win the game all on his own. And I remember thinking, "Well, he's got guts." But of course he couldn't do that every game.' Steve Curry of the *Sunday Times* apparently caught his first glimpse of the boy genius on one of Gazza's better days.

When I first saw him playing for Newcastle he was obviously a good player, a conspicuous player, barrel-chested, he had aggression and he used his upper body to great advantage. He had a great range of passing, vision, and he could manipulate the ball. But there was a naivety about him too.

Then I watched him in an England Under-19 tournament in the south of France. He was an entertainer, but highly strung, and he remained so through his career, but that goes with genius. You could see how much he loved the game; he would stay behind to practice. It was obvious he'd go far because he was exciting and because of his ability with a football.

The summer of 1986 was chiefly notable for his first knee injury, which he picked up in a pre-season tournament in the Isle of Man. His first trip to a knee specialist followed, and that set the pattern for the 1986/87 season. The tradition that most young footballers have a difficult second season is almost as much of a cliché in football as the 'difficult third album' syndrome is in rock. And Gazza's goal tally dipped to just five as he struggled with injuries and form.

It was a frustrating time; a new, more determined, perhaps over-eager Gascoigne emerged. Paul Parker has particular reason to remember his first match against Gazza. 'It was in 1987/88 at Loftus Road and I was shielding a ball off for a goal-kick and he tried to do me in. He attacked me and got sent off, it was a second yellow card. I'd heard of him of course, knew he was a good player.' And it wasn't long before people were beginning to call him 'the new Duncan Edwards'. (This was a tad unfair on the United legend because, at this stage in his career, when Gazza didn't have the ball, he simply didn't contribute.) But persistent rumours of what he was getting up to off the pitch left some wondering if he wasn't the new George Best, Alan Hudson or Tony Currie. How long before he pressed the self-destruct button in a blaze of newspaper headlines? McFaul asked himself the same question. 'There was a time when I feared he couldn't handle it and was going to disappear. I thought he'd lost it, and said to myself, "What a waste of talent." ' But Gazza came back, not for the last time. Comebacks, indeed, became part of what he was best at.

In May 1987 the England Under-21 coach Dave Sexton picked him for the summer tournament in Toulon. Gazza's immediate response was to ask if Newcastle would let him move to Sheffield Wednesday. Their manager, Howard Wilkinson, had made a bid but McFaul had told him Gascoigne was definitely not for sale. That didn't stop Manchester United expressing an interest. By that time Gazza's head had been turned. He refused to sign up to a five-year £1m deal at St James' Park, although his morale was lifted by the arrival of the brilliant (and equally unpredictable) Brazilian Miran-dinha.

Although the players named their goldfish after each other, when Ian Hamilton saw the two of them it was obvious theirs was not a striking partnership made in heaven. 'When Mirandinha was unmarked, Gascoigne tended to ignore him, preferring instead to set off on an intricate, inventive and usually doomed run into the heart of the enemy's defence. When Mirandinha was marked, Gascoigne liked to slip classy first-time balls into spaces where the Brazilian should never have been.' Mirandinha suspected that Gazza was taking the mickey out of him. Hamilton shared the Brazilian's suspicions, but after seeing the two players argue, Hamilton con-cluded that Gascoigne 'had been trying to impress him, as one Brazilian, one artist, to another'.

Against Wimbledon, Gazza came up against a differ-ent kind of artist: Vinnie Jones. The plan to psyche Gazza out of the game was carefully laid, as Don Howe recalled: 'I'd heard all about him and his ability when I first saw him at Newcastle. When we were due to play them in the Cup in 1988 Bobby Gould sent someone to watch them and he reported that Gascoigne was a very clever player and that he controlled the play for them, so we spent a whole week practising how to control him. We gave Vinnie the special job of man-marking him and that's where the famous picture comes from.' It was, in its own way, a kind of tribute. Not that a shell-shocked Gazza saw it like that on the day.

Although Wimbledon and Jones had been able to intimidate him out of the game, he could be streetwise. As John Gregory recalled: 'I "did" him up at Newcastle, when I was in my last season at Derby, and he turned to his big centre-half Paul Jackson and said, "Hey Jacko, make sure you do him." That was a response I recognised and I loved that. And I've loved Paul ever since.'

And against Tottenham, Gascoigne showed evidence, if not of maturity, certainly of the upper body strength and stamina which was the legacy of Suggett's exercise regime, and which Charlton had foreseen. Terry Venables recalled: 'I had put Terry Fenwick to mark him, as he was a strong tackler. Early in the game, as Gascoigne took possession, Terry tightened himself and really hit him as hard as he could, but Gazza just leaned into him and Terry bounced off.'

Even though he had to cope with the burden of being the young playmaker in a struggling side, Gazza played with the confidence of a much older player. He still paid scant attention to defensive duties, still tried to beat that extra player too often, but he played as if he believed he had it in him to be the best. But the talk of his being Britain's first £2m player, the stories about when (not if) he would leave Newcastle, began to wear him down. Coaches noted that off the pitch he was quieter, more subdued. Negotiations with Newcastle foundered when it became clear that Gascoigne really did want to go. To the top. And with a bigger club.

For all the talk in his ghosted columns in the *Sun* of his north-east roots, Gascoigne wanted to get away.

Newcastle felt claustrophobic; he probably felt (Hamilton suggests, probably accurately) that he had never quite won over the fans, and he wanted the issue settled. When he rejected that five-year deal to stay at St James' Park the club was left with little choice but to sell him before his contract ran out in a year's time. It was bitter news for the fans, and unrest over this sale (remember, Waddle and Beardsley had already left the club in the preceding two summers) eventually led to Sir John Hall's takeover of the club. In that respect (and that respect only) it was good news for Newcastle. The Magpies had lost their second clown prince, but he had reigned for slightly longer than the first one, Len Shackleton, who also left for a record fee (£20,000) after just two years. And that was to local rivals Sunderland.

Later, Gascoigne would look back fondly, and with the inaccuracy of nostalgia, on these days. He left St James' Park as Britain's most expensive footballer, but he was still primarily a footballer. Within two years he would become a celebrity, a product (in fact, a hundred spin-off products), a trademark, a brand which could sell a new pair of football boots as easily as it could sell a few thousand extra newspapers. Eventually he would be in danger of being remembered, as one manager would later warn him, as much for what he did off the pitch as on it. But all that was in the future. As he left St James' Park in the summer of 1988 he was, quite simply, Britain's best young footballer since George Best.

TOTTENHAM HOTSPUR
He'll be trouble.

Julia Masterson, Irving Scholar's PA

Paul Gascoigne's spell at Tottenham Hotspur began in chaos and ended in controversy. There are those (and

Sir Alex Ferguson is among them) who say that Gazza should never have joined Spurs in the first place. Ferguson, who went on holiday in the summer of 1988 with, he says, Gazza's pledge that he'd be a United player, was stunned to get a call later from his chairman Martin Edwards telling him that the player had signed for Spurs. As Patrick Barclay observed, 'He talks about giving Gazza a cuddle in his memoirs, but when he heard that he'd rather have given him a half nelson.' To this day Fergie insists that it all went wrong for Gascoigne when he didn't join the likes of Paul McGrath, Bryan Robson and Norman Whiteside at Old Trafford. 'The fact that he never wore the red shirt was his mistake. I wonder if his advisers ever consider what a boob they made. It is my belief that if he had signed for United he would not have had nearly as many problems as he had in London.'

The boob, if boob it was, did not become immediately apparent because, as his friend Chris Waddle remarked, within two years Gascoigne was playing for England in the World Cup semi-final. But Paul Parker, one of his team-mates in that World Cup and a former United player, concurs with Ferguson's view and still wonders if Gazza made the right move. 'Maybe if he had joined Manchester United his career might have been completely different. Fergie commanded respect and could have shielded him more. And London was too early for him. At United he would have been with players of a similar stature and he wouldn't have been the big fish that he was at Spurs.' Venables, in his memoirs, seems to regard all this as crying over spilt milk: 'Tottenham had kept an eye on him since he was seventeen. Liverpool and Manchester United were chasing him as well, but I think they were less sure about his talent and more worried about his reputation.'

So Spurs it was who signed him, thanks largely to the last-minute intervention of Waddle and, Fergie says, to the club's offer to buy his parents a house. His new chairman, Irving Scholar, on first inspection saw Gazza as 'looking very much like a country boy on his first visit to the Smoke'. It wasn't his first visit to the capital, but Gazza decided to enjoy it anyway, bringing his mates down to the hotel with him. Their main function, according to Garvie, was to sit in the hotel, eat and get drunk. Gazza tried to chat up Scholar's personal assistant Julia Masterson, who warned her boss about trouble ahead, and his friends famously threw paper darts at Scholar's head. All this was irritating, but it didn't threaten the move. Two demands which did nearly scupper the deal were the Liverpool clause and the fact that the afternoon before the signing, in the words of his then agent, Paul 'flipped'.

Gascoigne is said to have gone berserk when he heard how much Spurs were paying for him (£2m, which made him the most expensive player in Britain). In part, he seemed to appreciate the pressure the fee and the accompanying tag would put on him, but he also seems to have resented his old club getting anything for him. After all, he reasoned, they'd got *him* for nothing. When the deal was finally done, Gascoigne is said to have spurned the celebratory glass of champagne. After a while he sloped off to Madame Tussaud's to see his friends.

After such an inauspicious start, things could only get better. And they did. Venables recalled: 'When Gazza first came to the training ground, his reputation had gone before him. All the players were waiting to see what he could do. They did not have long to wait. When we started a practice game, he got the ball around eight players as if they weren't there and smacked it into the net. It was absolutely brilliant; just to see him play like that made the hair on the back of your neck stay up. Everybody stood there and applauded him.' It sounds too good to be true, as if a writer whose day job it was to dream up plotlines for *Roy of the Rovers* ghosted this part of Venables' memoirs. But there are enough witnesses to similar feats on the Spurs training ground to suggest that this incident has only been slightly embellished through recollection and pride.

Yet it was only three weeks before Masterson's warning came true, when Gascoigne and his friends were accused of behaving obnoxiously in a London night club and Venables had to insist that he withdraw from a team of car mechanics who were due to play a showbiz XI for charity. And even though on the pre-season tour of Sweden Gazza was confined to the hotel, that didn't keep him out of the headlines. He found himself the subject for the first time of a tabloid exposé after a model claimed he'd persuaded her to drive 180 miles to have sex with him. Who, besides Gazza and the model, knew if it was true or not? As the player was soon to discover, truth is one of the first casualties of the circulation war.

With Spurs' first fixture of the 1988/89 season called off because their ground didn't meet safety standards, Gazza made his debut for his new club against his old club at St James's Park. He bottled it. The betrayed home fans pelted him with Mars bars, hurled cries of 'Judas!' at him and jeered when he was taken off thirteen minutes from time because he was suffering from cramp. Fifty Newcastle fans did wait for two hours after the final whistle to get a glimpse of the player they still regarded as a hero, but he had left by an entrance on the other side of the ground.

The Newcastle manager Willie McFaul, sensing that Venables may have been wondering if he'd done the right thing, said to him: 'Terry, he can play, but he can be a bit difficult.' That sentence has to contain two of the greatest understatements in Gazza's career, as Venables would find out over the next three seasons. Yet it was also a remark of some generosity, because Gazza had left Newcastle with bad blood between him and the club chairman, who labelled him 'George Best without the brains', a comment George Best would subsequently almost agree with. Gazza responded in kind, calling Stan Seymour 'clueless' and inviting tut-tuttings and head-shaking from the FA.

Gazza arrived at White Hart Lane as the obvious heir to one of football's most publicised traditions. With his dead-ball skills, his range of passing and his ability to beat defenders, he seemed like a natural Spurs player. But the fans took a while to win over. While not being won over easily is another great Spurs tradition, Gascoigne had come to Tottenham at a fragile time in the club's history. The promise of the early 1980s (two back-to-back FA Cup victories in 1981 and 1982, and a UEFA Cup triumph in 1984 over Anderlecht on penalties) had been dissipated. Ray Clemence, Richard Gough, Glenn Hoddle and Ossie Ardiles had all recently been lost to the club through injury, age or transfer. The new manager, Terry Venables, was trying to rebuild, but some of the players he brought in (like Terry Fenwick and particularly Paul Stewart, who arrived the same time as Gazza and was so bad he got much of the flak which could have been directed at Gascoigne) didn't always impress.

Gazza didn't always impress either. He certainly gave notice that he was no ordinary personality, although his decision to wear a naked-lady tie to the press conference to unveil his new boot deal probably just reinforced the stereotypical view, as expressed by Scholar, that he was some kind of Geordie hick. After a Littlewoods Cup draw against Blackburn in November 1988, Colin Hendry slated Gazza to the press. When Spurs won the replay 2–1, Gazza took pleasure in taunting Hendry. It all seemed like the usual handbags at twenty paces, until Gascoigne decided to take it a bit further, turning up at a Blackburn night-club and asking, 'Where's the big mouth who said we were useless?' If he could sound like a thug, he could also defuse tension with a pratfall, as he did when irate fans taunted him at Ayresome Park. His response? To don an imaginary pair of glasses, walk into an imaginary lamp-post and fall over.

If he didn't set White Hart Lane alight in that first season, he did enough to suggest there were great things to come. His sloppy play was blamed for a handful of goals Spurs conceded, and there was always the chance that he'd get booked for something stupid like swearing (as he did against Charlton Athletic; altogether he earned himself 21 disciplinary points and a two-game ban). But there were enough good moments in his interplay with Waddle to suggest that in 1989/90 their partnership would really zing. He gave David Seaman (then at QPR) a foretaste of his power from a set-piece (his dead-ball skills actually merited the over-used word 'Brazilian'), and against Luton he left a couple of defenders trailing in his wake as he rounded the keeper to score. It was, as Hamilton said, a playground goal.

You had to be an unusual player to score goals like that. Unusual and rather good. Often when you're watching seriously great players, there is a point in a game where you can just see them changing gear, as if they've just said to themselves, 'I've had enough of this.' Romario did it against Sweden in USA 94; he just collected the ball and (you could almost see it from the way his expression changed) decided to score. Having done that, he relapsed into his earlier slumber. With Gazza, too, there was already that sense that he had another trick in him, that if he wanted it badly enough he could do stuff that would turn a match and turn your head.

The hype was already enough to turn his head, if he let it. The ghost of George Best was constantly invoked both as a comparison and a dire prophecy. Gascoigne told reporters: 'There's no way I'm not going to be able to handle the pressure. I've just too big a heart to let any problems get on top of me.' But in 1988/89 he only did just enough to placate the fans. On a wall near White Hart Lane a poster read 'Jesus saves', and underneath someone had scribbled 'But Gazza scores on the rebound' – small but tangible evidence that the faithful were being won over. That year he played in 32 League games and scored six League goals, which was roughly what he'd done the season before at Newcastle (for the record, in sixteen seasons Gascoigne has never yet managed to top the 35 League appearances he made in 1987/88, his last season at Newcastle). But even that was sufficient grounding to turn every game in the 1989/90 season into an argument about whether he should play for England or not in the forthcoming World Cup.

Gascoigne started the 1989/90 season by causing the police to be called out. Nothing too serious. They just had a quiet word in his ear about him shooting pigeons on the training ground with his twelve-bore shotgun. He'd started off firing at clay pigeons, and then got bored.

During the second match of the season he grabbed his team-mate Gary Stevens warmly by the throat. Stevens' crime was to try to stop Gazza from retaliating after Everton's Mike Newell had clattered into him. Gazza was on a yellow card at the time of the incident, and he later apologised to Stevens.

Sometimes, the scrutiny just seemed to throw him. He got booked ten times that pre-World Cup season and was pilloried by many football writers for his immaturity, his crudity and his habit of backchatting to referees. Was he going to be, David Lacey asked in the *Guardian*, 'an international footballer who was also a bit of a character or a character who might have been an international footballer?'

Waddle, who in the summer had been sold to Marseille, warned his old mate not to play the fool first and put the football second. Gascoigne promised to take heed, but he was seldom out of the headlines: a thrown punch at Chelsea, a cracked bone in his arm at Coventry, a tackle which prompted a mass brawl at Crystal Palace. And yet towards the end of the season he put together a run of performances against quality opposition like Nottingham Forest and Manchester United which almost seemed like throwing down the gauntlet to the England manager.

And this season, for the first time, he floated the idea that it might be better for all concerned if he were to go and play abroad. Mooted in his regular column in the *Sun*, this notion could either be taken as just something he and his ghostwriter had made up to fulfil a dream headline or the very first hint that he was getting just a bit fed up of all the pressure on the domestic front.

After the 1990 World Cup, of course, Gascoigne was a national hero, and in 1990/91 he finally became an undisputed hero to Spurs fans. That was, one Spurs fan said emphatically, 'his one great season'. But nothing is ever simple with Gazza and by the end of that one great season he would be sold and crocked as the club's financial crisis got almost as many headlines as Tottenham's performances on the pitch.

If the scene where the players applauded him for his tricks on the training ground owes something to the football comic strip, the 1990/91 FA Cup run is classic *Roy of the Rovers*. You have a boy wonder so naturally gifted that one of his goals could fill most of a week's comic strip. But, to increase the tension, he is carrying an injury so that every time a Neanderthal centre-half tries to clog him (because that's his job, and because the boy wonder has enraged the seasoned pro by playing fancy football) the reader can do nothing but wince. And this FA Cup run isn't just about glory under the Twin Towers, it's about the very survival of the club . . . it's the perfect *Roy of the Rovers* formula.

And in round after round the boy wonder thrills his team-mates, his manager and the fans. Against Blackpool, in the third round, it is his free-kick that sets up the winning goal. Against Oxford, in the fourth, he runs the game, scoring twice and prompting the Oxford manager Brian Horton to say, 'Gascoigne was so sharp it was unbelievable. We needed twelve men out there but he would still have done the things he did.' Against Portsmouth, Venables' assistant Doug Livermore comes in on the morning of the game and says to Venables, 'I've got bad news. Gazza was playing squash for an hour last night.' To which the gaffer replies, 'I'm not worried about him. He's got so much nervous energy he could play squash all night and still play football the next day – but find out who he's been playing with; he'll be shattered.'

Nobody ever finds out who Gazza's squash partner was, but when Portsmouth go 1–0 up, it's Gazza who scores 'two cracking goals' (the gaffer's words) to take Spurs through to a quarter-final against Notts County. To add to the drama, after Spurs beat Notts County on 10 March, with Gazza bagging the winner (Spurs had, again, gone 1–0 down), the player goes into hospital for an operation on his groin. He has a month to get fit if he is going to feature in the FA Cup semi-final. Will he make it? Of course he will – this is Gazza of the Rovers. And the draw has given the plot yet another twist: to reach the final Spurs will have to overcome their north London rivals, Arsenal.

The night before the semi-final Gazza is so hyper that the team doctor has to knock him out with an injection (for his own protection, you understand, and so the rest of the team can get some beauty sleep). On the day of the match, when Venables comes to do his team talk, he can't get a word in edgeways because Gazza is so pumped up and talking so loud.

The free-kick itself is hard to describe. If you saw it, words can't add much (even Henry Winter, the Arsenal-supporting football writer for the *Daily Telegraph*, describes it as 'the best goal I've ever seen. It summed him up; firstly, the technical skill needed to score like that and secondly, the sheer impudence and imagination of it. I thought at the time he would go on to dominate world football'). If you didn't see it, Venables, at least, put it into some kind of context:

> Curling or bending a free-kick is easy if you do not put much pace on the ball, but when he really concentrates Gazza has this terrific ability to put bend on the ball, but still hit it with great power. The free-kick was about 35 yards out and I could see he was concentrating hard. It looked a little bit too far, and I thought that for him to score from there, the shot would have to be something special. It was.
>
> The ball flew past Seaman into the net. To strike it from 35 yards with such ferocity, bending it at

the same time, was incredible . . . it was superbly struck, very fast and accurate. Gazza set off on a circuit of the stadium, while Arsenal's players just stood and gaped at each other. As he reached the bench, Gazza put his arms around my neck and laughed in my ear: 'The silly bastard only tried to save it, didn't he?'

Seaman's memories of that strike are, understandably, slightly different. 'It was a great strike, but I should never have been beaten from that far out.'

And so to the final, where the *Roy of the Rovers* plot went wrong. Gazza should have scored the winning goal *before* being stretchered off with an injury which appeared to be life-threatening but, when you bought the comic next week, turned out not to be anywhere near as bad as first feared.

Although there are various reports of him resembling a twitching bull before the teams ran out on to the pitch, there was no real evidence of this as he lined up with the other players to meet Princess Diana. He kissed her hand instead of shaking it, a gesture both courtly and cocky. And then the teams ran to their places. It was immediately clear, as soon as the whistle blew, that Gascoigne was, as Venables put it, 'wild'. You have probably seen calmer things running around farmyards with their heads cut off. One deranged chest-high challenge on Gary Parker should have earned him at least a yellow card, if not a red. But the referee, Roger Milford, only had a stern word with him.

On the bench, Venables (by his own account) was baffled: 'I do not know if he was angry or what, but he was doing himself no favours.' Forest's Gary Charles collected the ball on the edge of the Spurs penalty area. 'Gazza was chasing the ball and was outside his own box, so he only needed to stay on his feet and give Charles a problem by staying on him.' Instead, as Venables remarked, 'he went wild again'.

Charles seemed initially to have come off worse. Gazza got up gingerly and then, seconds later, slumped to the ground in obvious and immense pain. The Spurs physio, John Sheridan, knew it was bad and Gazza soon realised just how bad it was when he asked Sheridan and Sheridan couldn't answer.

Ironically, Venables felt the loss of their best player helped the team: 'There was one side-benefit. Until Gazza went off, I had not got the balance of the side quite right.' Later, one of his team-mates said that if Gascoigne had only got past the first twenty minutes he would have gone on to win the game. There was also the question of what the only midfielder not given specific defensive duties was doing charging around on the edge of the area anyway.

This is easy to say in retrospect, but there was a certain degree of inevitability about Gazza's performance in that FA Cup final. He had, after all, started that crucial April 1990 England game against Czechoslovakia (crucial because his very selection for the World Cup squad depended on his performance that night) in very similar style before he steadied his nerves by putting a ball through for Bully to score from. Venables did not believe 'any player has ever had to bear so much pressure in so short a time, carrying not only Tottenham's FA Cup hopes, but the whole financial future of his club on his shoulders'. Also on his considerable shoulders by then, and very much in Venables' thoughts when he made that statement, was a monster called Gazzamania. Since the tears in Turin, he had been surrounded, as a player and a human being, by a kind of madness normally reserved for pop stars. He had left

Newcastle partly because he couldn't stand the fans getting on his back; now, it seemed as if the whole world was on his back, a burden that would not be lifted until he checked himself into a clinic in October 1998.

In that final Gazza had crippled himself, in ex-Sports Minister Tony Banks' famous phrase, trying to cripple someone else. He would (and could) have expected no sympathy from the media, and he got none. There was a certain amount of self-satisfied arm-folding, self-righteous I-told-you-soing from a press which had, as Hamilton pointed out, only a year before praised his aggression as guts, fire and determination.

The reaction from fellow pros was more muted, probably best summed up by one of his opponents (and England team-mates). 'I certainly didn't rush over and ask him if he was all right. If I had spoken to him it would have been to thank him for the free-kick, which was right in my zone [as indeed it was: Stuart Pearce put Forest ahead from that very set-piece]. We had no idea of the extent of his injury and, in any case, sympathy was a bit short as he had tried to maim two of our players.'

Bobby Robson, alone, tried to put himself in Gascoigne's boots and imagine what must have been going through his mind. 'I can still picture it now. He was so hyped up, so desperately keen to show everyone he was worth every penny, wanting to run the show and be the star of the final. He wanted to be clever, score the winning goal and be the tough guy as well. I knew what was going through his head as if he had told me. He had wound himself up like a coiled spring, but instead of providing power it snapped.'

After the final, which Tottenham won 2–1 after extra time, the Spurs players piled en masse into the hospital to give Gazza his FA Cup winner's medal. They were laughing, he was crying. Glenn Roeder had already been in to try to cheer him up, but it was hard to do as both players suspected that his career might now be over. If he was lucky, he would be out for a year. The Lazio deal he had signed before the FA Cup final seemed to hang in the balance. Officials from the Italian club, Venables recalled, looked suicidal, yet they were surprisingly sympathetic. The Spurs manager even hoped the injury might help him keep Gazza at White Hart Lane for a while longer, but when he passed Lazio's medical even that faint hope evaporated.

Spurs fans are surprisingly equivocal about Gascoigne. The ambivalence is beautifully illustrated by three extracts from the fanzine the *Spur*, quoted by Hamilton in his book. After the FA Cup semi-final, the then editor, Stuart Mutler, wrote: 'When that big bastud of a free-kick left the right peg of Paul Gascoigne on 14 April 1991, you could have peeled me off the roof of Wembley stadium. Is Gascoigne going to crap on the Arse? He is y'know. GET IN THERE YOU F***ER. Boring I know, but that's the way it was.' After the final, Mutler wrote: 'Haywire City. Yeah, course I knew he was capable of such acts of stupidity. But for the Gaz to plummet from such a towering high? No, I could no longer defend the man. I had to expel him from my soul. Paul Gascoigne. You are a bastard. Get Out of my Life.' And then, finally, when he returned to White Hart Lane to play in a friendly for Lazio: 'I still can't get used to seeing him in that pale blue Lazio shirt . . . he's like some bird that's chucked you. I really thought, I really really thought I was over Gazza.'

Another prominent Spurs fan who asked not to be named (no, it's not Salman Rushdie) said, 'It was sad when he left but there wasn't a lot of fuss about it because he'd been out injured for a year and we got good money for him and it felt inevitable – the deal was arranged before the FA Cup final. In fact, we weren't as fed up as when Ginola left.'

Have some Spurs fans just been too successful at expelling Gazza from their soul? Hunter Davies confessed that he had never really taken Gazza into his soul in the first place:

> Of course I was excited when he joined, but I didn't think he was a great player for Tottenham. He was in his maniacal phase, twitching head and neck. Of course he was brilliant and original and an excellent player and he dominated games, but he would brow-beat players to give him the ball. They were brainwashed into giving it to him even when he wasn't in the best position and that made the team lop-sided. The tackle was typical of his daft-as-a-brushness. I was in the minority of Spurs fans, the rest loved him.

Some fans will admit they wouldn't put him in their all-time Spurs team, but can't quite work out why. Is it because he was so heavily associated with Newcastle? The fact that he didn't play that many full seasons for Spurs? Or, as one put it, 'We just got fed up that Stein and he made it pretty clear that season that he just wanted to go. It wasn't like Ginola who insists to this day that he was forced out against his will.' To quote another, 'In terms of all-time Tottenham greats, I'd put him somewhere at the top of the second tier, but mainly because he was only playing here for three seasons. The real greats stayed here ten years or so, but he was a Tottenham player in the sense that he was an entertainer.'

For sympathetic observers like John Gregory, however, the White Hart Lane years were the highlight of Gascoigne's career. 'I always think that for every player there is a three-year peak when he can do no wrong. Gazza's came very early. Tottenham had the best of him.'

3. SS LAZIO

Come on guys!

Banner from Lazio fans greeting Gascoigne

There has never been another transfer deal like Paul Gascoigne's move from Tottenham to Lazio. Any full account of the interminable machinations and complications which dragged this saga out for so long is likely to be, well, interminable. In Stein's authorised biography of his most famous client, *Haway the Lad*, the summarised tale of the Anglo-Italian negotiations becomes tiring to read, so you can imagine how the whole affair must have seemed in real life to the player involved.

The saga of the transfer itself has become embroiled in the recent chequered commercial history of Tottenham Hotspur Football Club, the incoming and outgoing chairmen (Scholar and Sugar) and the manager all retelling the story in a manner reminiscent of the Japanese film *Rashomon*, in which each of the witnesses gives a very different account of the same crime. Venables had, by his own account, 'begged him in private and through the press not to leave', assuring him that if he waited another couple of years, maybe even until after the 1994 World Cup, he could join one of the real Italian giants like Juventus. (There is some evidence that Juve's owner, Gianni Agnelli, was interested in the player but was dissuaded by club officials who questioned his temperament and his discipline.) At this time, the Spurs manager said, Gascoigne joining Lazio was 'like Pavarotti singing in the Copacabana Club at Cleethorpes'.

While Venables was warning him of the personal problems he might face, Gascoigne's old mate Waddle was encouraging him to go, saying (and this was some weeks before the FA Cup final), 'Why wait to break a leg?' The financial case for a move – there was talk of his earning £1m a year – seemed unanswerable. His PA, Jane Nottage, said that Gazza felt Spurs could have done more to keep him, but it's hard to see what more Venables could have done when the club was distracted by its own financial crisis. Simply put, Tottenham badly needed the money Gascoigne's sale would bring. Yet at the same time, his old England boss, Robson, could see why such a move would be good for the player too: 'The world was at his feet. Italy was the place to be in those days with big money and a pop-star lifestyle. It was inevitable that Gascoigne would be going there.'

Two points are probably worth making here: the Gascoigne transfer (despite Venables' reservations) suited both clubs involved and the player, and Lazio, even after the injury, never gave Gascoigne or his representatives any indication that they had lost faith in their new signing. They did, though, reduce the fee and the salary. When Gazza finally arrived in Rome, he was on about half what a star like Gullit was earning at Milan. Nor did he get the £1m one-off fee his advisers had asked Spurs to pay in return for his agreeing to the transfer.

The deal was both a corporate financial saga and a medical drama. The injury to Gascoigne's knee happened on the Jewish sabbath, a fact worth mentioning, because by the time Stein had walked the thirteen miles home from Wembley, Gascoigne had been on the phone four times, in tears. 'Do you think Lazio will still take me?' was his plaintive question. But at that point the question must have carried even broader implications than that: would *anyone* want to take him when the evidence of his self-destructive tendencies had just been broadcast around the world for hundreds of millions to see?

And it was a bad injury, one which had already ended other players' careers, notably Brian Clough's in the 1960s. Gascoigne had ruptured an anterior cruciate ligament, the ligament which controlled the movement of his knee. The details of the surgery required to put him right and enable him to play football again are not for the squeamish. John Browett, the player's surgeon at London's Princess Grace Hospital, took time out to explain what was going to happen for the TV cameras. He would, he declared, be rebuilding the ruptured ligament by cutting out the middle third of the player's patella tendon. He would attach a piece of bone (one grafted from his thigh, one from his kneecap) to both ends of this tendon. This would then, using keyhole surgery, be threaded into position behind the kneecap where it would be fixed with staples and screws. It was almost six-million-dollar-man stuff, except in this instance the patient would provide the new parts.

Grim stuff, and few were convinced that, even if Browett's rebuilding worked, the player would have the discipline required for the long haul back to fitness. The news that the player would be 'gated' for six weeks caused particular hilarity among those who had been exposed to his hyperactivity. They had a point, as Gazza would later prove, but ultimately they were wrong because they had completely misjudged his own determination. As the *Sunday Times*' Steve Curry remarked, 'You can blame him because so many of his injuries appear to be self-inflicted, but at the same time you have to admit that he showed tremendous guts, character and courage to come back from them.'

As Gascoigne lay in hospital, he took to writing poetry. Nottage quotes a typical poem from this time in her book on her employer: 'Now what is in my mind right now/No one will ever know/But when I'm given that big, big chance/It will be a one-man show.'

It wasn't long before there were signs that the old Gazza was returning. He'd spray the media outside his window just for a laugh. Whether or not you regarded this as an encouraging sign probably depended on what you thought of him before that tackle, but he soon seemed to make up his mind that he would play football again.

Browett and the Spurs physio, John Sheridan, sat down with the player to spell out what had to happen when he left the hospital. 'I gated him in his house,' Browett told Venables. 'And I sat down with him and explained that if the wound didn't heal it would be the end of his career and the wound wouldn't heal if it wasn't given time and rest. To his credit, Gazza took us very seriously and remained in his house in Hoddesdon [Hertfordshire] for six weeks. I understand he watched every single video from the local shop to try and relieve the boredom, but he stuck it out and that saved his career.' Impressed as he was, Browett's eyes remained wide open to Gazza's foibles. He said that having him as a patient was a 'bit like riding a runaway stallion bareback'. The constant big issue, he seemed to feel, with Gazza was persuading him to pace himself and not come back too quickly, damaging himself in the process.

If you had to draw up a list of Gazza's virtues (and for all the flak he's had, it would be a reasonably long list), pacing himself would not be one of them. In July 1991, when he appeared on crutches and fired a water pistol at reporters, it seemed like a bit of a laugh. But when he gallantly defended his sister and was arrested for 'alleged assault' in Newcastle, that sounded distinctly ominous. And when, in September 1991, Gazza's wounded knee smacked into the floor of a Newcastle night club, the press had a field day.

Again, as with so much in Gazza's life, the incident itself is lost in a fog of conflicting stories. Gazza's friend Jimmy Five Bellies put it down to jealousy. 'When Paul left Newcastle for Spurs, people in his home city turned against him. It was disgusting.' The official Gazza story is that he was attacked by a complete stranger when coming back into the night club bar from the gents. The *Sunday Times*, which at this point in its history was focusing its investigative journalism on footballers' night club brawls rather than breaking cases like the Thalidomide scandal, sent an intrepid reporter up to Newcastle to ferret out the real story. And, according to the newspaper, this was a story about a day-long pub crawl (Gazza had, one witness alleged, been 'half drunk' by ten in the morning), interrupted briefly by a trip to watch 45 minutes of the Newcastle–Derby match, which ended in controversial circumstances in that night club. There was even evidence, the report suggested, that he had left the club unharmed.

Amid all this confusion, one passage in the report did, at least, have the ring of authenticity. One local told the newspaper: 'He moves at the centre of his pack of minders and he tries it on with every girl who crosses his line of sight. He thinks it's all good clean fun – but their boyfriends are Geordie lads just like him and they don't take that sort of thing. The result is trouble wherever he goes.' This witness concluded by saying, 'He regards Newcastle as his personal domain.' Well, not after this (whatever 'this' was exactly) he didn't. This seemed to spell the end for Gascoigne's rather romantic idea that he could be just one of the lads. Back in hospital, his right leg lying on a support and his kneecap broken, Gazza seemed, Nottage said, 'pretty down . . . subdued . . . not his usual bubbly self'.

By this time, she reported, he was wondering if his career really was over. He must have been suffering from the realisation that he couldn't safely go back to his old stamping ground and cursing himself for being so stupid as to go into the night club in the first place. Browett said the good news was that the cruciate ligament had not been damaged, but the player's fitness programme would have to be rescheduled and a whole new set of exercises devised. The final blow came when his old Newcastle mate Glenn Roeder, who had been planning to move out to Rome with his family to act as Gascoigne's minder, decided that he couldn't base his family's future on a player whom, Nottage said, he felt had let him down.

This second injury set the player back another three months. He was gated for another eight weeks and, in the words of one Spurs physio, 'quietened down'. But not completely. He was still spotted at the Tottenham training ground, disobeying orders not to kick, just to run around. After he'd given a running commentary on a free-kick, a reporter asked him if his leg hurt. 'Why, aye, it does a bit,' Gazza admitted.

If ever a club knew exactly what they were getting for their millions, Lazio did. They had seen the demented performance in the FA Cup final, followed the affair of the Newcastle night club and even had to deal with his lawyer Stein's unexpected demand during negotiations that the club throw in a trout farm as part of the deal. But this was a very different Lazio from the one with which Sven Goran Eriksson won the Scudetto in 1999/2000. In 1991 they were still very much in the shadow of their upmarket city neighbours, AS Roma. And the club perhaps needed someone of Gascoigne's obvious star quality as much as he needed them.

They had, of course, originally signed the deal with the player before the 1991 FA Cup final, but it was

February 1992 before the club could show off the 'little king' (as he would become known) to the fans at the Rome derby. The Lazio fans seemed to know as much about him as the club officials, judging from the chant with which they greeted him: 'Gazza's boys are here/ Shag women and drink beer'. The chant and the fans' obvious adoration were music to the player's ears. Although he'd shown real determination in the past nine months, there must have been times when his self-confidence had all but evaporated. He had scaled the peaks of fame in July 1990, but less than two years later he was chiefly famous for what had been, what might have been and what might (and it seemed a pretty big 'might' at this point) be still to come.

Three months after this unveiling, and almost a year to the day since the original deal had been struck, the Serie A club was informed that the new, remade Gazza was ready for their inspection. After a practice match between Tottenham's A team and Tottenham reserves passed without any swelling of the knee, the Gascoigne party flew to Rome for the serious tests at a science institute near Lazio's Olympic Stadium. Gazza was attached to various machines (he even had his brain scanned), was told his heart was in good condition, was asked to pedal madly in a hamster wheel and finally to provide samples of urine and blood.

He remained perfectly calm through all this, but the doctors had not finished with him yet. Gascoigne was taken to a hospital in the centre of Rome by an American doctor, Jim Andrews, who specialised in sports injuries. Gazza took his trousers off (revealing, according to Nottage, that he was wearing no under-pants) and stood up. His legs were checked to see if they were the same height and he was told to do a few standing jumps to test the knee.

After that, Gazza and co. were allowed back to the hotel to rest. By this stage Gazza must have been wearying of all this, and when Vanessa Redgrave's ex-husband Franco Nero tried to engage him in conversation about the similarities of English and Italian, he just looked a bit baffled.

Sunday, 23 May was the crucial day. Gazza was given an MRI scan and an X-ray, and when the results arrived Nottage reported that the doctors gathered around one picture to debate whether the metal plate which had been placed in the broken kneecap had damaged part of the cartilage. They were trying to account for a mysterious black spot near his kneecap. Gazza then spent another hour with his right leg stuck in the chamber of an X-ray machine and his other leg stuck straight up in the air. By the time the machine was working, Gazza had a muscle strain in his good leg. Finally he was released, and he hobbled off for lunch rubbing his good leg.

Lazio had arranged a celebratory dinner for that evening so all was assumed to be going smoothly – until some journalists turned up, asking if everything was going to be all right as they'd heard there was a last-minute hitch. The dinner passed with no official announcement, and by the Monday morning Gazza was nervous. He distracted himself by eating a mozzarella breakfast and then, just before he ran on to the pitch, throwing up.

It wasn't until the Tuesday afternoon that the deal was officially confirmed. The American doctor, Andrews, proclaimed Gazza a 'superman'. But, as Hamilton remarked, this was a rather odd, unsettling business. The player had been given a clean bill of health, then after a scan of the knee (perhaps owing to the mysterious black spot) this was rescinded and the doctors were said to be undecided. Then, after all the talk of problems, Andrews told the press, 'He will be great. Not mediocre, great. Perhaps the greatest.' What remained, as Hamilton also pointed out, was 'an undercurrent of alarm, this fear that on the matter of his knee we had never been given the full story'.

This episode is worth recounting in detail because, judging from Nottage's account in her book, so many of Gazza's days in Rome seemed to be like this. Okay, most days there weren't career-breaking medical tests to get through, but there were other trials (the villa gates not opening, the telephone not working, the theft of £30,000 worth of clothes from the villa and, most of all, his relationship with Sheryl, her family and his family), and the star himself is portrayed as being seldom at ease in his surroundings or in his life. And whereas at Newcastle, Spurs and with England his confidence had rested securely on his relationship with a father figure (a Robson or a Venables) who had chided and encouraged him, here he was dealing with an organisation and one which behaved rather differently to the clubs he'd played for back home. There is a sense, in Nottage's account, of something always being not quite right, of a crisis which has just been smoothed over, or another in the offing.

His mentors had warned him. Venables had said that if he didn't 'take to Italy in the widest possible way' by learning the language and immersing himself in Roman life, 'if he is left to himself and begins to look inward rather than outward and just surrounds himself with his English friends, it could be a disaster'. Don Howe thought the Lazio move a different kind of challenge for Gascoigne:

He's from a working-class background and that's where he's happiest, in a working-class environment. In Italy he started to climb into other areas and he probably wasn't as comfortable. Whenever he needs a break or some comfort he seems to head back to the north-east, to his family and friends.

Lazio was a good move and a bad move. Good because he got to play at that level and because he got all that experience, but bad because he was stuck in a big house all on his own and you couldn't help but wonder, 'What is he up to?' He needed a proper home.

Two crucial types of relationship dominated Gascoigne's footballing career. One was with Sheryl, and Nottage's book showed just how the daily melodramas of that coupling could impinge upon his performance on the pitch (once, after another row with Sheryl, he had been found weeping in the dressing room and been sent home for a few days' rest). The other was with his coach, whoever that happened to be. Where that worked (Venables, Bobby Robson, Smith) Gazza was usually at his most inspired; where it didn't (Zoff, Taylor, Bryan Robson) he could, at his worst, play so far beneath what he was capable of that you began to question his commitment.

Gascoigne's relationship with Zoff was not brilliant, but it never broke down. The Italian certainly went out of his way, on occasion, to back his star player when the pressure was on, saying, when the press got on the player's back, that he did not expect to see the 'real Gascoigne' emerge until 1993/94. Till then he was content gently to ease Gazza into the club and into a new culture. This philosophy may be why neither Zoff nor the club came down too hard on Gazza when he popped off to Disneyland with Sheryl and the kids, or when he returned out of shape from a mid-season break. Indeed, even when he made his two most famous utterances in Italy – a fart and a belch – the club didn't publicly disown him (although they privately laid down the law). Invited to join in Anglo-Italian condemnation of the belch, Zoff said merely that it was 'not pretty'; Lazio's new chairman, Sergio Cragnotti, defended the player as 'an intelligent man who just likes to wind people up'.

But Zoff, given the pressures on every Serie A coach, and particularly on himself as the under-performing manager of a still under-performing team, could not be there for Gascoigne in the way that Venables and Bobby Robson might have been. He could and did hold meetings with the player. His advice to Gascoigne, certainly as it comes across in Nottage's book, is essentially a variation on a familiar theme: you should be concentrating more on your football.

The biggest difference facing Gazza when he arrived at Lazio, however, was that he didn't ever know if he'd be in the team. Once he'd settled in at Newcastle and at Tottenham he had been guaranteed a place as long as he was fit. Lazio had four foreigners (Gazza, Aron Winter, Karl-Heinz Riedle and Thomas Doll), and under Serie A rules only three of them could play in the same team. Zoff's method of selection was criticised, even by some of the other foreigners, as remote. It wasn't quite as mysterious as waiting for the right coloured smoke to come out of a Vatican City chimney, but it wasn't far off. Gazza found the waiting and the not knowing frustrating, especially as he was eager to prove to himself and to the fans that he still had the old magic. So his years at Lazio were punctuated by rumours of training-ground bust-ups – usually on a Friday when the bad news (if bad news it was) was more often than not delivered –

of sorrows being drowned and of the player himself beginning to complain that he was being treated like a seventeen-year-old again.

The club was also much stricter about Gazza's physical condition. He had no real problems with the exercises, as Howe pointed out, he'd usually be more than happy to do those; it was the attempt to shape his diet, to cut out the fast food, which he found harder to bear. That and the suggestion that he should rest every afternoon between two and five. And such regimes and diets would necessarily be a regular feature of his time in Rome because he rarely came back from a break in a condition which satisfied the club doctor, Claudio Bartolini.

There were also, Nottage recorded, certain institutional differences which put an extra load on the player. Italian clubs were not as paternalistic as English clubs and Gazza was left to deal with more of the bric-à-brac of everyday life, something he'd not done that much of when playing in his native country, let alone a foreign land. The club did, however, provide him with a bodyguard, Gianni Zeqireya, who had carried out similar duties for Madonna and Sylvester Stallone. Like many Italians he quickly grew fond of Gazza, once remarking, 'The thing about Paul is, although he may look like a man, inside he is a boy.' Zeqireya was particularly amused on one occasion to see Gazza with David Platt as they met at the airport to report for England duty. 'This David Platt,' he said, 'he looks like Gazza's manager.' Platt was indeed, as Zeqireya perceptively observed, twenty-something going on forty, whereas Gazza was twenty-something going on ten.

As Howe suggested, the move to Rome certainly threw into sharper relief the stresses in Gascoigne's background. A slightly more hysterical version of the usual parents vs girlfriend conflict was played out in a city where Gazza may never have felt at home (he is often quoted as asking friends to send out more videos, or watching *Postman Pat* videos with Sheryl's kids). At the same time, his friend Jimmy Gardner was often absent, either because he had problems with his girlfriend or because he was not encouraged to come out to Rome. It might have been different if the Roeders had made the trip with Gazza. Glenn Roeder had initially been pretty serious about the idea because he'd had an operation on a tendon so he could play, on the training ground at least, with the Lazio players. His family might have grounded Gascoigne and helped him come to terms with things, but Roeder, of course, had lost heart after the night club furore.

Gazza did, however, get on reasonably well with the players. His room-mate, Claudio Sclosa, tried to teach him Italian, but like most of the Lazio players Sclosa just seemed to end up learning how to swear in Geordie (Gazza, in turn, did learn to say 'Silenzio, bastardo!' which he found very useful when he was trying to stop a dog barking near his villa). He got a cheap laugh from Aron Winter one day by turning up at his hotel room wearing nothing but a pair of sunglasses. And those who, like Ian Hamilton, watched him train with the squad saw no evidence of tensions. There was the odd tiff, of course – like the row in November 1992 over bonuses to play in a friendly against Diego Maradona's Seville: Gascoigne wanted the players to ask for them, the other players couldn't really be bothered, and Gazza told forward Beppe Signori, 'You haven't got any balls!' – but generally the Italian players seemed amused by (and protective of) Gascoigne. The two Germans, Doll and Riedle, though, made it clear they weren't quite as amused. They felt he was getting preferential treatment over the other foreign players – i.e. them.

In England, pundits and the press always tried somehow to separate Gazza the genius from Gazza the tabloid celebrity and Gazza the yob; in Italy there seemed to be just a greater acceptance that geniuses are, well, not like everybody else. (Mind you, they had recently been entertained by Maradona, whose off-the-pitch problems made Gazza's look like minor peccadillos.) It was what seemed so different about Gazza which made him appeal so strongly to the Italian fans. Maurizio Concita, a long-time Lazio watcher for *Gazzetta dello Sport*, said:

> The fans are notoriously demanding but they always liked him. They even made banners for him with curiously worded English sayings on like 'Come on guys'. Whenever he returns to the Stadio Olimpico, if he is spotted in the stands the *curva norda* always applauds him. His irreverence, all that making faces and sticking his tongue out and cadging some chewing gum off a referee, we weren't used to seeing that. Even now, five years since he left, if you mention his name it's enough to get people talking about some of his goals, especially his famous one against Pescara.

The Lazio fans' memories of Gazza focus on such flashes of brilliance. Against Parma in October 1992 he played just behind the strikers, much as Graham Taylor wanted him to do for England, and inspired them to a 4–2 lead at half-time, leaving the field after 67 minutes to a standing ovation. A couple of months later, during a match against Pescara, he waltzed past three defenders before scoring. Against Torino in the Cup in January 1993 he was, the papers insisted, 'un lord' (this was the game where he did a dance-step like a shuffle called 'il passo doppio'). Against Milan in March there was a majestic string-pulling performance and a tap-in goal from a few yards out. And against Roma back in the winter of 1992 he probably saved Zoff's job (well, for a while anyway) when he headed an 88th-minute equaliser in the Rome derby. Afterwards, as you would expect, there were tears. 'Yes, it was the old waterworks again,' he said. 'I've never felt pressure like that, not even in the World Cup, because of what would have happened if we had lost.' His reward for this just-in-time act of heroism came three days later when he was punched hard in the arm by a marauding troupe of Roma-supporting nuns.

These were serious sides to be turning on the style against; it was not like dominating the midfield against a panicky Turkey where, however well you played, any assessment of your performance was always going to be qualified by the quality of the opposition. And such flashes of brilliance convinced the club (from the chairman down to Zoff and most of the players) that they hadn't made a stupid investment. But in January 1993 the club's director-general, Enzio Bendoni, gave Gascoigne's advisers, Stein and accountant Len Lazarus, a more forceful version of Zoff's advice: the player had to sort out his personal problems and concentrate on his football. It was soon after this that Gascoigne responded to a TV reporter's enquiry by belching into the microphone. Thus the 'commento gastrico' scandal was born, the English press, strangely, seeming even more hysterical than the Italian media (Gazza was now 'The Italian Yob'). In public the club largely stood by Gascoigne, but in private Cragnotti summoned him to lunch so he could be told how the club expected its players to behave. Gazza dug himself out of that one with that lordly display against Torino, but proceeded to throw away some of the credit he'd earned on the pitch when he replied to another journalist's question with a fart. Stein claimed the reporter had misheard – Gazza's stomach had rumbled. It was an excuse which left you fearing for the lawyer's sense of hearing.

The same pattern continued for the rest of the 1992/93 season: great performances followed by listless displays which would persuade Zoff to substitute him, although the club doctor, Bartolini, sprang to his defence, saying that he still wasn't fully match fit. Off the pitch there were fewer 'commento gastricos', and if he did offend, as when he was sent off against Genoa on 28 February, he had the cheek or grace to shake everybody's hand before strolling off.

At the end of the season the chairman of one of the Lazio fan clubs was still predicting that Gazza could be as important to the club as Gianni Rivera had been to Milan and Michel Platini to Juventus. These were pretty heavy comparisons to be making, but to many fans they didn't seem unreasonable. He had, after all, played 22 Serie A games and scored four goals. Surely, as Zoff had said, the best of Gascoigne was yet to come.

Gazza can be at his most self-destructive when everything's looking rosy, and he never did become Lazio's Platini or Rivera. There was no single calamitous event, like that ligament-wrecking tackle in 1991, just a gradual erosion of Gascoigne's relevance. In September and October 1993 he played four games and never stayed on the pitch for the full 90 minutes. Then, while his England team-mates were being destroyed by the Dutch in Rotterdam, he picked up the first of a series of injuries, individually minor but collectively major, because they kept him out of the team till mid-December. Whenever Zoff was asked what was wrong with Gazza now, he just shook his head. And the club began to leak details of the player's pranks to the press in a kind of 'this is what we have to put up with' kind of way. Turning up at training stark naked was hardly a hanging offence, but the frequency with which such stories appeared in the press made him seem less significant, more of a buffoon.

These jokes just didn't seem so funny any more, now that the prankster was increasingly unable to last a whole game and stay at the top of his game. The club was constantly aggrieved at the state he was in after any kind of break, when he seemed, as the song goes, to be popping in to see what condition his condition was in. The hope that at some indefinable point in the future Gazza would sort out his life and behave like a model professional had long since gone, and the exasperation and impatience became 'official' when one paper worked out that Gazza's appearances so far had cost £400 a minute.

The player hit back, saying, 'If Lazio are getting the hump, they'll just have to get the hump because I can't help these injuries. I've come through the thigh, I've come through the tendon, I can't joke about this any more.' (The club, though, maintained that he was picking up all these injuries because of his lifestyle and his general physical condition.) He hit back more eloquently on the pitch against Juventus, turning what the British press had dubbed his last stand into a triumph as he linked up with Alen Boksic to give Lazio a 3–1 victory. But then when he came back in January 1994 he was, contrary to what he'd said earlier, joking about his injury, a groin strain suffered after climbing out of bed (nudge nudge). Injuries and suspensions continued to combine to limit his effectiveness, although he could still turn in an inspired 50-minute cameo performance on his day. He did more than that for his 'second dad' when Venables, now the England manager, came to watch him on St Valentine's Day against Cagliari. That performance suggested that Gazza could do it if he felt like it – but also that he didn't feel like it most of the time because he had no support at the club.

When, come March, he returned from a surprise (to Lazio) appearance in an England friendly against Denmark, Zoff threw him out of training. More shenanigans followed, including a failure to turn up to watch the boys take on Napoli. Cragnotti scolded him in public. It was only a few days after this that the shin break occurred. The fact that the tackle had happened on the training ground seemed to confirm to Lazio that the player could no longer be trusted.

Venables tried to put as good a gloss on it as possible by saying, 'It was simply a clash of shins with a young Lazio player. The reason Gazza smashed his leg and the other guy didn't could be put down to age. Gazza was coming up to 27 and his bones were beginning to be a bit more set.' Browett confirmed that Lazio were 'very pleased with him'. He was down to 72kg in weight, which meant he'd lost 17kg. One of the reasons that Lazio might have been so pleased with his condition was that they had half-decided to sell him.

By the time Gazza fought back from this blow, Zoff had been kicked upstairs and Zdenek Zeman had taken over. Maurizio Concita regarded this as the final blow. 'His insistence on a rigid three-man midfield didn't give Gascoigne the space to perform or create in the way he liked.' On 6 April 1995 Gazza returned against Reggiana. The fans cheered what few touches he made and he lasted the game, but Zeman concluded that Gascoigne had provided the journalists with more entertainment than the spectators. After two more ineffectual substitute appearances, Zeman announced that 'Gascoigne can do no more for this club.' Indeed, Lazio were so keen to see the back of him that, initially, they were happy to sell him for appearance-related fees – some risk, given his record in Serie A.

Concita says that Gascoigne is still remembered fondly at Lazio and in the country as a whole. 'His career moves are still followed with great interest. He had a turbulent time with injuries and some faux pas, like the belch. When I met him at the airport once he pinched my luggage and put it on a carousel. He struck me as a friendly, generous character but it's felt that his generosity rebounded on him and he had a circle of exploitative hangers-on.' Steve Curry reckoned Gascoigne didn't have the guidance he needed to make it work. 'In Italy he needed support and protection the most, off the pitch, not on it. It was a culture shock for him and he was isolated, insecure and exposed.'

The person who was least surprised when Gascoigne's Italian career fizzled out may have been Giorgio Chinaglia, Italy's own spin on George Best, a wayward genius from the 1970s who had found it impossible to adapt to the discipline of the big Italian clubs. He had found Gazza in a restaurant fairly early on in Gazza's career, and over several bottles of champagne had warned the player not to throw his life away.

Could Lazio ever have worked? Reading Jane Nottage's account of the stress involved in a typical day in Gazza's life in his first few months at Lazio it is a wonder that he ever managed to focus enough to do the business. Open her book at random and you are very likely to find a sentence such as this: 'I talked to Sheryl and finally persuaded her to give it another go.' In this account, Sheryl seems to resent football, occasionally putting her partner in positions where it seemed he had to choose between her and the game. At the same time, relations between her and his family seemed, to use Concita's word, 'turbulent'. And towards the end of his time in Rome, there are reports that Gazza got so bored that he'd send his friend Jimmy Gardner down the bottom of the garden at Villa Gascoigne and take potshots at him.

To envisage Lazio working, you have to string together a lot of 'ifs': if he hadn't done his knee in, if he hadn't broken his shin, if the Roeder family had made the journey, if he'd had better support from the club, if he'd taken the club's strictures about his long-term fitness more seriously, if . . . In other words, the answer to 'Could Lazio ever have worked?' is no.

But always a redeeming feature remains, as captured by this eloquent summing-up of Gascoigne's impact on the fans, the tifosi, by Andrea Galdi, football correspondent of *La Repubblica*: 'How they love it when he waves to them at the Stadio Olimpico, mad with enthusiasm. The people who lock their avid gaze on him when he is playing. The people who carry his picture on their shirts, with the words "C'mon Gazza". The people who wait for him outside Lazio's training ground at Maestrelli to shake his hand, to get an autograph, to say to him, "Grazie, Gascoigne." In this, Gascoigne has been triumphant.'

4. GAZZA COME HOME

GLASGOW RANGERS

Go on, Gazza! Go on, give us something!

A Rangers team-mate

April 1996, Ibrox. Nine minutes to go. Rangers are drawing 1–1 with Aberdeen. One of Gazza's team-mates shouts, 'Go on, Gazza!' Gazza shouts back, 'Knock out!' The team-mate replies, 'Go on, give us something!' So Gazza goes for a fifty-fifty ball in the Rangers half. Goes for it and wins it. He starts to run with the ball, running like a demented spider. Except 'run' doesn't quite capture the magic of this movement. It's as if he's a kid scampering across a playground, only this isn't a school playground but Ibrox, and he has the ball at his feet and his side need to win today to clinch their eighth title in a row in front of 46,000 fans. He has already beaten two Aberdeen players right at the start of his run and without actually taking any players on he's got to the edge of the area with the ball at his feet. He's in danger of being sandwiched by a defender on either side; it's as if they're weighing up the pros and cons of bringing him down there and then, right on the edge of the box. But he holds them off with his arms, a final burst takes him into the penalty area, the ball is still at his feet, another defender tries a last desperate, lunging tackle, but Gazza rides it and slides the ball under the keeper. Glasgow Rangers 2 Aberdeen 1. If it stays like that, Rangers are champions. Except it doesn't stay like that, because Gazza converts a penalty with five minutes to go for his hat-trick. Although the second goal is the showpiece that lives in the memory, he had already scored an equaliser in the 21st minute, from a ludicrous angle, to steady the home side's nerves.

Fortunately, Gazza's second goal lives on in, among other places, the official club video, *Eight in a Row*. Even when you're watching it in your front room it gives you a glow. If it didn't seem so silly you'd be almost out of your seat. It's pure fantasy football, a work of improvised genius Wolfgang Amadeus Mozart would have been proud of. And it's entirely in keeping that, interviewed afterwards about the goal, the player said he was so knackered by the time he got to the penalty area that he was just glad there was no one left to beat.

For serious students of Gazza, the video is worth watching purely for moments of brilliance like that. The only other player on the video who comes close to his artistry is Brian Laudrup. But the highlights of Gazza's season are so thrilling that they don't need the *Last Night of the Proms* soundtrack so thoughtlessly provided by the director. They are too exciting, too unpredictable and too much fun to watch to be compressed into one of those canned highlights sequences. You might need such a dressing for the dourer stuff, but Gazza's flashes of inspired improvisation speak for themselves.

Glasgow Rangers were not the first name on everyone's lips when they were asked which club Gascoigne ought to move to from Lazio. Leeds, Chelsea and Middlesbrough were at the head of the pack chasing him. There was no interest from Liverpool or Manchester United, Ferguson not having forgotten or forgiven Gascoigne's change of heart seven summers before.

Lazio's flexibility on the matter of a fee disappeared when they saw how many British clubs were interested (including, oddly enough, Queens Park Rangers). Lazio chairman Sergio Cragnotti said, 'Paul needs to find himself as a man and as a player and will only do it by returning home.' Just as well really, as no non-British clubs expressed an interest.

The chase seemed to come down to Middlesbrough, managed by Gazza's old England team-mate Bryan Robson, and Rangers. Sports psychologist George Sik, who has met Gazza twice and got drunk with him once, thereby achieving a lifetime ambition, said, 'After Lazio, it was down to those two, and Walter Smith managed to convince him to come to Scotland by telling him about all the fishing opportunities up there.' And so the £4.5m deal was struck.

The new, slim, bleached Gazza was unveiled at Ibrox on 11 July 1995 and greeted by thousands of adoring, grateful fans chanting 'There's only one Paul Gascoigne!' There was rejoicing in one half of Glasgow, resentment in the other half and bewilderment south of the border. Somehow, the Sassenachs would never get used to the idea that the best English midfielder of his generation was playing for a club in . . . Scotland. Surely this wasn't what the *Sun* had had in mind when it ran its GAZZA COME HOME headline on the back page in February 1994?

Roddy Forsyth, who has written a critically acclaimed history of Rangers and has covered Scottish football for the *Daily Telegraph* and Radio 5 Live, defended the move.

I get really, really fed up of hearing that Scottish football is a lower standard. The leagues are obviously different, but there's not a lot of difference in the standard. I remember I asked Graeme Souness how many tough games there were in England, and he said, 'Man U, Arsenal . . .' and probably got to about six, and I said how many are there in Scotland, and he said, 'Three' (Dundee United and Aberdeen were quite good at the time).

They play twice in England, so that's twelve, and four times in Scotland, so that's twelve. He said, 'Ahh, but you prove anything with statistics.' Look at Paolo Di Canio, Pierre Van Hooijdonk, Mark Viduka . . . they all joined Scottish football on a low ebb and left for a lot of money and have gone on to better things.

While there were many who thought he was mad to go to Rangers, some people in the media thought it a wise move. The *Sunday Telegraph*'s Patrick Barclay, a Scot and a Dundee fan, like Forsyth has little time for those who slur his country's national league. 'I think Rangers was a good move for him because I think that Walter Smith knew how to handle him to an extent. He was slightly out of the limelight and he played some good football there.' As Forsyth remarked, 'Smith was a father figure to him but he also set limits so Gazza knew what behaviour was unacceptable.' Terry Butcher suggested that Smith's deputy, Archie Knox, played a part in this. 'It wasn't Walter Smith who got the best out of him, it was Archie Knox who would kill him. Gascoigne was physically scared of Archie who has a way of getting a point across. He sometimes had to resort to extreme measures.'

Gascoigne's first season at Rangers had it all: run-ins with referees, the annual disappointment in Europe, the row over his flute playing, the classic Old Firm games (for which Gazza always seemed to raise himself) and the League and Scottish Cup Double. And a meeting with Sean Connery. Gazza shakes hands with Connery before a pre-season tournament, tells the actor, 'You're bigger than I thought,' to which Connery replies, 'Always.' Asking for advice, Gazza is warned: 'You'll get a lot of rabbit.'

Sik thought 'The media spotlight was not quite as intense as it would have been in London. A lot of the English papers just forgot about him unless he was playing for England.' But it was intense enough to worry Smith. 'We get fed up of reading the constant trivialities about him in the papers, so who knows how he must feel. I worried that it might affect his game, make him think again about what he'd done when coming to Scotland, but credit to the lad he stuck it out,' he said at the end of the season. At that time, Smith was still blaming the papers for all the publicity; later, he would come to realise that Gazza shared responsibility for some of the hype.

The flute playing, he claimed, was an innocent mistake. He had heard the fans singing 'Gazza, Gazza, give us the sash', so he'd asked Ian Ferguson what they meant. Ferguson had showed him the action but hadn't, Gazza said, explained the significance. 'I was just trying to fit in,' he complained, half in bewilderment as he realised he'd walked into yet another controversy.

Pretending to be a Protestant marcher was a stupid thing to do in a city with such an intensely felt religious divide. Forsyth said, 'It's difficult to know what to make of that, whether he knew what he was doing or not. He did know it would please Rangers fans and team-mates. It's strange with the English players up here, in Old Firm games it seems to be them who are the ones who go over the top. Hateley was sent off. Sometimes the English players just don't know when to stop.' Butcher half-agrees with this. 'There is a tendency to get carried away. In the Old Firm derby when Frank McAvennie and Chris Woods and myself got sent off, Graham Roberts got caught up in it all and was singing Protestant songs and conducting the crowd like an orchestra . . . Paul probably thought it was a fun thing to do. He's the kind of person who acts first and thinks later.'

The second time Gazza did it he knew exactly what it meant. He used it to enrage the Celtic fans who'd been taunting him about beating his wife. This repeat performance, while far from admirable, was at least understandable.

The Rangers squad was a pretty harmonious bunch, but then, as club captain Richard Gough pointed out at the time, they were winning everything. Gazza arrived with a new haircut (short and bleached) and a new nickname ('Refresher mouth' – you had to be there really). The players socialised together, even Laudrup and Gascoigne. 'Laudrup certainly didn't fall out with him – he's not as quiet as people think,' Forsyth said. 'He got really annoyed that the press were writing that they'd fallen out. They may be different types of people from very different backgrounds but they got on well. Gascoigne got on with everyone.' Even, it seems, Russian striker Oleg Salenko, who lived near to Gascoigne and Jimmy Gardner at the Cameron House Hotel, by Loch Lomond. Salenko, who got paid in cash and kept his wages under his bed, used to take Gazza on in flare-gun fights.

The club indulged him to a degree, as Forsyth recalled:

It was Christmas, and the Rangers directors were entertaining some [potential] sponsors in the Blue Room, trying to impress them. It's above the home dressing room, and after a while they could hear someone singing – not just singing, really belting out Christmas carols. Of course, it was Paul Gascoigne. After a little while they had to stop and send somebody down to the players' showers to ask him to be quiet. There was silence for a while and they got on with their meeting. About ten minutes later there was an almighty loud sound of carols again, 'Away in a Manger', that type of thing. The meeting was stopped and when they got downstairs there was a whole choir – Gascoigne, the tea ladies, the ground staff, catering staff, he had gone and rounded them all up.

Indulgence had its limits, though. Smith once dropped him for drinking too close to a game, although even with this the odd exception was made. 'I remember before a cup final, he came into the boardroom full of directors and he was in all his kit, it wasn't long before kick-off. He poured himself a large whisky and downed it and out he went again, to the obvious astonishment of everyone in there. That was for his nerves.' Later, there was talk that he had drunk the occasional whisky at half-time.

After a slightly rocky start, due in part to the continued absence of his wife-to-be and her children, Gascoigne seemed to relish his new life. 'He'd laughed at Terry Butcher for playing in Scotland,' said Forsyth, 'but Terry would say, "Don't knock it till you've tried it." Then Gazza was saying to everyone, "Terry was right, you know." He loved it up here, the fans loved him – they adored him – and he responds to that.' He became a real hero to the club's young fans. 'He's brilliant with children,' added Forsyth. 'I'm not sure I'd want him as a next-door neighbour but I'd leave my kids with him without any hesitation. I remember once when he was practising chips and lobs with a couple of ball boys and when he'd finished he gave one of them a £50 note. The boy couldn't believe it.'

Apart from some of the publicity, Smith's only cause for complaint about his new signing was that Gascoigne never really wove his spell in the European Champions League. (This wasn't entirely down to his unfortunate habit of getting sent off in key games; Forsyth reckoned that most teams who faced Rangers had a very simple plan to nullify them. 'They all know that Gascoigne and Laudrup were the two playmakers so they put two men on each of them. That was how they stopped them, and it usually worked.') Nevertheless, that first season was a good one. As the Channel 4 *Gazza's Coming Home* documentary closes, Gascoigne talks about doing up his house so that Sheryl and the kids can move in. On the video, there's extra footage of the wedding which took place that golden (for Gascoigne) summer of 1996, after England's successful run in the European Championships. The documentary, in which Gazza comes across as a surprisingly sympathetic figure, details the heroic phase, if you will, of Gazza's career at Rangers.

The following season, 1996/97, will be remembered for the wrong reasons, specifically his admission that he'd beaten his wife. 'There were a lot of people who thought Rangers should sell him after that,' Forsyth recalled. 'I remember saying at the time that I'd stuck up for him many times but even I couldn't find anything to say in his defence that day. He got sent off against Ajax the day before it all came out, and I don't think he was ever really the same player after that.' Although Rangers clinched their ninth title in a row that season, it was not a vintage one for Gazza.

When Smith signed Gascoigne for Everton, he stated that the player needed a fresh start every two years. At Ibrox, Gazza seemed to need a fresh start after just a year and a half. But in the summer of 1997, commendably, he turned down lucrative offers from English clubs and, at financial cost to himself, chose to stay at Ibrox, out of loyalty to Smith. However, a famous exchange between manager and player at the time sums up the changing mood. After another of Gazza's misdemeanours, Smith turned to him and said, 'Do you like being in the papers?' When Gazza replied in the negative, Smith shouted angrily, 'So what do you do it for?'

Two more incidents, an alleged assault and his appearance in a New York bar in Celtic colours, left Smith wondering what he'd got himself into and talking about his player's 'deeper, darker side'. 'Every time something happens with him I feel it myself,' he said. 'Believe me, there have been many times when I've sat down and thought I'd made a mistake. When I signed him I was 100 per cent clear about my judgement, but the percentage drops with every incident that happens. And so too does the level of backing at the club.' It was hard not to conclude that the place where the percentages were dropping fastest was in the boardroom.

By the autumn of 1997 Rangers were so desperate to keep him out of mischief that they gave him a job for a few hours a week in the commercial department. It seemed to work, although the need to employ him profitably became more acute when he was banned for five matches after racking up 21 disciplinary points. The sending-off which had triggered the ban, not to mention the ban itself, had seemed unduly harsh, but Gascoigne would at least be back for the New Year's Old Firm game. He came on eighteen minutes from the end, just in time to be taunted by the Celtic fans. Just in time to play the flute again.

Over that New Year holiday there were unconfirmed reports of Gascoigne breaking the club's ban on booze 48 hours before a match, although again it was impossible not to feel he was being singled out. He can't have been the only player in Scotland to have had a few drinks over Hogmanay. Still, it was a less than promising start to 1998.

Why or when Rangers went sour, only Gazza and Smith know. But as early as October 1997, after England's World Cup qualifying triumph in Rome, it had become an open secret that the club wanted to sell him. There is little evidence that Gazza actually wanted to go. Forsyth reckoned 'Rangers fans were very sorry when he left, but perhaps he had milked the seam as far as it would go. Smith managed him superbly and got the best out of him. He's a wise, older man who doesn't take a lot of messing about. He told Gascoigne he was going to sell him and he got very upset and cried. Gascoigne loved it there.' For Butcher, it wasn't hard to see why Gazza appealed to the faithful: 'The Rangers fans loved him because he was one of them, he was a punter who was playing. And they still love him now.'

And yet, in that documentary, and in interviews he gave to the British press, there were clear hints that although he loved Rangers he wasn't necessarily loving the life he was having to lead. Sheryl and the kids never moved into the house. His own family didn't seem as much in evidence as they were when he'd been at Lazio. His flare-gun fighting partner Salenko had been sold. Odd as it may seem, when he wasn't socialising with his team-mates, telling jokes on the training ground, fishing or boating in Loch Lomond or on the phone to Sheryl, he found, as Ian Hamilton wrote, the solitude oppressive. Too much time to think and too many worrying things to think about.

To those like Forsyth steeped in the club's history, the outcome came as no great surprise. 'He was sold by David Murray, but he didn't want to go. He wouldn't have worked under Dick Advocaat. The team work very, very hard for each other now and he wouldn't have fitted in. And Rangers wanted to get some money for him while they still could. They're always ruthless with selling players, like Andy Goram and Chris Woods.'

Gascoigne left Rangers with one consolation: he had, at last, found a club where the fans really did revere him, as they continue to do to this day. When he scored his wonder goal against Scotland in the group stages of Euro 96, a few fights broke out at the Scottish end between the Rangers fans who felt compelled to cheer the goal (after all, he was one of theirs) and those Scots (and other Rangers) fans who took exception to the cheering.

MIDDLESBROUGH

Anything can happen with him. That's for sure.

Mark Schwarzer

Leaving Rangers to join Bryan Robson's Middlesbrough was one of those wrong turns which seemed like a good idea at the time. Just as the *Sun* had mounted a 'Gazza come home' campaign when his career seemed marooned in Italy, there was a muted call, in some parts of the national press, for Gascoigne to really come home and play for an English club.

Some of the motivation for this was based on sheer snobbery over the alleged quality of the so-called weaker teams in the Scottish Premier League like Dunfermline. The nation's cab drivers, whose specialist subject on *Mastermind* could have been the life and times of Paul Gascoigne, told any passenger who was meek or interested enough to listen that at Rangers he only had to play four games a season (the Old Firm games). Even some of the smarter footballing scribes, like Henry Winter at the *Daily Telegraph*, were referring to Scotland's top flight as a 'jaded repertory theatre'. Most of

Rangers' games, Winter declared, were a 'sprint and turkey shoot' compared to the marathon of the English Premier League.

Winter and co. did have one very obvious ulterior motive: they wanted Gazza in the best possible shape for the 1998 World Cup finals. Hoddle had also been dragged into the debate; it was implied he'd be much happier if Gascoigne were playing south of the border. Rangers were also set to change managers at the end of the season, the Smith era ending with the arrival of Dick Advocaat, and the player seemed to feel he'd be better off jumping before he was pushed. Certainly the Rangers chairman David Murray had made it clear that he had little interest in keeping Gascoigne, who was, as the press put it rather ruthlessly, 'a declining asset'.

The club initially wanted to sell him to Crystal Palace for £3m, but the deal foundered. Rangers blamed Palace's new chairman Mark Goldberg, which in the light of his subsequent performance is not an implausible suggestion. But the only thing going for such a move for Gazza seemed to be the probability that he might be reunited with Venables. Once the Palace deal had evaporated Gascoigne did what must have seemed the next best thing: he signed for Bryan Robson, a disciple of Venables during Euro 96 and a former England team-mate.

At a press conference on 26 March 1998 to mark his arrival on Teesside, Gascoigne seemed, once again, overwhelmed by the welcome. 'I've only been here two days and the reaction I've had from the fans on the street and the letters and faxes I've had, it's been incredible.' His new boss declared, 'I know that when he's fully fit and he's had a few matches under his belt, that I've bought the best midfielder in this country.' Returning the compliment, Gascoigne said, 'It's not just the pull of the north-east, I'm playing for a guy I idolised. He was my favourite player as a youngster. I've played with Bryan, or "gaffer" now, and I'm just pleased to be part of his plans.' One of his new colleagues, Boro keeper Mark Schwarzer, told reporters, 'Anything can happen with him. That's for sure.'

Boro were heading back into the Premier League after an unlucky relegation the season before. Robert Nichols, editor of the Boro fanzine *Fly Me to the Moon*, said fans were ecstatic when they heard the news. 'It was a strange time when he joined. We were buoyant anyway because we were in the Coca Cola Cup final and he'd been unveiled at the stadium a few days earlier. We were hoping he'd recreate the form he'd shown for England. His goal against Scotland was still fresh in our minds and we hoped he'd be in that kind of form for us.' Nichols claimed that even at that stage in Gascoigne's career the signing was regarded as a coup. 'We'd had some big names – Juninho, Ravanelli – and there was only one name who could top them really and that was Gascoigne, and we got him.'

The Coca Cola Cup final on 29 March was made for Gascoigne to do his stuff, but he only came on as sub after 64 minutes and was booked within six minutes. A second bookable offence, a trip on Dennis Wise, was ignored by the referee and he stayed on the pitch. His most influential act was to start an attempted one-two with Paul Merson which broke down and led to Chelsea's second goal. But his behaviour on that day is still remembered with affection by Boro fans because he gave his loser's medal to Craig Hignett, whom he had replaced on the subs bench. Hignett said that it was that day which convinced him he had to leave Middlesbrough, admitting he had been a tad apprehensive when he heard about Gazza's signing because he 'didn't know what to expect', but he had no axe to grind with the player who came in for him. 'He's nothing like you read in the papers, a beer-swilling, pie-eating monster. He's great to have around. One day he turned up naked in the canteen just to get a laugh. Paul was incredible,' he added. 'He asked the manager not to pick him. Then after the final he wanted to give me his medal. I refused at first, but then he insisted and I've got it at home. He signed it for me as well. We were both in tears, we were like a couple of blubbering women.'

With Gazza, Middlesbrough were suddenly a more attractive package, particularly when, says Nichols, things went wrong. 'We lost the next two games and Radio 5 Live phoned me up on the Friday and asked if I could do an interview on Monday at 7.30 a.m., but only if we lost. They wanted to do one about how Middlesbrough had started losing since Gascoigne had joined. We did lose and I did the interview – it had nothing to do with Paul, the whole team played badly.'

To most outsiders, Gazza's performances for his new club seemed singularly unimpressive. Ian Hamilton thought him 'wearily peripheral most of the time, easily exasperated when his attempted tricks did not come off'. Nichols did not quite agree: 'He contributed a lot to our promotion push and he looked very strong.'

There was understandable apprehension about what shape, mental and physical, he would be in for the new season after missing out on France 98. The day before the 1998/99 season kicked off, Merson recorded in his diary: 'Then there's Gazza. He's got better in training and he's still got all the old magic in his feet, but I do fear for him because he's still living to excess off the field and his body is going to rebel at some point.'

It was, in some ways, a miracle that Gascoigne was playing at all that first weekend. He had been out on the Thursday with Jimmy Gardner and another close friend, David Cheek. Gardner and Cheek were sharing a room at the Marriott Hotel. At five o'clock in the morning on the Friday, Gardner rang reception for medical help. Cheek had died of a heart attack; a post-mortem proved inconclusive. Robson told the press that he'd told Gazza to join in training to get his mind off it. Gazza played the following day against Leeds, having assured Robson he'd only had 'a couple of glasses of wine' on the Thursday night.

A week later, the club got an authentic glimpse of the Gazza of old – unfortunately of the off-the-pitch variety. The club had just taken delivery of a new state-of-the-art team coach. Left behind by some of the players at the training ground, Gazza saw the keys in the coach and decided to take it for a spin into Darlington, where he could meet his team-mates. Everything was going smoothly until he tried to turn on the main road. As Merson recalled, 'He tried to turn it like he would a car.' The predictable result was that he scraped one side of the coach on a couple of concrete bollards. His repeated attempts to extricate himself and the coach only made things worse; eventually, when it stalled, he just decided to leave it there. The players still managed to squeeze into it and drive down to Birmingham for the Villa game, but the driver had to explain away £15,000 worth of damage. Hignett mused, 'Sometimes he doesn't know where to draw the line. If someone else had done that I'm not so sure they'd have got away with it.' But then, he added, that was the essence of Gazza. 'Maybe someone could have tried to calm him down when he was younger but I don't think you could do that . . . That's his personality and the personality makes the player. If you turned him into someone who ate his broccoli and pasta and said "Yes boss" you wouldn't have the same player out on the pitch.'

Nichols says of those first games in the new season that although Gazza 'came back from the summer [looking] twice the size he had been . . . he played well for us'. It still took a good month for him to find his form, thanks to a calf injury, among other things. After Robson had taken him off on 23 August as Boro lost 3–1 to Villa (because, he said, he was worried Gazza was going to get sent off; maybe he was still upset by the memory of his inadequate coach-driving skills), Merson noted, 'Andy Townsend and I agreed that Gazza is not going to make any real impact until he stops drinking.'

Merson left Teesside soon afterwards in controversial circumstances with the press blaming his decision on the club's 'drinking and gambling' culture and, by extension, on Gascoigne. Merson and Gazza talked about all the stories and, so Merson said, Gazza told him 'he didn't have many mates in football but I was one of them'. Gascoigne could see Merse had to leave to make sure he didn't slip back into bad habits. He then added, poignantly, 'I'm still there. I can't get out of it yet.' Four weeks later, Gascoigne was admitted into the Marchwood Priory at Hampshire. 'Paul took it on himself,' Robson reminded the press, before adding that alcohol was only 'part of it. What people have got to realise is that Paul has had a lot of stresses, a bit of depression and personal problems which he's found difficult to cope with.'

Gascoigne returned three weeks later against Nottingham Forest and collected a fifth booking which earned him a one-game ban. Nichols recalled of this period: 'His best game was away at Southampton. We had two players sent off, but Gascoigne seemed to shoulder all the responsibility and he played superbly and we drew 3–3. He played like two or three men that day.' By December, Gascoigne had hit a run of form good enough to persuade Hoddle to send John Gorman to watch him against West Ham, where he was man of the match. Was a possible England recall on the cards? The press thought so. The prodigal's return was tipped for a certain friendly in February· 1999 against the world champions, France.

In the event, Howard Wilkinson would be in charge of that game and the cries for Gazza's return had faded. 'When he came back to Middlesbrough we were wondering if he'd come back too soon,' recalled Nichols. 'He had two or three good games, like the one at West Ham at home, but he was inconsistent. He seemed to have a mysterious dead leg for ages and there was a wall of silence from the club.' In the fanzine's end-of-season poll for 1998/99, Gascoigne was voted the most disappointing player of the season. Nichols said: 'It was all over the media. It was probably only about ninety people who had voted for him, but it was fair, he was – he hardly played.'

The following season, 1999/2000, his appearances were even rarer: a total of seven League games and one appearance as a sub was reminiscent of his darkest days at Lazio. Yet as the season started the new England manager, Kevin Keegan, was determined to cast his eye over Gazza and Ince. After a good performance at Selhurst Park against Wimbledon on 10 August, Gascoigne missed the Derby match because his mate Jimmy Gardner had got into bother. 'I don't think any other manager would have allowed it,' opined Nichols.

But the next week Keegan came up to the Riverside to watch him play. From the coach's public remarks, it sounded as if Gazza had earned himself an audition for a supporting role with England. Pumped up, Gazza ran out on the pitch with his silly head on and after charging around for twenty minutes limped off. I interviewed Bryan Robson a few weeks after this game for *FourFourTwo* magazine and he said, 'I don't think Kevin did Gazza any favours that day.'

From then on it was an on–off season for Gazza, with the emphasis very firmly on the off. After a few more games and a two-month lay-off, he returned against Villa in February to stage a rerun of his FA Cup final madness. He never played another League game for Middlesbrough. By then, though, the fans themselves had begun to wonder. 'The Wrexham match [Boro had lost 2–1 to Wrexham in the third round of the FA Cup] was the lowest point. He was absolutely . . . sh*t,' Nichols recalled. 'He was too slow. We knew he had lost some pace before he arrived, but it was like he couldn't accept that. We thought he'd play a different type of game, sit back a bit more and spray the ball around, but he didn't. He was trying to do the same things he used to do, charging forward, trying to beat people, and he couldn't do it.'

Throughout his time at the club rumours floated around about what Gazza was getting up to off the field. He'd shared a house with Merson on his arrival but his habit of always having something to drink in the house had got to his team-mate. Then he roomed with Andy Townsend, but he left too. 'Paul was left rattling around in a big house on his own,' said Nichols. 'He would phone up local TV programmes if he was bored. Once he turned up for training in his dressing gown. That was just before he went to the Priory.' Tabloid news-desks heard other rumours, none really substantial enough to print. But the general feeling was, as Nichols said, 'If this had been anyone else but Paul Gascoigne he would have been sacked.'

There were brighter moments, though. In late September 1998, when the presenter and journalist Brough Scott arrived at the training complex to interview Gazza, a month after that Villa game, it was inevitably Gascoigne who tried to dominate the training session. He soon had to stop to have a gash on his left leg tended, and jokingly knocked Alun Armstrong flat. It wasn't long before Robson was shouting, 'For f***'s sake, don't f*** about, Gazza!'

So spectacular was Gascoigne's decline during his tenure at the Riverside, however, that it raised a huge question mark over Robson's judgement. 'I think it was one of Robson's biggest mistakes,' said Nichols. 'It hadn't paid off and a lot of the baggage he brought with him was harmful to the club.' Specifically, Gazza's arrival and subsequent decline seemed to justify the charge that Middlesbrough was a pub team full of thirty-somethings. 'Robson was too soft. Gazza needed someone like Walter Smith to be firmer with him. There was a collective sigh of relief when he left. I think it's great he's having an Indian summer, but we can't believe it's the same Gascoigne playing for Everton that was here.' Hignett isn't convinced that Robson handled Gazza badly. 'It's a difficult question. He had a lot of injuries, occasionally Gazza didn't help himself, but he never had a minute's peace. He was always being slagged off in the papers.'

George Sik just thought Gazza made the wrong move, full stop. 'I don't think Middlesbrough was a good club for him to join. They're not a happy club, they don't seem that united. And Robson couldn't handle him. Besides, maybe one of the reasons he is doing better at Everton is because he signed on a free.'

EVERTON

I have ambitions – mainly not to give the manager any problems.

Paul Gascoigne

The crowd was smaller than usual. Everton fans, still seething over the sale of Nicky Barmby to Liverpool, were hardly likely to be immensely cheered by the arrival of a player who, for all his fame, had only played nine games in the previous season for Middlesbrough.

One reporter estimated that there were, at most, 30 Evertonians gathered outside Goodison to welcome Gazza. He made the obligatory jokes – announcing that he'd be buying the then England manager Kevin Keegan a season ticket to Goodison. But he seemed to realise that he had just bought his own season ticket to the Last Chance Saloon: 'What I have to do is work hard, keep my nose clean and stay out of trouble.'

He sounded realistic but defensive ('I am fit, I must be, otherwise I wouldn't have passed the medical') as he started, in July 2000, what was supposed to be a two-year contract at the club. Everton (and manager Walter Smith) had covered themselves: a clause in the contract gave them a get-out if he got into trouble off the pitch.

He looked thinner than ever as the season started, too thin some said – worried that he might be up to his old dieting tricks. But there was evidence of maturity: up against his nemesis Glen Hoddle, he simply shook his old manager's hand and said: 'All the best Glenn.'

He was – and this is not a word used often to describe him – omnipresent as Everton started the season inconsistently. He bossed the midfield against Leicester, prompting talk of an England recall from Smith, But Gazza, looking at the squad for the 7 October World

Cup qualifier against Germany, was more accurate: 'I think England is gone now.'

Harry Pearson, writing in the *Guardian*, put the boot in, saying Gazza had 'huffed and puffed like an actor auditioning for a part in a Thomas The Tank Engine movie'. Pearson, though, was in a disgruntled minority. Sky Sports pundit Andy Gray, no sentimentalist, drooled over his vision as he led Everton's midfield against Aston Villa on 5 November. And then, suddenly, Gascoigne took a free-kick near the right touchline and collapsed in a heap. At first, the club believed the thigh injury would keep him out only for a few weeks but, after three operations, he never played another game that season.

Such inactivity had, in the past, often signalled a return to what Graham Taylor referred to as refueling. And on 4 June 2001, fans were saddened – if not surprised – when, under orders from Smith, he checked himself into an Arizona clinic for treatment for drink and depression. In September, as he returned to the Everton first team, he confessed all – not to the tabloids for once but to the *Observer*'s Ian Ridley. 'If I wasn't playing, I would drink Saturdays, then Sunday, then Monday. Then I would try and train and it was no good, then have another drink to pass the day, it was a horrible cycle, I felt so close to having to pack the game in.'

Like Merson and Adams, he made a public mea culpa: 'When it comes to drinking, I don't think of the future, I live day by day. I had to accept I was an alcoholic [at the clinic] but I try not to say I am an alcoholic, I prefer to say it's a disease I've got.'

Three months after he had recovered to the point where he justified his selection and won several man-of-the-match awards. And against Southampton, in early

December, he electrified Goodison with a second-half display that, team-mate David Weir noted, 'made the team come alive'. Smith was delighted that his protégé had silenced the cynics – for a while: 'Gascoigne upsets teams by having the confidence to have the ball and take responsibility.'

Yet Ridley, at Everton to interview Smith, noted that Gazza's zeal was almost excessive. The player was 'usually in long before everyone else at the training ground . . . after lunch, when his adult playmates had gone, he would stay to train with the reserve squad. Then, after tea, with the youths – and the eight, nine and ten-year-olds in the evening. Only when someone had taken the ball home would he return to his rented flat in Quebec Place in Liverpool's Waterside Village.' Ridley, looking out of Smith's window, saw Gazza, sitting on a ball on a flat roof, unfazed by the rain, watching a youth team game.

The determination faltered in February, possibly because another hoped for reconciliation with Sheryl fell through. His eating disorder returned (he would eat a whole packet of corn flakes for breakfast and then vomit them up) and he began to worry that, as he told Smith, it wasn't worth struggling to get fit if you were just going to get injured again. Everton lost an FA Cup quarter-final against Middlesbrough, a result which cost Smith his job and made Gascoigne's exit seem inevitable. And in March 2002, he joined Burnley on loan with his new manager Stan Ternent hoping Gazza could ignite the Clarets' faltering charge to reach the Division One play-offs.

The assumption was that new Everton manager David Moyes had squeezed him out but, initially, this seemed not to be the case. Moyes tried to persuade the player to stay but admitted: 'He was upset with a few things not to do with Everton and maybe he felt it was right to play his football elsewhere.' And Gazza, mysteriously, would say only that he had left because 'Someone at Everton has been stabbing me in the back'.

BURNLEY
He did things other players could only dream of
Mitchell Thomas

Gascoigne's spell at Burnley can be boiled down to two negatives: the Clarets didn't make the play-offs – and Gascoigne didn't revive his club career. So far so predictable yet, as his Clarets team-mate Mitchell Thomas noted, it needn't have ended that way.

'When we knew Gazza was coming, there was a real buzz about the town and the club. The first training session we had was a really good one. In the five-a-side, everyone was looking to get on his side. He did things other players could only dream of. He did look a lot thinner than I had ever seen him [Thomas also played alongside him at Spurs], in an almost drawn way. His fitness was there but he was a bit thinner and going bald.'

A sell-out crowd of 20,000 watched his debut at Turf Moor against Bradford in March 2002. He hit a curling free-kick in a 1–1 draw which Bradford 'keeper Alan Combe just saved. Gazza couldn't believe it ('David Seaman wouldn't have saved that') but almost scoring on his debut proved to be as good as it got for Gascoigne and Burnley.

After three games, Gazza was on the subs' bench again. 'He just got caught up in one or two games because it was a bit quick,' Thomas told Ian Ridley. His last appearance was an eight-minute cameo in the last game of the season as Burnley beat Coventry City 1–0 but didn't make the play-offs. 'There was definitely a sense when he came on that this would be his last appearance in English football,' recalled Thomas. Ternent, certainly, didn't seem inclined to keep him: 'I don't think Paul will stay. He has a lot of offers on the table.' Given Ternent's reported offer ('If you've been on the piss all night, tell me, I'll pick a team to suit you for 30 minutes'), the parting may have been for the best. Ternent and Thomas, like the player and his new agent Ian Elliott of First Artists, assumed that in the summer Gazza would be bound for Dubai or America.

So, just a few weeks before his thirty-fifth birthday, at an age when veterans like Paolo Maldini were still prospering, Paul Gascoigne played his last first-team game in English league football.

5. FROM HERO . . .: GAZZA FOR ENGLAND 1988–90

Look at that silly bugger. He's as daft as a f***ing brush.

Bobby Robson

Alan Smith used to like to watch *Coronation Street* in his hotel room on England trips. His room-mate, Paul Gascoigne, didn't. 'By the time I'd watched that, he'd played table tennis and done a few lengths of the pool,' Smith recalled. 'He just couldn't sit still. I remember waking once at four a.m. to find him sitting up, flicking through the pages of Ceefax.'

This was 1989. Gazza and Smudger were both relative new boys to the England set-up. Smith still remembers the player's prowess in training. 'We used to do these competitions in training, two against two or three against three, and I remember how quick he was over two or three yards. I'd never seen anything like it. It could make you feel quite sluggish.' But few had any doubts that Gazza could play, certainly when he had the ball. He was, Bobby Robson remembered, all 'cockiness and arrogance on the pitch and dizziness off it. The question then was whether we could get the dizziness out of him and get the best from him. He was right up there with Bryan Robson, even a bit quicker through the space and furnished with a bit more trickery. But where Robson scored over Gascoigne was discipline. He never did daft things or risked the ball in an attempt to please the crowd.'

The press had been talking up Gascoigne's England prospects since the spring of 1988. Robson had seen him score twice in Newcastle's 5–0 thrashing of Swindon in the fifth round of the FA Cup that season and had been impressed. But a bit daunted too. 'He had a lot of talent, but it needed to be harnessed and one would have to build a team to suit him.' After the game, in the club lounge, Robson pored over Gazza's game with Newcastle boss McFaul. The player came in later and watched the England manager from a distance, as if in awe. Robson had a quiet, encouraging word with the youngster. 'Forget the European Championship this summer,' he told him, 'and set your sights on the World Cup finals in 1990.'

Robson is clear that in his own mind he had decided after that one display that there was no way he could not take Gascoigne to Italy. But at that time he saw him as a squad player, someone who could come on twenty minutes from the end and change a game. Building a team around a player who, when Robson saw him, was not even 21 wasn't the kind of thing experienced international managers did, especially when you already had talents like Bryan Robson, John Barnes, Chris Waddle and Peter Beardsley to call on. Besides, it was not that obvious how (or where) to play Gascoigne. Robson's coach, Don Howe, said, 'He was an inside forward really, not a midfield player. He was more like Jimmy Hagan, Wilf Mannion and Johnny Haynes.'

Publicly Robson kept his own counsel, even though, almost from the moment Gascoigne joined Spurs in July 1988, the tabloids campaigned vociferously for his inclusion. He says now his silence was deliberate: 'I took a lot of criticism for not picking Paul earlier, but that was deliberate on my part. I wanted him to value his England place and not to believe that it came easy or that it was there for the asking.'

Gascoigne was named in the England 22 for a friendly against Denmark at Wembley on 14 September 1988.

He wasn't in the starting line-up but he came on five minutes from the end. He had a longer run out against Saudi Arabia in the 'IN THE NAME OF ALLAH, GO!' 1–1 draw in November 1988, but missed another friendly against Greece in Athens the following February. And, even though he was in the squad, he didn't play at all in the World Cup qualifier against Albania in Tirana a month later.

For the return match on 26 April at Wembley, he came off the bench when England were 3–0 up, completely disobeyed Robson's instructions not to distort the shape of the team by running over to his friend Waddle, and scored one goal and made another. As Gazza scampered over to the wrong part of the pitch, Robson turned to Howe and said, for the first time, 'Look at that silly bugger. He's as daft as a f***ing brush.' Afterwards, Robson criticised the player for not doing what he'd been asked: 'We needed two balls out there. One for Gascoigne and one for the others.' He tempered this rebuke, however, by saying that managing Gazza was an exciting challenge because he had the potential to be another Michel Platini. Paul Parker, who came on as a sub to make his England debut, observed: 'He had more confidence than someone with 40 caps. I was timid when I came on. He scored a goal. He had a swagger and he wanted more touches than everyone else had had in the entire 90 minutes. I just wanted an early touch.'

The tabloids (and the player himself) might have felt teased by this stop–start progress. But managing the player psychologically was essential, although far from easy. Robson would usually explain to Gascoigne in advance that he wouldn't be picked for such and such a game. He would reassure him that he was in the squad and advise him to watch and learn from players like

Robson, Shilton and Butcher. Yet he also had to avoid undermining the player's confidence or alienating him entirely. Gascoigne was already convinced he could do the job. Robson said, 'He used to come up to me on the training ground and tell me, "I can do it you know, boss." I'd just smile and say, "I'll tell you when." He was really saying, "When I get in, I'll be in and you won't want me out." '

The manager soon decided to ignore the press because they were usually focusing on one pass or one goal whereas, to him, it seemed obvious that for all Gascoigne's talents, he would often only be in the game for twenty minutes in each half. Nor did it help that the player either didn't seem to understand his instructions or didn't seem to feel obliged to take them seriously. England's Under-21 coach Dave Sexton had harboured similar doubts when he'd introduced Gascoigne into his squad in 1987. Robson's most famous predecessor, Sir Alf Ramsey, even chipped in with the advice that Gazza was a 'free spirit' who probably would never do the business but had to be controlled or he'd let the team down.

On 16 May 1989 Gazza played in an England B team against Switzerland. The B team had been revived partly so that his fitness for international duties could be assessed. That night he scored a virtuoso goal, dribbling and double-shuffling past three Swiss defenders. The clamour from the press got a few decibels louder. He made his full debut a week later, wearing the number eight shirt in a 0–0 draw with Chile at Wembley. It was a dull game, but Gazza played reasonably well and, maybe more importantly, didn't do anything daft or disobedient.

With nine months still to go before Italia 90, Robson named Gascoigne in the squad against Sweden, but warned him publicly to mature as a player and a person. He came on again as a sub (this time for Neil Webb). By this stage, nearly a year to the day since Gazza first appeared in an England shirt, Robson's treatment of the £2m player was being seen not as a calculated ploy to ease Gazza into the international set-up but as evidence of the England manager's procrastination. When he was left out of the team to face Poland in Katowice in a crucial World Cup qualifier that October, Gazza's nerve cracked and he began to complain publicly about a campaign to keep him out of the England team.

The problem was, of course, the exact opposite: the tabloids had been campaigning for, if not demanding, his inclusion in the England team. After the debacle of the 1988 European Championship (when Robson said pre-tournament 'We are about to find out how good we are' and England finished bottom of their group) the press had lost some of their faith in Robson. But the manager, as England managers will, may well have decided he was not going to give in to such a campaign. He was too shrewd a manager to pick a player just because the press said he should, and anyway, the media hadn't yet convinced him that Gascoigne had learned how to play football when he didn't have the ball at his feet. Steve Curry, who was with the *Express* at the time, thought Robson handled all this well: 'Bobby Robson was very clever with him, holding him back before the 1990 World Cup, although he was criticised for it. That was important, he knew what he had.' Besides, here was Robson asking for the player to show maturity and there was Gascoigne in the tabloids pulling a funny face with his tongue sticking out, looking (in Ian Hamilton's words) 'oafish and deranged, not the man to whom you could entrust a nation's pride'.

Not for the first or last time in his career, Gazza began to suffer from false memory syndrome, talking (via the *Sun*) about the good old days at Newcastle when all he did was 'think, eat and drink football'. In his moment of outrage, he had conveniently forgotten how often he'd badgered his then agent to get him a move to another club.

There was another outbreak of press hysteria after Robson was quoted, after the player had turned in a superlative performance for the B team, as saying he couldn't trust Gazza. Robson protested that he had actually said he couldn't trust Gazza to fill the same kind of disciplined role in midfield as Bryan Robson, which was, as he pointed out, a slightly different kettle of fish, but he should have been wise enough in the ways of the media to know his remark would be truncated into a sensational headline.

Ultimately, the decision about whether Gazza would be in the World Cup squad or not came down to a friendly against Czechoslovakia at the end of April 1990. By that time Robson's attempt to ease Gazza in gently had come perilously close to backfiring, partly due to the player's own eccentricities. Just before an England friendly against Brazil the month before, Robson had dropped in to Stamford Bridge to see Spurs (and Gascoigne) play Chelsea. Like most of the player's admirers, even he had been left a little speechless when Gazza punched John Bumstead. So David Platt played against Brazil and Gazza had another four weeks to wait. Four weeks to get pumped up for the Czechs.

So pumped up, Pete Davies wrote in his book, that 'he nearly decapitated me, bouncing a ball off the wall barely inches from my head with a really manic aggression'. But then, as Davies went on to say, 'He knew this was his ticket to Italy tonight.' Tony Dorigo, who came on as a sub that night, said of the pressure on his team-mate, 'I don't know any player who has had so much expected of him as Gazza had on that night.'

For the first ten minutes Gazza played as if he were deliberately trying to prove Sir Alf right. It was manic, stupid football. The referee told him to cool it, but, like so much of his manager's advice, it seemed to 'go in one ear and out the other'. And then he hit a beautiful pass with the outside of his foot, over and through the Czech defence, for Steve Bull to score England's first goal. That done, he seemed to settle down, relishing the challenge of making Bully look like a deadly international marksman.

England won 4–2; Gascoigne had a hand in three of the goals and scored the last one himself. Twice, in the words of commentator Barry Davies, he glided past Czech defenders without appearing to change pace, just as, as Smudger recalled, he used to leave England players behind in those two against twos on the training ground. For his goal, he collected the ball on the edge of the box and mysteriously, without any noticeable increase in effort, passed the Czech defence and sent the ball into the roof of the net. Did he know that Robson was thinking of taking him off at the time? (Six years later, he'd score another wonder goal as another England manager, Terry Venables, prepared to replace him with Steve Stone.)

The game was treated as a kind of referendum on Gazza, but it was a strange kind of referendum because the only person whose vote really counted was Robson, and he had now become convinced (he told Sexton) 'that we have a player'. He also had a player who was liable to turn up on the back page of the *Mirror* in a clown suit, as he did the morning after the match. Perhaps out of embarrassment, or perhaps because the press had (in his word) 'slaughtered' him and his family, he would only say four words to the press the day after the game: 'I hate the press.'

He was still in this mood after a less convincing performance (by player and team) in a friendly against Denmark on 15 May. He asked the *Sunday Mirror*'s Bob Harris how he thought he'd played and got the usual non-committal 'you did all right' response. For some reason this enraged Gazza, who stormed off after telling Harris he was a f***ing c**t, that he was never going to talk to him again.

To no one's surprise (except possibly Sir Alf's), Gascoigne made it into the squad, but at number nineteen, which left some suspicious hacks smelling a plot. Was Robson just going to take Gazza to Italy and not play him? Robson wouldn't comment.

Manager and player had bonded, as Hamilton said, like a wise father and a dodgy son, fellow victims of the press. Robson had always liked the lad but could still be perplexed by him. Rushing down for dinner with the team one night, Robson 'bumped into Paul in his England tracksuit going through the revolving doors on his way out. I was somewhat nonplussed and asked him where he was going. "I'm off down the pub to meet me dad," he replied. I was stunned. I told him, "You cannot do that, man, especially in an England tracksuit." ' Gascoigne's weight could also still be a problem, but Robson's view was that 'he was conscientious about losing it, and if he'd put too much on he'd ask me if he could miss a meal'. Moreover, Robson was bemused by how hyperactive Gazza could be. 'I thought he was resting in his room watching television, and then he'd pop up here, while I was talking to one lot of players. And then I'd go to talk to some of the lads playing table tennis or something and he'd be there as well.' As the manager soon discovered, even if Gazza was in his room, he wasn't necessarily sitting still.

John Barnes recalled one incident, evidence of the lengths to which Gascoigne would go to avoid the tedium of squad get-togethers.

Gazza, Chris [Waddle] and myself were on England duty once [in Albania in March 1989], just killing time in a foreign hotel which overlooked a farm. Our room was twenty floors up and Gazza was hanging out of the window trying to hit the chickens with bars of soap. Suddenly Bobby Robson walked through the door. Chris and I stood up straight, like naughty school boys. 'What are you doing?' Robson asked Gazza, who continued lining up some poor bantam with a bar of Camay. 'I'm throwing soap at these chickens,' replied Gazza, almost surprised that Bobby should pose the question.

As Barnes went on to say, anyone else would have made up a feeble cover story. But Gazza's reply intrigued Robson, who retorted, 'You're doing what?' Gazza repeated that he was trying to hit these chickens with soap. Robson walked towards the window, peered at the chickens and said, 'Can you really hit them from here?' Gazza said, 'Yeah. Of course.' Robson insisted that Gazza prove it, at which point the player took aim and scored a direct hit on a chicken. As Barnes recalled, 'Bobby just walked out of the room, laughing and shaking his head.'

After reading that, it's easy to understand why, throughout Italia 90, the one question the England players heard from their manager with ever-increasing frequency was: 'Where's Gazza?' Usually the answer would be playing table tennis (sometimes with himself if he couldn't find a partner), playing volleyball in the pool, kicking the ball around with some kids or driving a buggy across the greens on the golf course next to the Is Molas Hotel in Cagliari (indeed, he almost ran over the manager in just such a buggy the day before the World Cup kicked off). Sometimes, though, the answers were a bit more unusual, as Stuart Pearce recalled: 'We were relaxing by the swimming pool one day and Gazza disappeared inside yet again, only to reappear minutes later having covered himself from head to foot in toilet paper. He dived off the board into the pool. Only he knows why.'

Chris Waddle was dismayed to find that he had been designated Gazza's World Cup room-mate. Part of the reason for his shock was the fact that Gascoigne still slept with all the lights on and woke at dawn, intent on cajoling his friend into an early-morning swim. Waddle was also Gascoigne's preferred table tennis partner and the victim of an endless stream of gags. Waddle once said his cappuccino was a bit frothy, whereupon Gazza revealed that it was actually bath foam. Waddle put the cup down, probably wondering how he had ended up sharing a room with English football's answer to Basil Brush. He even got lumbered with Gascoigne as his partner in the golf tournament. 'It was fine until the TV cameras caught up with us,' he recalled. 'He started singing and insisted I did a duet with him. That wasn't so bad, but when he began to dance with me and then lay flat on his stomach to try and push the ball into the hole with his nose, I'd had enough. There are times (most of the time, actually) when a little of Gazza goes a long way.'

You can understand why, then, one of the highlights of Waddle's World Cup (or so it seems from his memoirs) was the day someone brought Gazza a birthday cake and Waddle shoved it into his room-mate's face. Barnes recalled: 'All the players stood about laughing as Gazza sat there, covered in sponge and cream. He licked some off his face, then some more. Finally, he spoke. "Great chocolate," he said, which made us laugh all the more.' He also gave a speech that day which had the squad almost helpless with laughter. Recalling his amazing life story, he told the players and staff: 'I was great at seven . . . at seventeen I went to Newcastle and showed them how to play . . . at twenty I was the greatest player in the League . . . at twenty-one I was earning thousands a week.' This display of chutzpah and wit earned him a standing ovation.

But it wasn't all play. In the final friendly before the tournament began, against Tunisia on 2 June, it was Gazza whose miscued pass allowed the opposition to equalise. Howe and Robson worked on him in training, telling him not to react to tackles, to cut out the back-chat to referees, and Robson would often pull the player to one side after a team talk just to reiterate: 'You know what I'm saying applies to you too?' Invariably, Gascoigne promised that he wouldn't let his boss down. They worked on his stamina too. For a player who could drift out of games if he wasn't doing the business, he racked up, as Robson said later, a 'hell of a lot of mileage'. Sometimes he would have to be told to calm down, to stop chasing.

England's campaign began, somewhat inauspiciously, on 11 June with a 1–1 draw against the Irish, managed by Jack Charlton, Gazza's old Newcastle boss. Charlton believed his opposite number picked the wrong mid-field with Bryan Robson, Waddle, Barnes and Gas-coigne.

It would have been fine if Bobby had left Bryan to anchor midfield but he was also expected to get forward and get the odd goal. Because of that, it was hard to find the right partner for him. Gazza certainly didn't meet that requirement. Gazza, a strong runner and a superb passer, is at his best on the edge of the opposition's box. But at the other end of the pitch he can be as much of a liability as an asset. He tries to be too clever, aiming to nutmeg people or pull the ball down, when a defender would just hoof it. I reckoned the more pressure we put on him the better.

He had similar reservations about Barnes and Waddle, and set his team's game plan accordingly.

Despite the pressure, Gazza had a reasonable game, showing a few nice touches, striking a free-kick just past Terry Butcher's head and almost punching Ireland's Chris Morris. You could see the intention there, but you could also see Gazza remember that this was the World Cup, and the punch quickly turned into a hug and a handshake. The press, while blaming the Irish for the quality of the game, slaughtered England. Gazza, for once, thought it was fair enough, telling Pete Davies that the press had a point: the team had played badly. But that didn't stop him going down to the Forte village complex, where the press were staying, and cycling into a flock of peacocks.

Against Holland five days later, Gazza and England played with more finesse in a 3–5–2 formation. They may or may not have been inspired by the Gazza-led rendition of 'Let's all shag a hostess' and the official team anthem 'World in Motion' on the coach on the way to the ground.

Nobody can say for sure whose idea the sweeper was. Robson still says he wasn't pressurised into it by senior players like Bryan Robson and Gary Lineker; rather, he decided it was the smartest way to play against the Dutch. 'I'd got it wrong in 1988 against Holland [when England were trounced 3–1 in Dusseldorf] when I had two against two against Gullit and Van Basten. And then I decided I would play with a sweeper to cover myself against teams like the Dutch and the Germans.'

Whoever came up with the idea, it worked. Gazza, in only his second full competitive game for England, outshone Gullit. Early on, he slid past two Dutch defenders and placed a perfect cross on to Bryan Robson's head; the header flew just wide. When Barnes won a free-kick on the left, Gazza whipped the ball across the penalty area but Mark Wright and Lineker just failed to get on the end of it. After half an hour, he beat three men and was brought down. Frank Rijkaard struggled to contain the England midfield, but especially Gazza, who continued to jink, feint and pass his way through the Dutch team. There was another just-missed cross after he'd turned on a two-penny piece, then, with one minute to go, he won a free-kick which Pearce slotted home without anyone touching it – a pity, because it was an indirect free-kick.

Despite the goalless scoreline, Robson was bubbling with enthusiasm after the game, describing Gazza as the best player on the pitch and adding, 'He played as if he'd been in the team for five years.' His only minor complaint was the player's 'slight over-exuberance', possibly referring to the incident where Gazza walked up to Ronald Koeman and asked him how much he got paid. It must have been a good England performance because the chronically under-impressed scribe Brian Glanville wrote that it gave England a realistic hope of winning the World Cup.

Off the pitch, Gazza was having trouble finding other players to join him in his high-energy approach to rest and relaxation. He could always distract himself by betting on the horses (Gary Lineker and Peter Shilton were the squad's bookies), but even that began to pale. One afternoon Barnes, after much pestering, told Gazza, 'You can't play table tennis in your flip-flops, the manager said.' He had, by this stage, become bored with normal table tennis and had invented his own repertoire of strokes, of which his favourite was the double-handed backhand. When no one else wanted to play, he would just try to hit the ball into a glass of water. He often got it in first time.

Amid all this frenetic activity, he also found time to accidentally damage Bryan Robson's toe. Officially the toe was injured in training, but Barnes revealed that 'Bryan threw Gazza off the bed, but Gazza managed to hold on. The bed somehow went full circle and took the top off Bryan's toe. Gazza started laughing.' The situation was, however, more serious than that: Robbo was now out of the World Cup. It was a bizarre way to lose a captain and none of the players fancied having to explain things to the manager. 'For some reason Gazza couldn't stop laughing so we locked him in the bathroom,' Barnes added.

A cover story was duly concocted (Bryan had hurt his toe walking across the lawn, catching it on a sprinkler hidden in the grass), the manager was sent for and Gazza was released from the bathroom. The manager's face was like thunder when he arrived. Before the players could launch into the cover story, Gazza explained that Bryan had caught his toe in the bidet. All the other players, the plan in ruins, reluctantly piped up to support this transparently absurd story. The manager contented himself with saying, 'That was really bad luck, Bryan.'

Against Egypt on 21 June England reverted to 4–4–2 and continental sophistication gave way to meat and two veg. Although the tabloids insisted afterwards that England had given Egypt a 'pharaoh stuffing' (geddit?), Gazza's free-kick curling over the Egyptian defenders for Mark Wright to head home was the difference between the two sides. That and a superb save by Peter Shilton. The defensively minded Egyptians showed England what would come to be known, in the late 1990s, as 'too much respect'. Their goalkeeper, Shoubeir, was so hysterical when the final whistle went and he realised his country had lost by a goal to nil that he had to be given medical attention.

Before making that goal, Gazza had shimmied his way through a helpless Egyptian defence a few times, but he lacked the support up front to make them pay. Robson, as England managers are wont to do after such games, said the result was more important than the performance. In this case, he might even have been right. England finished top of their group with four points, the only side with a win, and Belgium were due next in the second phase of the competition. As the squad prepared to leave Sardinia, where they had played all their group games, Gascoigne turned to his room-mate and said, 'You know, Waddler, we can win this.'

Provided, of course, that his own manager didn't strangle him first. During the team meetings a bored Gazza would amuse himself by making noises. 'Real schoolboy back-of-the-class burps and hums,' said Barnes. 'Robson would be in the middle of his tactical stuff and the noises would start again. He knew it was Gazza of course but he couldn't bear to tell him off.' The manager's patience didn't even snap when he was holding an impromptu press conference and Gazza fired a ball into the middle of the throng of reporters.

The England party left their hotel in Cagliari some-what reluctantly. It had come to seem like a home from home for most of the squad (the obvious exception being Waddle, whose sleep patterns had been disturbed, to say the least, by his room-mate). Jane Nottage, the liaison manager for the England team, observed that the mood changed the day the squad departed for Bologna, especially with Bryan Robson, the England skipper, flying home prematurely for the second tournament running.

The squad had to share the new hotel in Bologna with other guests, which wasn't ideal; Robson, like most international managers, preferred to keep his players in a more isolated set-up, like that at the Is Molas Hotel. Nottage thought there was a 'strange electricity' in the Bologna hotel, but David Platt said the squad enjoyed the change. Something, though, was in the air, and relations between the England party and the press were semi-officially at an all-time low. The air of fear, loathing and mutual distrust was typified by the now notorious incident in which Gazza threw a cup of water at Paul Parker because he was talking to a reporter. 'That was blown out of all proportion,' said Parker. 'I was chatting to a friend who was a journalist. I'd known Steve [Stammers, who now works for the *Evening Standard*] for a while; he was the first person to give me a bit of press and he was from near me. I was chatting to him as a friend when Gascoigne came over and poured water over my head. It was just a practical joke, tomfoolery really. But the press needed a story.'

Belgium, second in their group behind Spain but with six goals already under their drawstrings, were a completely different proposition to Egypt, so Robson switched back to the sweeper system. A matter of hours before kick-off Gazza was still playing the fool. The

England manager looked out of a window and saw him playing tennis. Even Robson felt this was too much. He was probably right, because Gascoigne wasn't his usual effervescent self against the Belgians. The most creative player on the pitch that night wasn't an Englishman at all, but Enzo Scifo. The game was one of the best of the tournament with both sides feeling they could have won it in normal time, Barnes aggrieved that his perfectly good goal was disallowed for offside. Platt admitted that 'if it had been a boxing match, Belgium might have won on points'. But in the 119th minute, when penalties seemed inevitable, Gascoigne got dumped by Eric Gerets and won a free-kick on the left. Platt later recalled:

> It seemed like every player was in the area as Gazza stepped up to flight the ball into it. In these situations I always try to find a yard of space and hope the ball will get to me. I moved, the defender didn't, and the ball was heading in my direction. Instinctively, as it dropped over my shoulder I swivelled, and in one sweet movement volleyed it goalward. It flashed past Michel Preudhomme in goal and came to rest in the back of the net. Both teams knew the game was over.

The only downside was that Gazza had picked up a booking, for a late tackle on Scifo, but as it was his first of the tournament there was no great alarm in the England camp or the press post-match. Robson later admitted that he'd resigned himself to penalties. 'Gazza had gone negative five or ten minutes before the end; he was treading water.' A journalist asked about the kiss Gazza had given the manager. Was that a thank you for his advice about free-kicks? Robson joked, 'I was complaining about his after shave, that was for sure.'

So England were in the quarter-finals against Cameroon. Another game, another change of venue. This time, Naples beckoned. On the first day there, Gazza, Waddle, Bull and McMahon took Jane Nottage's driver and car (apparently with Bobby Robson's permission) for a drive to the beach. Nottage began to worry, especially when her driver returned alone over an hour later. She and the driver drove down to the beach again in a bit of a panic and scoured the sea front. 'After a few minutes we came across the miscreants.' Bully and McMahon were in the shade sipping cold drinks. Gascoigne, reported Nottage, 'was basking in the sunshine, red as a beetroot, while Chris Waddle tried to persuade him to cover up before he was burned to a cinder'. Gazza eventually came out of the sun and started to play pinball. When word got round that some of the England team were on the beach, a crowd started to gather. 'Gazza started to entertain the audience by playing card tricks.' Nottage was struck by how at ease he looked.

The day before the match, the last day of June, Robson joked that he was going to strap Gazza into a chair so that the rest of the squad could get some rest. Gazza still managed to persuade John Barnes to play squash. Barnes tried to talk some sense into his colleague: 'Don't be daft, Gazza, you have a match tomorrow and I have an injury.' But Gazza was not to be dissuaded. 'It was like the kid next door coming round for a kickabout. I couldn't refuse.'

Even that wasn't enough to stave off boredom, so Gazza squeezed in a few TV interviews as well. When asked if the pressure was getting to the players, he said, 'Nah. It's just eleven of us against eleven of them kicking a little white pill about.' What image did he want people to have of him? 'Mesel.' Pete Davies, watching this, realised who Gazza's face reminded him of: Michael

Palin. Again, this is one of those things where you probably had to be there.

Cameroon midfielder Jean-Claude Pagal remembers Gazza's antics while the anthems were being played. 'Aaah, Gazza!' he said, when interviewed for *Four-FourTwo* Online in the summer of 2000. 'During the national anthems he was sticking his tongue out and grabbing his crotch. So I did the same, giving him the finger and doing rude things.' Pagal insisted that England held no great fear for the Cameroon side. 'We felt we were better technically than them.' Except for Gazza, of course. 'During the game he did one really good dribble past me and I ran after him and shouted, "Hey, man, are you trying to kill me?" ' It was Pagal's job to take Chris Waddle out of the game, which he did by the simple but effective method of kicking him really hard on the left leg every time he got the ball. But, although he swapped his shirt with Lineker at the end of the game, it is Gazza he remembers best, and he gave a brutally succinct resumé of Paul Gascoigne's career: 'He was one of the best players in the world, but he drank too much beer.'

McMahon and Waddle decided that to lose against Cameroon would be a disaster, but not a disgrace. And lose is, of course, what England very nearly did, trailing 2–1 with eight minutes of normal time left. Although England were 1–0 up after just seven minutes, playing the Cameroon team was not, as England scout Howard Wilkinson had suggested, like having a bye to the last four. Indeed, Platt reckoned that their very unpredictability made it harder for England to control the game.

Gazza started badly, spending too much time talking to the referee. Robson observed, 'In the first half he played very poorly, losing his discipline and his common sense. The composure went and he chased after the ball like a cat chasing a ball around the back garden.' As the first half ended, he came off looking not endearingly daft but dangerously loopy. Gary Lineker's wife Michelle was heard to remark, 'He'd better cool his jets.' In the dressing room, Robson had a word: 'The obvious thing to do was to take him off, but I had confidence in him and I just told him he could not play like that in international football unless he wanted to get destroyed.'

After an hour, Gazza was chasing Roger Milla around in the England penalty area. A foul, a penalty, and Cameroon were level. Four minutes later, Ekeke ran on to a chip from Milla. It was 2–1; the Indomitable Lions were a pile of bodies by the corner flag. Although it was Cameroon who would be punished for their clumsy challenges, England were mixing it too: Pearce got booked, Butcher thumped Milla.

Gazza finally came to life, perhaps inspired by a sense of guilt at conceding the penalty. A lovely pass which didn't so much split the defence as make them irrelevant and Platt was through, but the shot slipped inches wide. Still, it was a good sign, probably the first time Gazza had put a foot right all night. With just eight minutes left, Lineker ran on to a ball from Wright, was clattered in the box, and England were awarded their first penalty since a friendly against Israel in February 1986. Pagal remembered the pain when Lineker equalised from the spot: 'Too much, man. My buddy Roger Milla gave the ball away and England equalised. Eight minutes. That was our World Cup, man.'

In extra time, though, England looked like they were falling apart. Wright was on the wing because he couldn't defend with a bloodied head (that's what you get for clashing heads with Milla). The ball kept bobbling around the England goal. Gazza, his socks down, hit passes to nobody and into nowhere. But then he got the ball, looked up, set off and put Lineker through on goal with another pass of precision engineering. Again, Lineker was hacked down. Again, he got up and scored from the spot, shooting straight this time because he'd remembered how early the keeper had moved on the last one. England were through – just. As Waddle came off the pitch he turned to Robson and said: 'Some f***ing bye that.'

Turin and the Germans now beckoned. Gianni Agnelli, owner of Fiat and Juventus, paid a visit to the dressing rooms of both teams. When he dropped in to wish England luck, Gazza assumed he was just an old fan popping in to say hello, grinned and gave the magnate a thumbs-up salute. 'All right, mate!' Agnelli, said Nottage, was captivated. The Italian would later come up with one of the most famous and appropriate descriptions of Gazza, referring to him as 'the dog of war with the face of a child'. When David Platt signed for Juventus, Agnelli would often ask him about Gazza.

The Germans were favourites, which, after that 'bye' in the quarter-finals, probably suited England. Robson recalled talking to Gascoigne before that semi-final, emphasising the importance of neutralising Lothar Matthaus, arguably the best sweeper in the world at that time. 'No problem, boss,' said Gascoigne. 'Just leave it to me.' And, as Robson admitted, Gascoigne was better than Matthaus that night. He won his own personal battle just as, with the blithe confidence of a cocky adolescent, he had assured his manager he would.

This cockiness has often been mistaken for immaturity, but the video evidence of Gascoigne's warm-up that night suggests otherwise. In the pre-match kickabout he looks urgent, fidgety even. There's a sense in which he seems sure of his right to be in that stadium in that World Cup semi-final (and remember, he'd only just turned 23), but at the same time he looks as if he's aware of his own tendency to lose control. It's almost as if he's telling himself not to screw this one up, not to do what he'd done in that Under-21 game against West Germany when his pointless aggression had forced Sexton to take him off at half-time. Except that Gazza seldom looks back that far, so maybe he was just reminding himself he was already on a booking.

The German coach Franz Beckenbauer has always maintained that he'd rather have played England in Turin than Cameroon. As Platt had said, the African side's very unpredictability made more established sides nervous, and it was hard to construct a game plan to defeat them. Beckenbauer thought he knew all about the English. In one of his memoirs, entitled, with simple immodesty, *Me*, he wrote:

> With the British, you know what you're going to get. They have remained true to their style for decades now: fast, powerful, straight ahead, strong in the air. It is honest football, they rely on their strengths, and these are not rooted in technical perfection. Also, the English are unsuited for calls for an ambulance and life-saving measures. It cannot be that their pain threshold is so much higher, rather it seems to be that self-pity and attempts to deceive the referee are not in accordance with the way they understand their job. Of the team that reached the semi-final, only Paul Gascoigne was unpredictable.

He did, however, admit that 'England are hard to beat, they never give up'.

This rather patronising assessment does not quite square with the reality of the game on 4 July, the night after which Beckenbauer turned to Robson and said, gracefully, 'Neither side deserved to lose.' The Germans, as Beckenbauer made clear, thought they knew what to expect: a twenty-minute cavalry charge from the English which would tire them out. If the Germans could withstand that without conceding a goal they believed a place in the final was probably theirs. But the match didn't go according to Beckenbauer's plan. Or anyone else's for that matter.

The England fans easily outsang the Germans before kick-off and England began as the Germans expected, but with more punch. A first corner in the first minute; the ball came out to Gazza who volleyed it, probably just wide, but the German keeper Bodo Illgner got a hand to it. A second corner, then a third . . . Gazza tangled with Brehme, got another shot in, won a free-kick. The fans were singing 'Let's all have a disco'. Gazza began to fulfil his pledge to Robson by nutmegging Matthaus. The cavalry charge was going on for too long and was too fierce for the Germans' comfort. And Gazza was everywhere, making Matthaus look like a club footballer, putting Stuart Pearce through. Then the Germans hit back, the game's momentum reversed and England were glad of the half-time whistle. Gazza and Brehme had tangled again just before the interval, but Gazza ruffled his opponent's hair and smiled.

Matthaus came out for the second half as though stung with shame for the way he'd let Gazza play. The Germans poured forward and got the break – that deflected free-kick. In English minds that goal is in perpetual slow-motion replay, the ball spinning agonisingly slowly off Parker and past Shilton into the net.

But, as Beckenbauer had foreseen, England didn't give up. Gazza came back into it. His free-kick glanced just wide off Pearce. Another jewel of a pass put Waddle through. And then Gary Lineker equalised. He ran back down the pitch, insane with joy, and the fans began to sing 'You'll never walk alone'. It was still level at 90 minutes. During the break, Gazza came over to applaud the fans.

At the restart it was West Germany's turn for the cavalry charge. But when one attack broke down, Gazza struck another brilliant pass to Peter Beardsley, who lost the ball. Gazza stretched out, trying to snatch the ball back from Brehme, missed, and made contact with the player. As Gazza would later describe the event for a video, 'Look at that: one roll, two rolls, three rolls.' The German bench was up en masse, gesticulating indignantly. Robson complained:

> It was nothing more than a mistimed challenge, but the entire German bench leaped to their feet and, I am sure, influenced the referee, José Ramiz Wright, in his decision to give him the caution that would keep Paul out of the final. Gazza was aware of the implications immediately as he pleaded with the referee. He was distraught, and tears began to wash down his face with the cameras showing every moment to a captivated television audience. It was heartbreaking.

Lineker pointed to his temple, as if to indicate to the bench that Gazza had lost the plot. At the time Robson assumed Lineker wanted the manager to talk to him, but, as Robson later said, 'I couldn't talk to him so I shouted at Lineker, "You talk to him, make sure he doesn't do anything daft." ' There was a question mark over whether or not Gazza ought, at this point, to be substituted, but Robson didn't want to disturb the balance of the team and, he said, 'gambled he would not get himself sent off'.

The tackle itself still looks innocuous on replays, an error of judgement rather than an act of evil intent. But the referee later told Nottage that he hadn't booked Gazza for that tackle but for his cheek all night. And Gazza and Brehme had already had a few tussles by then. The referee might have had a point. He might also, having looked at the replay, have decided he needed a better cover story.

The purple mist which Lineker and Robson had seen was beginning to lift. Gazza had been gulping for air, his neck jerking, his face (for once) devoid of any emotion as if he didn't know where he was. Then you could see him, on camera, shouting for the ball. He was back in the game, although, Tony Dorigo noted, he was still liable to burst into tears when, for example, he tried to tackle Matthaus and the sweeper just soared straight past him.

The cry of 'There's only one Paul Gascoigne!' filled the stadium. Brehme crunched into Gazza, far harder than the earlier tackle, and got a yellow card too. Gazza simply got up, walked over and shook Brehme's hand, an act of extraordinary magnanimity in the circumstances. As Pete Davies observed, 'Six months ago he'd have hit him and got sent off.' England came back again, had a goal disallowed, and then it came down to penalties.

Robson walked over to the weeping Gazza and tried to console him. In London, the other Robson, his old England skipper Bryan, was pleading, 'They should take the cameras off him.' Gazza was crying primarily for himself, but later the tears seemed to symbolise what had happened to the team. As Ian Hamilton said, 'it was Gazza who'd shown the way, who'd been the first to sense how badly this defeat would hurt'. For Gazza, it was probably a blessing that his room-mate blazed that penalty over the bar. He had, despite his booking and his tears, insisted on putting his name down as the sixth penalty-taker.

Dorigo went over to Gazza in the dressing room afterwards to tell him he'd been magnificent. Gascoigne's eyes were bloodshot, his face bright red and soaked with tears and sweat. All the players sat there stunned, especially Peter Shilton, who knew he'd just had his last shot at the World Cup. Waddle, Robson recalled, 'looked as if he'd had the spirit flattened out of him'.

And then someone, possibly McMahon, began to sing. Gazza didn't react at first, but he soon shook himself out of whatever pit of despair he was in, and joined in. After a while he was even telling jokes. It had hurt, but by the time the third-place play-off was played in Bari, three days later, the suspended Gazza was, with Terry Butcher, leading the crowd in a mini-Mexican wave.

If you talk to Robson today about that semi-final, he will probably mention the shot from Waddle which came back off the post in extra time, measuring the distance the ball was from the goal with his hands, as if to say 'we were that close', that close to winning the semi-final and the World Cup. There were so many reasons for the nation to feel both proud and desperately unlucky, and both those reactions seemed to be contained in Gascoigne's tears. As Hamilton observed, the childlike innocence of Gazza's tears struck a chord; the less-than-childlike Stuart Pearce cried later, but, maybe because the whole nation was grieving by then, nobody really noticed. It was Gazza's tear ducts which, finally, sold football to the watching millions. That balmy July night in Turin the idea that football was indeed 'the beautiful game' didn't seem so absurd.

But putting the tears to one side, Gascoigne's performance in that semi-final (and, indeed, for the whole of the tournament, with the exception of that first half against Cameroon) was immense. Here, at last, England had a genuinely world-class midfielder in the way that Lineker was a genuinely world-class striker. And, as Hamilton said, it was the fact that he dared to be world-class, that he dared to try it on as if opponents like Gullit, Matthaus and Scifo were just kids he was playing against in a backstreet game in Gateshead, that endeared him to the nation.

Looking back, his team-mate Terry Butcher said, 'That tournament showed that Paul Gascoigne was one of the greatest footballers England has ever produced. England could do with someone half as gifted as him in midfield now.' Parker added his verdict: 'He was the player of the 1990s. If you asked a hundred people the same question they would all have him in their top five without a doubt, or they know nothing about football.' Robson's coach in Italia 90, Don Howe, said simply, 'He was just one of the best midfielders in the tournament.' Robson himself said after the tournament that 'Gascoigne came out of that as the best young player in the world.'

We had heard this kind of stuff about English players before, and often it turned out to be self-deluding hype. What was different about Gazza was that these views were being reflected, these words were being echoed, by other, less patriotic, judges. Soon after the tournament was over, one of Agnelli's most trusted executives, Luca di Montezemolo (who became vice-president of Juventus), invited the *Daily Mail*'s Jeff Powell and Jane Nottage to lunch to ask Powell's opinion about David Platt, Des Walker and Gazza (all of these players would subsequently move to Italy). The Napoli coach, Alberto Bigon, said publicly, 'Gascoigne may be the only player who can replace Diego Maradona.' That said, Gazza still missed out on selection for the team of the tournament, and more cautious pundits, like Powell in the *Daily Mail*, were hedging their bets a bit, predicting that with maturity (that word again) he could become one of the 'truly great' England players.

Back home, over 200,000 fans greeted the squad at Luton Airport. Gazza, who had shown his feminine side in Turin, turned up with a feminine front – a huge pair of plastic breasts – and a fake beer belly. With a grin that seemed uncomfortably close to a leer, he seemed, as Hamilton said, to be convinced he had pulled off a 'stylish comic coup'. Was this Gazza proving that, as he'd said during the tournament, 'I just want to be mesel'? Or was this reading too much into it? Was it just another of his pranks (like spiking Bobby Robson's orange juice or booking sun-beds for black team-mates) to be greeted with a grin or a groan, depending on your sense of humour?

Gazza was back, although he was, in a foretaste of what was to come, hiding from the crowds in his dad's Dormobile. They slipped away up to Dunston, accompanied (another harbinger) by the *Mail on Sunday*, who had exclusive rights to his homecoming in the northeast. They had paid a fortune for a piece in which the best line was Gazza's 'I'm gagging for a pint.' The journalist tried to dress it all up by alluding to Thomas Hardy's *Return of the Native*. It was thin stuff, but it made the front page. But then everything Gazza did would make the front pages from now on.

The honeymoon with fame lasted days, not weeks. By 12 July, just eight days after that semi-final, Gazza met with his lawyer Stein, accountant Lazarus and Chris Waddle, who was represented by the same management team. Gazza seemed, so Stein said in Waddle's memoirs, 'a somewhat confused young man'. His mate tried to give him some helpful advice: 'Enjoy it while it lasts.' But looking back later, Waddle said, 'Only I didn't realise then exactly what was going to happen, although I'm not sure what Paul could have done to stop it. I don't think I could have coped the way he did and I've never been surprised when things became too much for him.'

Henry Winter, football writer for the *Daily Telegraph*, said, 'I remember seeing him at QPR a couple of games after Italia 90 and he was treated like a pop star. I'd never seen anything like it.' The only thing which remotely resembled it was the season in the late 1960s when George Best became the fifth Beatle. But the media scrutiny had become so much more intense in the twenty years or so since Best's heyday. Gazza's long-time girlfriend Gail Pringle lost him, according to the headline on her exclusive story, to the world. His life, she said, had become like living in a goldfish bowl, which was almost accurate. To the player himself, it probably felt like being on the wrong end of a microscope with the rest of the world on the other end staring down at you.

This is not to say Gazza was a purely innocent victim in all this. He and his advisers were happy to turn Gazzamania to his financial advantage, but the phenomenon soon span out of control and the player began to feel the pressure. He talked longingly of 'doing a runner', admitted he feared the pressure could only get worse, and probably privately agreed with Kevin Keegan, who said, 'He's a breath of fresh air for football but in ten years' time he could either be on skid row or top of the pile.' Nottage reckoned that it was over this summer that Gazza began to try to blank out the pressure with alcohol, drowning his sorrows in a quiet pub.

On the first day of September, Gazza turned up for Spurs' game against Arsenal and admitted he was tired. His club manager, Venables, then decided limits would have to be set on the player's off-the-pitch activities. On the Monday evening, Gazza appeared on *Wogan* and let it be known that, after 57 days, Gazzamania was officially over.

By then, though, it was already out of his control.

6. . . . TO ZERO (AND BACK): GAZZA FOR ENGLAND 1990–96

The boy was in a state, and I was concerned about his health.
Graham Taylor

By October, when England played their first competitive game since the World Cup, a European Championship qualifier against Poland at Wembley, Gazza's mate Waddle had been consigned to the subs bench and Shilton had been replaced in goal by Chris Woods, but the Italia 90 team had not yet been turned into a footballing diaspora by the new incumbent, Graham Taylor. Gascoigne lingered behind in the dressing room and came out to tumultuous applause from the fans. After the game, which England won 2–0, it became apparent that Taylor might not be as impressed by Gazza as the crowd had been. England had, he said, played with ten men against the Poles. The missing man, the press quickly decided, was Gascoigne, who hadn't made much of an impact on the game. Still, fingering a player in such a way seemed counter-productive, if not cruel (it was not yet apparent that this was to become one of Taylor's most familiar gambits as England manager; Gary Lineker and Carlton Palmer would later be singled out in such a fashion).

Taylor, however, wasn't alone in harbouring such doubts. The next month, three days before England were due to play the Republic of Ireland in another European Championship qualifier, *The Times*' Stuart Jones asked the question: 'What should Graham Taylor do with Gazza?' This was, as Hamilton remarked, not a question anyone would sensibly have raised three months before. Jones' report of one of Gascoigne's displays described it as a 'private excursion'. He now stood accused of failing to feed Lineker, just as, a few seasons back, he had failed to supply Mirandinha. It all seemed ludicrous proof, if it was proof of anything, of the extraordinary fickleness of the media.

Although a growing number of people were agreeing with some of Jones' criticisms, it still came as something of a bombshell when Gascoigne was dropped for the Republic of Ireland match. Taylor's 'official' explanation had some merit: this would not be Gazza's kind of game, he said. Fair enough. Even Robson had admitted that Gazza had not been in his natural element against the same opposition in the group stages of Italia 90. But then why replace Gazza not with a tough-tackling, box-to-box midfielder but with Gordon Cowans, a player past his best who seemed to possess some of Gazza's delicacy but without much of his bite? Taylor, helpfully, tried to explain:

> I would find it very hard to believe that the things that are written about Paul don't affect a boy of 23. Because he is such a gifted footballer, it has to be of concern to me as England manager, but it is not something I can control. It was not a question against the Republic of playing Cowans instead of Gascoigne, it was a question of the team. You can talk about the flaws you may believe are in his character, but I won't. Whatever I think has to be left to me and the player to discuss privately. Throughout my career, when I have had something of a private nature to discuss, it has remained private between the player and me.

It was an answer of the type which raises more questions than it resolves. What flaws? What, if anything, had Taylor said to Gascoigne in private? Jane Nottage, whose book is consistently sympathetic to Taylor's difficulties in managing the player she worked for, wrote: 'Gascoigne was in no state to go out on the pitch and play. Graham took one look at him and realised he couldn't manage it. His eyes were darting about nervously and he was incapable of stringing a sentence together or concentrating on what was said to him. In Graham's opinion, he was simply unable to last 90 minutes.' To Nottage, Taylor seemed to be protecting Gascoigne, which is probably how he saw it too. Unfortunately, the new England manager's loquacious-ness had simply fuelled the very speculation he had hoped to damp down. If Gazza was in such a state that he couldn't string a sentence together, how come his club manager hadn't noticed? (There is another possible explanation for the player's omission: there were ru-mours that the player had received death threats.)

England drew 1–1 in Dublin, neither a good nor a bad result. For Gazzamaniacs, though, there was a disquieting sense that a point of no return had been passed. Gascoigne duly returned in the new year for England's friendly against Cameroon on 6 February, but was substituted. It didn't seem particularly sinister; he was carrying an injury at the time and his appearances for his club had, by then, been largely restricted to the FA Cup. But another 21 internationals would pass by before Gascoigne donned an England shirt again. Owing in large part to the damaged cruciate ligament suffered in the 1991 FA Cup final and subsequent injuries, Gazza appeared in a less-than-grand total of 11 (out of a possible 38) games under Graham Taylor.

More than the referee in Rotterdam, Gazza's unavaila-bility was probably Taylor's biggest slice of ill luck as England boss. For all his misgivings about Gazza's 'flaws', he had hoped to build a team around him, and in the opinion of Patrick Barclay doesn't quite get the credit he deserves for making good use of the player.

> I think Graham Taylor was the only England manager who really understood where to play him. He usually tried to play him up front, just behind the front two. His thinking was to keep Gazza as far away as possible from the defence. And if he was up that end of the pitch, he couldn't be distracting the back four, chatting to them and demanding the ball in all sorts of situations. That has always been one of Gazza's flaws, that he tries to play too much of his football in the wrong part of the pitch.

In mid-August 1992 Taylor flew out to Rome to meet Gazza and to see if Lazio would release him for a forthcoming friendly against Spain in Santander. In the end, he found himself, Nottage said, telling the club that the player had strained a thigh muscle in training. But Taylor left Rome satisfied that he'd begun to build a relationship with the player around whom he still hoped to build the team which would qualify for USA 94.

Gazza did join the England team in Spain to 're-acclimatise' himself, and made all the right noises in an impromptu press conference. The leg was fine, 'except that the right leg doesn't bend as far as the left. It stretches a certain muscle in your leg and that muscle has been very hard lately. Every time I kick a ball I split the thigh. I can run, I can do everything, but I'm not kicking the ball with my right leg at the moment. All I know is that I want to give everything I have for England again.' When he'd been 'gated' he'd tried to distract himself by watching old England videos, but he just 'upset mesel'. Watching David Platt's winner against

Belgium, he said, 'just made it worse. I've just missed it all: English voices, the banter, the jokes. Yes, I have been lonely.' The hack pack left impressed by his fitness, his charisma (which after the European Championship that summer – drew two, lost one, on the plane home – England seemed to need more than ever) and his 'maturity'. His presence, however, didn't give the England team quite the lift Taylor had hoped: the result, in tabloid terms, was Spanish 1 Onions 0.

Taylor made another flying visit to Italy a few weeks later to watch Gazza inspire Lazio to a 5–2 victory over Parma. Gazza came off after 67 minutes to a standing ovation, and Taylor quickly reassured him that he would definitely be in his next England team. He was true to his word, and Gascoigne made his England comeback at Wembley in a World Cup qualifier against Norway on 14 October.

News of his return added 30,000 to the gate. Post-turnips and swedes, the fans and the press needed cheering up. Gazza was encouraged in the *Mirror* to GO GET 'EM, but for much of the first half he didn't manage to go get anything as high and inaccurate passes flew over him to the front men. He was probably under strict orders to stay just behind the front two and not go back into his own half, a ploy which might have worked had the team's passing been better. Frustrated, he got booked for elbowing a Norwegian in the face. There was a widespread assumption that he would be taken off at half-time, but he wasn't, and for ten minutes in the second half he reminded everyone why Taylor was right to try to build a team around him.

Stuart Pearce was lining up a free-kick and about to take it when Gazza reminded the referee that the offence had taken place five yards further forward. The ball was moved, and Pearce hit a screamer which Platt got on to the end of to put England 1–0 up. Soon afterwards, Gazza struck a low in-swinger of a corner which Alan Shearer should have scored from. By the 76th minute, when the Norwegians equalised with a long-range shot, Gazza looked spent. Still, it was a promising return, although he didn't quite justify the post-match hype about Gazza rolling back the years.

Gascoigne's sister Anna got married the Saturday before England's second World Cup qualifying match, against Turkey on 18 November. Taylor rearranged the England training schedule so that Gazza, who was due to be best man, could attend. Gazza was told to be back at training the next morning, and Lawrie McMenemy was sent along to keep an eye on him. Taylor drove Gascoigne from Lilleshall to Burnham Beeches so he could have a chat with his player before he went off with Sheryl to Newcastle. While they were waiting for Sheryl, Gazza asked Taylor if he could have a brandy. Taylor, thinking it would be the friendly thing to do, said yes, and insisted that he'd have one too. Five brandies later, Taylor could hardly stand. 'I'm just not used to drinking that much on an empty stomach in that short space of time,' he explained. He staggered back to the hotel, considerably the worse for his bonding exercise, and, as Sheryl announced she wasn't going to the wedding, Gazza and McMenemy set off together, with the player's Italian security guard, Gianni Zeqireya, in tow. Gazza behaved himself all day, apart from spiking his body-guard's drinks.

Four days later Gazza excelled against inferior oppo-sition, scoring twice and making a third as England won 4–0. He bossed the midfield for the whole match, helped partly by the Turks' habit of retreating en masse when he got the ball. Afterwards, Lee Dixon said that just having Gazza in the team had given England a lift.

Gazza had almost missed the game with flu and been told to wrap up; with a hint of his old ebullience, he'd turned up at training wearing fourteen shirts.

Taylor, delighted, spoke of the 'warm feeling' in the dressing room. But he did not stop there. On the subject of Gazza, he said, rather mysteriously, 'Please God don't let anything go wrong for this lad.' Probed a bit further, Taylor said, 'This fellow has got something about him which, if we're not careful, can still bring him down. You're on edge all the time with him. He's probably at his most vulnerable now he's back playing. He has time to think about other things and it could be that people may suggest he get involved in all sorts of things.' The press then asked the obvious question: what kind of things? Taylor replied, as if speaking in some kind of code, 'He enjoys life to the full and might get sidetracked.' It's possible that at this point Taylor was thinking of the brandy-fuelled bonding session. But his answer gave the press the excuse they needed to ask the blindingly obvious question: so, Graham, why did you leave him out against Ireland then? Taylor went a little further than his previous statement: 'It was my first experience of seeing somebody who looked glazed at times. The reasons to drop him were not tactical. There were certain incidents before the game. The boy was in a state, and I was concerned about his health.' It sounded like the kind of thing which a couple of years back Taylor had suggested should remain private. Some football writers wondered if the manager was feeling that whatever he'd said in private was not having an effect.

San Marino at Wembley in February 1993 looked like being another Turkey shoot, but four of England's six goals came late in the game. John Barnes was booed every time he touched the ball, although there was a theory, as Hamilton pointed out, that Barnes was getting the boos the crowd really wanted to direct at Gascoigne, who looked tense, petulant and slow. Taylor said that Gazza was not himself, a statement few could disagree with. On the basis of that performance, it looked as if someone had knocked him on the head and told him he was Carlton Palmer.

Taylor's post-match psychoanalysis was that Gazza was 'having a struggle with himself. In his mind he had won the battle to prove us all wrong and get back on the pitch.' There was more than a grain of truth in this; Venables would always say the player was better with a specific short-term goal in mind. 'Since Turkey his fitness has slipped away.' At this rate, 'Crikey, we may be able to get fifteen minutes with him.' Asked if Lazio were to blame (the *Sun* had started its 'Gazza Come Home' campaign) he suggested instead that Gazza 'seems unhappy with himself and within himself'. And when he was unhappy, the manager added, he ate too much of the wrong kind of food.

Indeed, the week leading up to that San Marino game had been another turbulent week for the 'private' Gazza. His girlfriend's visit to Rome the week before had ended in yet another fight with photographers. He had also played four games in eleven days. Taylor probably ought to have taken him off after 60 minutes, as his coach Zoff was doing at Lazio, but he left him on right up to the final whistle.

After the game, Taylor rang Nottage to talk to her about Gascoigne. He started off saying almost the very same thing Bobby Robson had said about him before the World Cup: 'Sometimes you talk to Gascoigne and you don't know if he's taking it in or not. Sometimes you wonder if he cares what you're saying.' According to Nottage's account, Taylor was saddened by what was happening to Gascoigne and worried for the player and for the team. 'Last August/September he had been fighting to get fit . . . now he seemed uninterested and flabby and it seemed to be down to the booze. In the days leading up to the match, he was drinking a lot of brandy. I really shouldn't have played him at all, but it's difficult to drop Gascoigne quietly.' Nottage asked him why he thought Gazza was drinking. 'The sad thing is, I think he does it because he can't stop.' He added, 'I can't carry Gascoigne, and if I drop him, I'll have to say why. I feel for the lad, but I can't do anything. I have a World Cup to qualify for.'

This conversation, as reported by Nottage, does at least put Taylor's later public remarks into context. He must have felt he'd done all he could behind the scenes. He may also have been preparing press and public for that controversial moment when he'd have to drop him. Press and public, of course, had little inkling of this at the time, Lawrie McMenemy trying to steer the media's analysis of Gazza's problems back to football, saying, 'It comes from the frustration of a person of such great natural ability who is wondering why he is unable to produce it such as he would like.' The tabloids had their answer: blame the Italians. They were, in the *Sun*'s words, letting one of the greatest talents in the game 'evaporate like the fading flares of a half-spent Roman candle'.

But Lazio could hardly be blamed for the ease with which, in Izmir at the end of March, the Turks marked him out of the game. Luckily he scored with a looping header (England won 2–0), which postponed another burst of post-match psychoanalysis from the boss. But if he was largely invisible against the Turks, how would he fare against the Dutch at Wembley in four weeks' time?

The omens were not good when he pulled up for Lazio with what looked like a knee injury. Fortunately, it was only a thigh strain. Ruud Gullit then gave Gazza some free advice the day before the game, telling him to realise that he had to play a different game, accept the limitations placed upon his game by the knee injury and adapt accordingly. Gazza may have felt the Dutchman's words gave him something to prove; certainly he (and England) played as good a half as he had ever played under Taylor. Had England gone in at half-time 2–0 up, they might have won. And had Wouters not smacked Gazza in the cheek, they might still have clung on to a 2–1 win. The 2–2 draw and the accompanying dropped points meant that England now could not lose on their May/June away trip to Poland and Norway.

On 1 May Gazza went into hospital for an operation 'to strengthen a depressed fracture of the cheekbone', which it was thought would put him out of action for three weeks. The game in Poland was four weeks away, and he made it, although he had to take his 'Phantom of the Opera' face mask with him. But in Katowice it was clear something was very wrong, not just with Gazza but with the team.

Tony Adams said that Carlton Palmer's pre-match motivational techniques left something to be desired. Instead of rousing his own lads, he went up to the Poles and insulted them. Whatever Palmer had said to them seemed to do the trick – for the Poles. They were 1–0 up at half-time and should have had the game sewn up, but a late strike by Ian Wright rescued an undeserved point for England. It was not a disaster, but it threatened to become one because of Taylor's post-match reaction. He publicly lambasted his players for running around like 'headless chickens', Gazza earmarked as the most headless of them all. He also dismissed Gazza's talk of how hard he was training in Italy, saying it was also a matter of 'how you feed and refuel yourself between training sessions. This is something Paul has to come to terms with.'

Taylor's talk sparked a refuel crisis. The media was soon focusing on binge eating and booze as the refuelling techniques Taylor had been alluding to. It was a remarkable thing to say to the press rather than to the player himself, but with knowledge of that conversation with Nottage it's easy to see this, as Barclay said, 'as a way of firing a warning shot across the player's bow, trying to warn him of the dangers ahead'.

When the team flew on to Oslo for their second away match in four days, Taylor hosted a post-mortem on the Poland match, thereby torpedoing team morale days before the vital fixture. Adams reckoned this session probably destroyed Chris Woods' confidence. He felt that there was already too much negativity about the squad, saying the only person with the squad who sounded optimistic was Trevor Brooking, who said he'd been in teams which had been in far worse positions and still qualified.

Taylor compounded matters by changing his tactics. His innovations in this area had already come under some unwelcome scrutiny. Specifically, his varying approaches to the kick-off. He once told Crystal Palace's Andy Gray that he was to kick the ball as far upfield as he could and to make sure it went out for a throw-in. That way, England would quickly be close to the opposition's goal. Gray couldn't believe this; most of the other players were dismayed. Now he'd decided on a new approach to this pivotal issue: for the Norway match, he told Gazza it was his job to dribble the ball upfield as far as he could go. The ploy would work, Taylor thought, because the Norwegians would be expecting them to kick it into touch. Alas, David Seaman remarked, 'somehow the Norwegians found out about our plans and had four or five players waiting for Gazza. It was embarrassing schoolboy stuff straight out of the *Roy of the Rovers* book of big-match tactics.'

If Taylor's switch on the kick-off was stupid, his change in the team's formation, with only one day to try it out in training, turned out to be suicidal. Gazza was to play behind the front two of Les Ferdinand and Teddy Sheringham, Carlton Palmer and David Platt would be in central midfield, and the three centre-halves (Gary Pallister, Tony Adams and Des Walker) would be the last line of defence with the full-backs (Lee Dixon and Lee Sharpe) pushing forward to help out in midfield. It was the formation which had taken Taylor to his finest hour as club manager, the season Villa finished second in the championship.

The players were worried enough just talking through the formation at the hotel that evening. On the day, the full-backs stayed back, picking the ball up from the keeper, and the centre-halves got stuck in the middle. Platt said the team ended up defending so deep that they were inviting the long ball to Jostein Flo, the very thing the system had been designed to prevent. It was a terrible performance. Although Platt insisted the players should shoulder all the blame, it was and is hard to see how Taylor thought such a change was going to work with so little rehearsal (and, to be frank, with such uneven quality running through the team).

Having been sidelined through injury for the turnips and swedes fiasco in 1992, Gazza had returned to a side whose performance was greeted as 'Norse manure' by one tabloid. His performance stank almost as badly as that of his team-mates. He slipped back into Rome admitting, 'I felt sorry for him [Taylor], we all let him down.' Taylor also felt let down (the Oslo encounter was the game before which Taylor is alleged to have caught Gazza trying to sweat off weight in the shower), according to Nottage, as he discussed, again, the pitfalls of dropping the player. But Gazza felt obliged to remind the press, in a remark which showed how bad morale had become, that he couldn't do things all on his own. Point made, he said he was looking forward to a summer of beer and pizza.

In September England dragged themselves back into the race with a 3–0 stuffing of Poland at Wembley, with Gazza back to something like his best. And, alas, his worst. He got booked, which ruled him out of the winner-takes-all tie in Rotterdam, scheduled for 13 October. Gazza blamed the Poles for needling him, Robson and Howe's advice about not retaliating now forgotten. Once booked (and suspended), he got the elbow out, kicked the ball at a prone Polish player and generally did enough to get himself sent off. But he did score the best goal of the game.

Rotterdam, of course, ended Taylor's unlucky reign as England manager, although he didn't go until after San Marino had embarrassed us in Bologna by scoring seconds after the kick-off. Another referee in Rotterdam and Taylor might have survived, although Teddy Sheringham, a Venables loyalist, said that would have been a disaster for English football.

Gazza, inadvertently or otherwise, may have done as much as anyone to bring him down. The relationship was not, perhaps, as bad as you might suspect, judging from the media coverage of Taylor's remarks. Alan Smith thought that 'Gazza liked Graham Taylor. They got on.' Indeed, Stuart Pearce recalled the night, some time in 1992, when the squad went to watch the musical *Buddy*: 'I have memories, or is it nightmares, of Graham Taylor, with his shirt open to the waist, singing a duet with Paul Gascoigne of "Singing in the Rain" while some of the players poured water over their heads.' (Taylor obviously liked the musical. After Holland had fought back to 2–2 at Wembley in April 1993, he turned up at the press conference the next day singing 'Oh, misery, misery'.)

But what Gazza made of some of Taylor's tactics, including his innovative approach to the kick-off, can easily be imagined. It's probably fairest to say that, despite some sincere effort on both sides (especially on Taylor's), the relationship between player and manager never really clicked. Taylor was never quite the father figure Robson and Venables, as his club manager, had been.

Pearce reckoned that Taylor's big mistake with Gascoigne was that he tried to change his life. That's possible. But the real problem Taylor had to wrestle with was that, after the 1992 European Championship and what some saw as his vindictive substitution of Gary Lineker, he did not have the support from press or public he needed to confront the Gascoigne issue. A manager whose face had recently been superimposed on to a turnip on the back page of a national newspaper was not really in a position to take on England's most popular footballer without a damn good reason, and ultimately he knew that he could only justify such a decision by spelling out the details as he saw them. But, as he said once, 'If I told you everything about Gascoigne all hell would break loose.'

Maybe if he had dropped Gazza, the player might have taken heed. Taylor toyed with the idea but ended up sending out coded messages at post-match press conferences. But Gazza was often immersed in his problems with Sheryl, and, as another England manager would later discover, if that relationship wasn't working, he was a lot less likely to be functioning as a footballer.

Terry Venables' appointment as Taylor's successor must have been greeted with a certain amount of relief by Gascoigne. Here, at least, was a manager who had understood how to handle him in the past. And Venables, with his roguish charm, was hardly likely to start delivering lectures in public about how players should behave. The new England boss flew out to Italy in February 1994 to watch Gascoigne and Lazio beat Cagliari 4–0. Gazza played with controlled aggression that day and scored with a banana kick in the last minute. The celebration was even more spectacular than the goal: he swung like Tarzan from the Cagliari crossbar, kicked the Lazio bench (in fun, you understand) and struck what Ian Hamilton described as a 'ludicrous Chris Eubank statue pose'. The next day, master and pupil relaunched their mutual admiration society at a press conference. Venables praised Gazza's maturity; Gazza voiced his relief when he said that with Taylor 'I always felt I had something to prove'.

It sounded too good to be true, and it was: after leaving the Rome derby with cracked ribs, he surprised his club at the beginning of March by playing for England against Denmark. Upon his return he was thrown out of training for not trying, which gave rise to a 'nervous fit' from the player. Further trouble prompted the club chairman, Sergio Cragnotti, to give him a public telling-off, and then he fractured his shin in a five-a-side game against the club juniors.

This latest folly kept him out of contention for England until the spring of 1995, although Venables made sure he was invited to training camps. He was also on hand at the beginning of April to watch Gazza's second comeback for Lazio against Reggiana.

Sitting in the stands, Venables decided: 'He certainly hasn't lost his nerve. Although he wasn't trying to get stuck in himself, he put himself into positions where he could have been hit; he wasn't holding back and trying to protect himself.' He was, Venables heard, working out three times a day and had lost three stone. There were even rumours, which Venables couldn't confirm, that Jimmy Five Bellies hadn't got his usual complement of bellies.

Venables said later that he'd have been interested to see how Gazza would have coped as a fit player in Serie A for another season. But it wasn't to be. After a couple of less impressive performances, when his 'second dad' wasn't watching, it became clear that the Italian club (and new coach Zdenek Zeman) had lost their patience with, and faith in, Gascoigne. This was good for Rangers, Venables and Gascoigne himself.

When the move to Rangers was being discussed, *The Times* published a profile of Gazza which Venables read with interest and agreed with. The profile concluded: 'Gazza's football says more about him than any amount of psychoanalysis. The joy, the freedom, the exuberance, the craziness, the crudity. It is all right there on the field . . . whatever else has changed in his life Gascoigne's love of football has not. He will always play expecting to see coats on the ground instead of goalposts.' The piece reminded Venables of Ron Greenwood's old comment, that 'the ideal player would be an extrovert on the pitch and an introvert off it'. Gazza half-fits that bill.

Venables deserves much of the credit for the way Gazza's international career subsequently revived under him. As the *Daily Telegraph*'s Henry Winter noted, 'Terry knew how to bring out the best in him. It was under him that Gascoigne really flourished.' Stuart Pearce said that, whereas with Taylor Gazza felt restrained, Venables' approach was to 'let him have his head and then rein him in'. But his job was made much easier by other circumstances in Gascoigne's life. For a start, the player had a new, fresh challenge at club level ahead of him. Scotland was also a lot nearer to Hertfordshire (and Sheryl) than Rome, and Gascoigne had hopes that she would move the family up to Scotland to be with him. So he was happier all round and more motivated, to a degree unseen since his comeback from that first knee injury.

Moreover, Venables' backroom staff was stacked with people with whom Gascoigne felt at home: Bryan Robson was the de facto number two and Don Howe came back in as coach. Howe reflected on Gazza's commitment at this time: 'When Venables took over Gascoigne was injured but he would invite him along anyway and he'd train with David Butler, who used to work with injured players. Christ, he used to work, and he would never, ever grumble, he would just get on with it. He had a fantastic attitude, he really did. He almost got too fit – he was so fit one time he pulled his shirt up and . . . his stomach was like a wash-board, it really was. When he put his mind to it he had incredible dedication.' His former Italia 90 team-mate John Barnes watched Gazza in training and, like Howe, marvelled:

Gazza is the hardest trainer I have ever seen. His problem is that he does not understand the concept of pacing himself, whether in a match or in training. Gazza gives everything from the start; he began every match at Italia 90 at whirlwind pace and was fit and young enough to maintain it. Training under Terry, he still started at lung-busting speed despite the fact that he was older and had suffered all these injuries. In practice matches, the day before a game, I would tell him: 'Stop making these runs, otherwise you'll be knackered within fifteen minutes of this match let alone for tomorrow.'

He added that Gazza ran 'more in an hour than many do in the entire match . . . When we were holed up in an England hotel together, I often felt like giving Gazza some advice but he never sought it and wouldn't have heeded it anyway. Gazza wants to listen, learn and change his life but finds it difficult to do.'

Gascoigne's reintroduction to the England team was gentle. During the Umbro Cup in June 1995 he was a bit player, a substitute to be used, almost as Bobby Robson had envisaged back in 1989, when a game needed changing. He came on 22 minutes from time against Japan, who England just beat 2–1 (when Venables got home, his wife Yvette, whose post-match remarks were normally confined to 'Tough luck' or 'Well done', said, 'Why didn't you put Gazza on earlier?'). Against Sweden five days later, in a 3–3 draw, he took the free-kick from which David Platt scored and was 'absolutely gutted' to discover that he'd broken Magnus Erlingmark's nose with his elbow.

In November Gazza was part of the England team which beat a second-string Swiss side 3–1 at Wembley. He played well enough, but Venables did tell Peter Beardsley to warm up at one point. Asked why later, he said, 'Well, it was to give Gazza a warning that I wanted him to stay in midfield and just concentrate on what he was supposed to be doing. He is getting better, but he needs to be more disciplined and not complicate matters.'

Things took a slight turn for the worse, as far as Gazza's international future was concerned, when Venables revealed in January 1996 that he would not be staying on as England manager after Euro 96. He seemed uncertain of the strength of support he had at the FA, and knew he'd soon be spending too much time in various courts to focus on the England job. When he offered his resignation the FA accepted with what to most of his players seemed indecent haste. Gazza made a heartfelt public plea for Venables to stay on, but, although most of the players (and most of the public) agreed with him, the decision had been made.

All Gazza had to focus on now was making sure of a place in Venables' Euro 96 squad – which essentially meant avoiding injury for five months. He did more than that, and his exceptional form meant that no one was surprised when he was named in the squad Venables took on a pre-tournament tour of China and Hong Kong. The idea, ironically enough in the light of what happened on the tour, was to get the players away from the pressure-cooker atmosphere of a nation preparing to host its first major football tournament since 1966, and to, er, keep out of the headlines.

Gazza had been celebrating Rangers' Double the night before the England party were to fly off to the Far East. Pearce recalled:

He hates flying so he topped up on the night's intake before boarding. We were not even off the tarmac at Heathrow when he was asking for a Budweiser. The steward was quite patient with him, finding him a beer, but when Gazza wanted another one he began to get a bit irritated and asked him to hold on. He was standing just ahead of Gazza, looking after the row in front, so Gazza reached forward and to attract his attention patted him on the bum. The steward turned round and punched him straight in the face. A classic right to the side of the head. I was sitting close by with Steve Stone and we just fell about laughing.

Pearce said Gazza's 'crumpled face' and 'quivering lip' made him look just like he had when he cried so memorably in Turin. A couple of Gazza's team-mates began to wind him up, saying things like, 'You're not going to take that from him, are you?' To which a nearly weeping Gazza replied, 'If Jim [Five Bellies] and my dad were here . . .'

There was a stopover in Copenhagen, by which time the captain of the plane was threatening to have Gazza removed. He made this threat in public and Gazza got wound up even further. The captain then repeated the threat, only this time he suggested leaving Gazza on the tarmac in Russia. Pearce noted that at this stage both Gazza's lips were quivering and he was whimpering: 'They're going to put me off in Moscow.' Pearce went on, 'Watching the entire episode unfold was far better than watching any inflight movie.' With no journalists on the flight, Gazza's antics didn't make any headlines. He would not be quite so lucky on the way back.

The football scheduled on the trip was secondary to Venables' main aims of keeping the 'news bastards', to use Gazza's heartfelt phrase, away from the players and of making a bit of money for the FA. All that was overshadowed, though, by Gazza's birthday party. Venables had told the lads they could have one last night out before the serious business started, and Bryan Robson was sent along as a chaperone. Stuart Pearce and Gareth Southgate were among the players who stayed in the hotel, Pearce convincing his team-mate that it was not worth the risk. Steve Stone, Pearce's room-mate, was not to be persuaded, although he escaped lightly

azza clenches his fists in triumph as England squeak through against
ameroon in the 1990 World Cup quarter-finals, a match scout Howard
Vilkinson had assured them would be a bye

Above Gazza, two months after the World Cup and a few weeks after he'd tried to call an end to 'Gazzamania'

Right Gazza points out the trajectory of his free-kick against Arsenal in the 1991 FA Cup semi-final, a kick David Seaman was stupid enough to try and save

bove Gazza had a hand in two of the goals in England's 4 – 1 romp against
olland at Euro 96, arguably the best England victory since a certain 4 – 2

op left Gascoigne's distinctive hands-on approach to the Rome derby
ndeared him to the Lazio faithful

ottom left Gazza and Venners have a laugh; the player described his
entor as his second dad

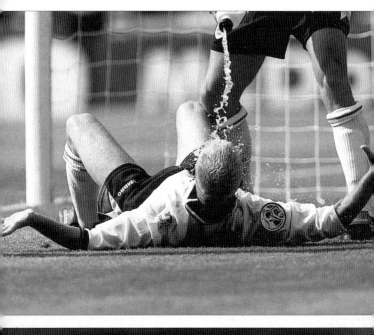

Above Gazza, like Shakespeare's Caesar, liked to be surrounded by fat men, in this instance the contented Jimmy 'Five Bellies' Gardener

Top left Gazza's dentist chair celebration after his wonder goal against Scotland was his revenge on the tabloids that had called him a disgrace after the England party's pre-tour antics

Bottom left Gascoigne exercises his stomach muscles at the Rangers training ground and tries to exorcise the ghost of wasted years at Lazio

Gazza prepares to go on *Stars In Their Eyes*: 'Tonight, Matthew, I'm going to be . . . Ronald McDonald.'

because, as a relatively unknown member of the squad standing to one side when the infamous 'dentist's chair' photograph was taken, he was cropped out of the picture.

According to Sheringham's account, it's clear a good time was had by all, except Bryan Robson, who had his Versace shirt cut to ribbons by the players. The chance to have 'fun with official approval', as Sheringham put it, was too good to miss. The night out at the China Jump Club began to take a more serious turn when the players started drinking Flaming Lamborghini cocktails in honour of Gazza. Robbie Fowler, talking to a girl at the bar, used the immortal phrase 'Do you come here often?' (or so Gazza claimed) to great hilarity. Somebody's shirt got ripped; pretty soon all the players' shirts were in shreds (including Robson's). The players then began joking around with a pair of outsize boxing gloves which were hanging in the bar. Some pictures were taken and, as Sheringham later recalled, 'I suppose the alarm bells should have rung.'

Then somebody noticed the 'dentist's chair'. If you sat in it, two barmen would come over and pour three different bottles of spirits down your neck. It was Sheringham's misfortune to have his picture taken in the chair which made him (Pearce said) 'look more like Ollie Reed than a professional footballer'. The photos soon found their way into the appropriate hands and were plastered all over the tabloids. Gazza had a drink in his hand and his face had that glazed look of which Taylor had spoken a few years back. Perhaps because of that earlier refuelling crisis (and perhaps due to rumours about Gascoigne's own lifestyle), Gazza was singled out as the DISGRACED FOOL in the *Sun* and vilified in the other tabloids.

The England squad seemed split between those (like the participants Les Ferdinand and Tim Flowers) who could see no harm in a lads' night out with the tournament kick-off still a fortnight away and those, like Pearce, who thought 'The players should have known better. It is not asking a lot to keep your heads down for two weeks. After the tournament is the time to go berserk and have a drink and celebrate.'

Venables resisted calls to sling Gazza out on his earring, even when disaster struck again on the flight back. Flowers and Sheringham have subsequently maintained an 'I know nothing' stance with regard to this incident worthy of Manuel in *Fawlty Towers*. David Seaman said that a seat tray was broken when a card player sat on it and two small TV screens were cracked when another card player knocked into them (he also pointed out that the inflight card school included Cathay Pacific staff). Pearce clearly knows who did it but in his memoirs doesn't name names.

The truth, innocuous as it sounds, may possibly be found in Dennis Wise's autobiography. On the way out, Gazza's attempts to sedate himself ahead of the flight led to unforeseen consequences. 'Gazza had just had a few drinks to calm his nerves, as many people do. When we were airborne he tried to slide out the television attached to his seat. He pulled it the wrong way and it broke.' Wise and Gazza were both, accidentally, involved in the next bit of damage when they had a bit of trouble trying to pull Gazza's holdall out of the overhead locker. In view of the recent newspaper headlines suggesting that the entire England squad had gone on the rampage, it was obvious that no explanation (no matter how innocent) involving Gazza could be made without running the risk that England's most naturally gifted player would be tried and convicted in the press and forced out of the squad. Adams asked the squad if anyone wanted to own up, nobody volunteered, so they agreed to take the rap together. Venables came up with the concept of 'collective responsibility'. Every player put a sum, probably around £1,000, towards the airline's damages and the matter was closed.

Such was the ferocity of the media onslaught that it created in the squad the very thing Fergie has always tried to foster at Old Trafford: a conviction that it was them against us, or, in this instance, us against the world. The implications of that celebration of Gascoigne's goal against Scotland were clear: it was a gesture of defiance and derision to the rest of the world.

The media might have mattered more if the mood in the squad had been different, but most of the players felt at ease with Venables and confident that if they did make suggestions or remarks no grudges would be held. And Gazza relished working with his old boss. As the *Sunday Times*' Steve Curry pointed out: 'Although his best spell for England was probably Italia 90, Euro 96 showed that he could respond and play well for people he liked, and Terry accentuated his talents. If I had to pick one Gascoigne moment for England, it would be that goal past Colin Hendry against Scotland.'

Gascoigne had some reason to be apprehensive about that clash with the Auld Enemy. As he never tired of telling his team-mates, he wouldn't be able to hold his head up in the Rangers dressing room if England lost. But before that fixture, England had to face the Swiss at Wembley in the tournament opener.

It is fashionable now, partly because of Venables' oblique - semi-retirement, to deconstruct England's achievements in Euro 96. Okay, so they got to the last four, the revisionists' case goes, but England were playing at home, they didn't have to qualify, won only two of the games in open play (and one of those against a Dutch side who weren't speaking to each other) and would never have reached the last four if the linesman hadn't disallowed a perfectly good Spanish goal. The myth of England's success, so the argument goes, is based on one game against a disunited Dutch side and that Gazza goal. And Gazza did nothing else of note in the entire tournament.

There is something in this, of course: England had qualified automatically, the players did get a lift from the 'Football's Coming Home' phenomenon and they did get the rub of the green against the Spanish. But England still, for the second time in six years, only went out of the semi-finals of a major international tournament on penalties to the eventual winners. And Gazza, although he wasn't the fizzing, energetic force of old, gave, as Pearce said, a good hour in all those games in Euro 96. His performances in that campaign repay close scrutiny, if only because they suggest that he probably performed at a higher level for longer than many of us now realise. When most of us recall Gascoigne it is for individual moments of breathtaking brilliance or tragic stupidity, but in the summer of 1996 he gave the lie to pre-tournament tabloid talk that he was 'burned out' as a player.

Against the Swiss, Hoddle reckoned that Gascoigne had a better all-round game than he did against Scotland. Watching the game again, on video, you can get some idea of what Hoddle meant. Early in the first half, he takes three opponents out with one run and then another two with a pass which Teddy Sheringham just fails to get on the end of. Later in the first half there's another flash of brilliance when he hits an instant return pass with the 'wrong' foot (he lets the ball come on to his back foot before hitting a pass which leaves the Swiss defence chasing the play) to put Steve McManaman into space. But, like the team, his performance lost momentum after half-time as the Swiss came back into it.

Then, on 15 June, came Scotland, the goal and the 'dentist's chair' celebration. Just when it all seemed about to go badly wrong against the Scots, when the whole nation could sense that this was a passage of play which could change the course of the team's tournament once and for all (and when, indeed, the England manager was considering replacing him with Steve Stone), it was Gazza who passed the ball to himself over the head of a bewildered Colin Hendry and volleyed into the net.

If you're not Scottish, it's almost impossible to watch that footage without being exhilarated. And the little extras are wonderful to savour: the woman in an England shirt jiggling forward to kiss her boyfriend; Bryan Robson sitting on the bench next to Venables, leaning back to the gaffer with a triumphant smile on his face and saying words to the effect of 'Can you f***ing believe he did that?' And there's something in Robbo's expression which says that he knows how hard it is to do that. In a crucial international. Against the Scots. Minutes after David Seaman had saved a penalty.

Flushed by that success, England destroyed the Dutch three days later, Gascoigne providing an assist in that glorious third goal (Alan Shearer's second), the one England move in recent memory which suggested that the nation which had invented the game really hadn't forgotten how to play it. Less well remembered is the corner struck by Gascoigne from which Sheringham got England's second.

After three games England had scored seven of which Gazza had bagged one and had a hand in two others, and against Spain in the quarter-final on 22 June he came as close as any England player to breaking the deadlock with a fine shot which Antonio Zubizarreta parried to safety. And against Germany it was his corner which was perfectly placed for Tony Adams to flick on and for Shearer to head into the net. And twice in golden-goal time he came very close to putting England in the final. The margin of England's defeat was, ultimately, not Gareth Southgate's nervy penalty but the inches by which Gazza's outstretched foot missed the ball rushing past him.

This time Gazza did get to take a penalty. But later, when the England players were in the dressing room in stunned disbelief that it had happened again, it was the skipper Tony Adams, not Gazza, who broke the silence. He turned to Southgate and said: 'You have to admit it was a sh*t penalty, Gareth.' Southgate burst into laughter and the tension was broken.

For Gazza, Euro 96 was his second coming. The build-up to the tournament had hardly been auspicious: a smack in the face from an air steward, a whiff of scandal in Hong Kong, tabloid insistence that he was 'burned out'. But he had proved them all wrong. Again. As he set off for his post-tournament wedding to Sheryl, for which *Hello!* had paid £150,000 for exclusive rights, he had been securely reinstated as the reigning, undisputed genius of English football.

Yet one anecdote, recounted by Bobby Robson in his autobiography, gives a measure of the concern Gazza still aroused in those who knew him.

Three days after the German game, I went to a dinner party at the Hilton Hotel in London on the night of the final, and I spotted Terry sitting at the bar on his own, with his head bowed. I went up to him and patted him on the back and said, 'Hi'. He was clearly in great distress. Naturally I asked what the matter was. He looked up at me and said, 'Bobby, I have some terrible news for you, something awful has happened.' I knew that he shared my liking of Paul Gascoigne and I put two and two together and came up with five. 'Gascoigne?' I said. Back came Terry's reply: 'No, Bobby Keetch is dead.'

7. THE AGONY: GAZZA FOR ENGLAND 1996–98

If the manager comes to me and says 'Your time's up', I'll say 'Fair enough'. Simple as that.

Paul Gascoigne

There seemed no particular reason why Paul Gascoigne should fear Glenn Hoddle replacing Terry Venables as England manager after Euro 96. True, Venables had indulged Gazza and probably got the best out of him more consistently than any other manager, with the possible exception of Walter Smith, in the player's career, and Gazza had understandably been as out-spoken as any player in the Euro 96 squad about the fact that the players didn't want Venables to resign. But amid the happy glow which surrounded England's performance that summer, the question of Gascoigne's age (he was 29) was ominously raised as a substantive issue for the first time. Raised and almost immediately discarded.

The player himself was honest enough to admit that the only judge he couldn't dazzle with sleight of feet was Father Time. He told the press that August, 'I'm 29. There are all these young lads coming through. It's tough. You've got to keep your fitness up, keep producing the goods, because there are so many kids coming through. Touch wood, I'm involved, but there's a great future for English football.'

But touching wood didn't really seem to come into it, at least as far as Gascoigne's place in the England team was concerned. The Swiss striker Stephane Chapuisat had said, after the drab 1–1 draw during Euro 96,

'When Paul Gascoigne is OK, England are strong. Take Paul Gascoigne out, and England are nothing.' While Gascoigne's team-mates might have disagreed with Chapuisat's verdict, its broad thrust was not one either the fans or the people in the game would have violently opposed. The nation was firmly in the grip of what the *Sunday Times*' Steve Curry would call 'the Gazza complex', the belief that with him England were a better team than without him. Each of the last three England managers had based his team selection on this complex, and although it hadn't always paid off (especially for Graham Taylor), it had succeeded often enough to seem worth persevering.

The new manager also seemed far better placed than any of his predecessors to understand the pressures placed on a creative midfield genius. Hoddle's own inclusion in the England side had been a subject of national debate for most of the 1980s. He had been given an early foretaste of the uncertainty which would mar his international career when, after a striking debut in a European Championship qualifier at Wembley against Bulgaria in November 1979, he was dropped by manager Ron Greenwood who, when asked to explain, replied cryptically, 'Disappointment maketh the man.' So Hoddle knew that what Gascoigne needed above all was reassurance. The last thing he required was to be in and out of the team and to be fobbed off with explanations which sounded as if they had come off the back of an England's Glory matchbox.

Hoddle's post-Venables reconstruction of the England camp was more radical than injuries required, as radical as (if more successful than) Graham Taylor's post-1990 rebuild. But there was no suggestion in any comment made by Hoddle or any of his coaching staff (John Gorman, Peter Taylor, Ray Clemence and Gazza's former mentor Glenn Roeder) that the replacement of Gascoigne had been entertained. Not even one heretical whiff, floated in debate so it could be shot down. Most of Hoddle's staff had their roots at the same north London club as Gascoigne, and the player himself would go on record, before that first vital World Cup qualifier in September, saying, 'I nearly had the chance to play with Glenn Hoddle at Spurs. I'm pleased that his ideas of the game are similar to Terry Venables' and I enjoy the way he wants to play football.' Even if Hoddle had wanted to drop Gascoigne, there was no obvious successor. Players could replace parts of his game, but nobody had his range and unpredictability. Apart from his obvious qualities as a footballer, he was one of the few England players who could change the pace of a match, something England, under Venables, had only just about learned to do.

So when Hoddle announced his first squad as England coach in August 1996, Gascoigne was duly selected, with an assurance from Walter Smith, his manager at Rangers, that 'England can rest assured they'll have him fit and ready for his opening World Cup tie. He won't need a lot of training to get himself back to peak fitness.'

There seemed only two real pretenders to Gascoigne's throne in that first squad: David Beckham and Matt Le Tissier. Venables had, almost against his will, been forced to select Le Tissier for the aborted friendly with the Republic of Ireland at Lansdowne Road in February 1995. There'd been some speculation that Le Tissier would be unable to show off his undoubted skill on a surface scarred by too many rugby matches, but in the event nobody found out how true this assertion was, and Le Tissier spent the next eighteen months in limbo. Hoddle had certainly made his admiration for the

Southampton midfielder clear (he was rumoured to have tried to buy the player when he was managing Chelsea), but he was not widely seen as Gascoigne's natural heir. The tragic flaw in Le Tissier's game, so the consensus went, was that he lacked pace, even compared to a post-cruciate Gascoigne. As for Beckham, he had at that point made just 39 appearances in the Premiership for Manchester United and there was, as yet, no debate about his best natural position. He was on the wing at United, and that, broadly, was where he was expected to play for England – if, indeed, Hoddle picked him in the starting eleven.

Of those more on the periphery, Jamie Redknapp was deemed to offer at least some of the quality of passing which was part of Gascoigne's game. But he didn't have Gazza's eye for goal and he missed that first squad because of injury, the same reason he would miss out on so many occasions to come. Besides, he seemed most at ease as a sweeper, someone to pass the ball to Gascoigne but not to replace him. Furthermore, neither Steve McManaman or Darren Anderton, as attacking midfielders, had Gascoigne's breadth. On the Britannia Airways 740A which flew out to Kishinev, the Moldovan capital, for the World Cup qualifier which was Hoddle's first game in charge, the spine of his team seemed to be David Seaman, Paul Ince, Paul Gascoigne and the new captain, Alan Shearer.

Hoddle's England did an efficient job in Moldova, winning 3–0, Gazza heading the second goal from a move started by Nick Barmby and Ince. The same trio had combined just after half-time to give Shearer the chance to break his duck away from home for England. He spurned it, but went on to score the third. Hoddle seemed satisfied and, just as importantly, so did the press. Ince, not Gascoigne, had acted as the team's heartbeat, but with Incey's wholehearted brand of play, that did not seem ominous for Gazza. He'd played well enough, although subsequently Hoddle would say, 'He was not a hundred per cent fit, but he was worth the gamble because of his ability. We got away with it.'

As England away trips went, it was almost flawless. Unfortunately, Gazza was responsible for the 'almost'. Just 24 hours before the game the England players had watched the Under-21 team; as they'd scampered out of the rain into the covered press box, Gazza had pulled down Ince's shorts, the bare bottom a gift to the Sunday tabloids. Hoddle didn't get too heavy over this, but after the qualifier was won he made it clear that he did not want his England reign to be remembered for such jolly japes. (He had already, quietly, instructed the players with a strict code of conduct and the FA wanted him to take a hard line if there was any repetition of the antics which, somehow, caused thousands of pounds worth of damage in the Club Class cabin of that Cathay Pacific flight before Euro 96.)

For a player who, rightly, found England managers' willingness to speculate about his state of mind somewhat distasteful, Gascoigne surprisingly (and probably unwisely) confided to the press at this time that a Glasgow motorist had wound down the window on his car and threatened to cut Gazza's throat if he celebrated another goal by playing the flute – Gazza's recent gesture during an Old Firm derby which had outraged the city's Catholics. To the press, he admitted, 'The training session didn't go too well that day . . . I was running around and you could see the pap out of my underpants all day.' It was one of the countless times in Gascoigne's life and career when you wanted nothing more than for someone to stand up and shout, 'Too much information!

Too much information!' Harry Harris, in his book *Hoddle's England*, suggested that this was the revelation which first set Hoddle wondering about his star player's mental fitness. But Gascoigne put a more positive spin on such speculation by allowing his name to be used in an emergency appeal by the European Children's Trust to raise £40,000 to fund a local orphanage for 200 children.

Poland were next, at Wembley on 9 October. It was Hoddle's first home game in charge against a side reputed (largely on the evidence of that notorious 1–1 draw at Wembley in October 1973, when Tomaszewski's acrobatics between the sticks denied the England players a trip to West Germany the following summer) to be our bogey team, although the Poles, who had since played England seven times without a single victory, were said to consider us as their bogey team. But hallowed as the Wembley turf undoubtedly was, it didn't seem to be intimidating the opposition as much as it once had. The Germans, Swiss and Spanish had all looked less than overawed for most of their games at Euro 96; before that, in a long series of friendlies, it was possible to spot the point in a game, usually around the 60-minute mark, when the opposition stopped thinking about the hallowed turf and began thinking about turfing into Harrods. In this context, the atmosphere in the run-up to England home games could best be described as a mixture of excitement, anticipation and sheer nervous dread.

Some distraction was provided, inevitably, by Gascoigne, who was the subject of a TV documentary which, equally inevitably, raised the 'R' word with its spotlight on the player's refuelling habits. Hoddle, like Taylor before him, felt obliged to comment: 'He is a married man now with a baby son. He should look at the little child and realise a baby needs looking after. It's special. When you get to 30, so does your body. You have to take care of it. Do things properly. Don't abuse it. And I include drinking in that.' This clear but measured warning was accompanied by a fairly lengthy analysis of Gascoigne's personality and prospects. 'I have spoken to Paul about a lot of things and I get the impression he wants to change his life. There has been a "Grim Reaper" around Paul for too long. Now there is no need for him. Paul can pull back the curtains on a whole new career. When you get to his age, if you have skill, life should get easier, not harder, provided that you look after yourself.' The England manager went on to mention Gordon Strachan and Ray Wilkins as footballers Gazza could emulate, and suggested, 'Maybe it's taken him this far in his career to realise how good he is. He can play on longer than he thinks he can. Go on until he's 35. This World Cup and even another. He is the kind of player who can dominate matches, with knowledge, skill and ability. Gazza should get up every morning and feel ready to take on the world.'

For a man whose command of the English language was described as being almost as good as Franz Beckenbauer's, this was quite some speech. While laying out fairly clearly what Gascoigne had to do, it also offered him what sounded like something halfway between a possibility and a guarantee that if he did play by the rules he had years of international football ahead of him. Few players can have been offered such reassurance by an England manager. Indeed, in the light of this narrative's grotesque denouement, it has been suggested that Hoddle went too far. Such handling has been compared, unfavourably, to the carrot-and-stick approach employed by Walter Smith at Rangers and Everton. But at the time, this was just the kind of reassurance most England fans wanted to hear. Certainly Hoddle had gone as far as he could, in the circumstances, to build up Gascoigne's confidence.

Some of the Polish players watched the documentary, and one of them confirmed 'there has been a bit of chatter about it among the squad in training'. But for the first 25 minutes it was the England defence which played as if they had an almighty hangover. Ince was left isolated in midfield, the back three were exposed and Gascoigne was semi-continually fouled, eventually making the gesture of giving his shirt to an opponent who seemed prematurely keen to take it home with him. That was almost the only point at which Gascoigne imposed his personality on a match which was decided by Shearer's excellent finishing and Poland's failure to make their chances count. After the game, Polish skipper Piotr Nowak said that he thought England were a one-man team, only this time, four months after Chapuisat had made the same claim, the player who made the team was Shearer. Still, England, despite not playing brilliantly in either game, had six points out of six. But Gascoigne still didn't look, in Hoddle's grand phrase, as if he was ready to take on the world.

Two weeks after England beat Poland 2–1, Gazza was sent off for kicking Winston Bogarde in Rangers' Champions League match against Ajax. The very next morning, Sheryl Gascoigne's badly beaten face appeared on the front page of the *Daily Mirror*. There were no excuses for such behaviour and, slightly to his credit, the player himself didn't offer any, saying simply, 'I deeply regret what has happened with my wife. It will live with me for ever.' He also issued another apology, saying he'd disgraced himself against Ajax and admitting that he had taken what he described as a 'domestic problem' into the match.

Neither apology cut much ice. A letter from a Mrs D. Thackeray-Hayes of Chesterfield to a national newspaper was typical of the general view on this matter: 'When the great dealer deals out the cards, some people come out at the bottom and stay there. Gascoigne is talked of as a LAD. He is 29 years old. Even at that age, my parents would have made my life a misery if I'd behaved as he does.' And Rodney Ward of Battersea spoke for millions when he wrote that Gazza was a 'pea-brained and pathetic' man.

Surely, everyone from women's groups to football writers like Henry Winter was saying, Hoddle can't pick Gascoigne for the tie against Georgia? Jack Charlton, launching his autobiography in the midst of the latest media frenzy to surround his former player, admitted he was stunned by the revelations: 'There are some lines you don't cross as a human being, and Paul went over this one.' Yet, he concluded, Gazza was 'basically a nice lad who is constantly under pressure', and he added that if he was Hoddle he would not drop him.

Incredibly, that seemed to be almost identical to what Hoddle was thinking. FA big cheese Graham Kelly informed the country that Hoddle 'had spoken to the player three times' and that Paul was having counselling. 'Glenn was impressed with Paul's determination to sort himself out and so picked him for the squad to go to Georgia.' Nevertheless, it was, as Kelly wrote with some understatement in his autobiography, 'a tricky one'. Hoddle talked his decision through with Kelly and FA chairman Keith Wiseman, but ultimately, Kelly implied, it was not so much a case of the FA agreeing that Hoddle had definitely made the right decision as feeling that they could not overrule him so soon into his reign.

Hoddle had contacted Gascoigne quickly, explaining, 'My first concern is for him and his family.' For someone whose man-management was later to be ridiculed, he handled Gascoigne adroitly in his hour of need. Like Charlton, he made it clear he did not condone the behaviour, but wanted to help. And Gascoigne, with the world seemingly united against him, might easily have cracked at this point without such support. Gascoigne's accountant Len Lazarus told the journalist Harry Harris: 'He believes his only redemption is football. He would be absolutely devastated if England dropped him. He told me, "Football is my life. If I've not got football, I'm finished." He has been desperately upset by what happened.' In Harris's account, Lazarus then went on to say, 'He feels that he has been crucified about the sending-off at Ajax.' With everyone from Julie Burchill to Joan Bakewell calling for him to be made an example of because of what he'd done to Sheryl, this seems a rather odd reaction. He must, surely, have known for which particular offence he was, as he put it, being 'crucified'. It may well be that his behaviour was so abhorrent to himself that at first he couldn't bear even to think about it.

Hoddle, though, was determined not to be the one to hammer home the first nail. He tried to deflect some of the outrage which greeted his decision to include Gascoigne in his next squad by saying that Jesus had spoken about forgiveness, adding, correctly, 'If Joe Public had done exactly the same thing, that man wouldn't have got the sack and his capacity to earn would not have been taken away from him.' Colin Malam, in the *Sunday Telegraph*, thought Hoddle was wrong, but not for the obvious moral reason, rather because, like Mrs D. Thackeray-Hayes of Chesterfield, he didn't think Gascoigne would ever change. 'How often have we been over this terrain before?' he asked, noting the recurring pattern of 'indiscretion followed by contrition' which had marked Gascoigne's career and predicting that the player would 'blithely transgress' again.

But Hoddle's faith in the 'incorrigible sinner' was far from blind. Once again, he made it clear to the public and to the player the terms under which he had been forgiven. After offering some tactical advice ('Paul needs to find out just what he can and can't do physically in his game'), he said, 'I'm hoping that in two years' time we can look back and this will be a focal point where everyone will say that, off the back of something dreadful that happened in Paul's life, he's turned it around.' He added the rider: 'He knows he's got to change and that's the first point of recovery in many ways. If you want to call it a last chance – and I'm not calling it a last chance – but the ball's in his court. There are a lot of things I've found out – which I can't go into – that explain a lot about Paul Gascoigne when he's on a football pitch. If we address them and get them right, then there is the Gascoigne of old, perhaps with a more sensible head on, which would make him an even better player.' Hoddle, who travelled to meet Gascoigne three times in a fortnight and even went as far as taking part in some of the player's counselling sessions, concluded with the sensible advice: 'It's down to him now.'

Hoddle wasn't just making a footballing decision here; he seemed to the *Telegraph*'s Henry Winter to have 'embarked on a personal crusade to rescue a wayward soul'. For Gazza aficionados like Ian Hamilton, Hoddle's conduct seemed to suggest 'a near promise that he would stick with Gazza all the way to the World Cup'. Gazza was, some columnists reminded their readers, always at his best when he was aiming for a specific goal, even if in this case the goal was personal and professional redemption. Few seriously speculated on

Hoddle's likely reaction if he felt that his forgiveness had been abused and that his crusade had failed.

The football itself was almost an anti-climax. Hoddle, for instance, recalled Ian Wright for the game in place of the injured Shearer, which in less emotional times would have been sensational news. And there was still one instalment of what had by now almost become a national soap opera to go, when Gazza turned up at an England press conference for fifteen minutes. He defended his form as a footballer but not his behaviour as a human being. 'The game in Moldova I wasn't really fit, and I still scored. The second game I worked really hard, I did my midfield duties where I was supposed to. For Rangers, eleven goals is not bad for a midfield player.' Admitting that 'hopefully' he had fallen as low as he could go, as a footballer and a husband, he even suggested that he would revise his approach to diet and fitness. 'When I was young, I used to binge and do daft things. I'm on a more controlled sort of thing now. I like to think I eat the right sort of things. I look after my body more, I'm doing more in the gym. When you get to my age you sometimes have to do two sessions a day, work in the morning, have a break and then sometimes again in the afternoon. It's things like that which I've been doing, and I feel physically good.' It almost sounded as if he was now bingeing on exercise and counselling, but it seemed he'd heeded Hoddle's warnings. He left saying, 'Thanks lads, take care.' There was a smattering of applause. But the psychoanalysis was not over. Asked if he thought making Gascoigne a normal person would make him less of a footballer, Hoddle mused, 'I don't know. Paul has been given a gift from an early age.'

After all this, Hoddle seemed genuinely torn about playing Gascoigne in Tblisi on 9 November. Les Ferdinand chipped in, saying that he wanted 'Gazza behind me if I'm picked. He's still the best at opening defences.' Georgi Kinkladze obviously agreed: 'He is still a very good player on the pitch and our biggest danger.' At the final, secret, two-hour training session in the Boris Paichaidze Stadium, the biggest danger seemed to be that Gazza would, yet again, over-compensate. He was reported to be, in a phrase used so often to describe him it has become almost a trademark, 'bouncing off the walls', acting in a manner Rangers team-mate Trevor Steven had described as 'frantic', releasing what he called 'unusual' amounts of energy and having to be calmed down by his team-mates.

In such a mood, it would have astonished almost nobody if he had staged a repeat of his 1991 FA Cup final performance. For once, though (Hoddle did pick him), he lived up to his pre-match promise that he would channel his aggression. A first-time flick started a move after a quarter of an hour which saw Teddy Sheringham score, and after 37 minutes he ran 30 yards before releasing the ball to Sheringham who passed to Ferdinand to score. By his own standards it was not a great performance. He had been efficient, in the manner of footballers of much lesser talent, rather than inspiring, but he had stayed on the pitch and, crucially, he had played to Hoddle's orders. Arrigo Sacchi's Italian spies, assessing this performance, were more impressed with Andy Hinchcliffe than with Gazza. Still, it was Hoddle's opinion that counted.

Good job really, because Gascoigne's first England boss, Bobby Robson, ruminated publicly on the decline of a great talent, saying, 'When I left Paul after the West Germany game in 1990 he was just like Ronaldo is now – the best young player of the lot and incredibly cocky about his talent. His potential has been unfulfilled.' He could, Robson suggested, have been up there with the Gullits and Van Bastens, yet here he was being found wanting by Italian coaches alongside the likes of Andy Hinchcliffe. The problem, Robson said sadly, was the player's lack of 'self-control, to reflect what was right and what was wrong'. Not all Italians were unimpressed, though: Gianfranco Zola still saw Gascoigne as a 'potential match winner' alongside Shearer and McManaman when the Italians came to Wembley in February 1997. His Chelsea and Italian team-mate Roberto Di Matteo also hoped Gascoigne wouldn't play because then 'maybe our job will be a little bit easier'.

Characteristically, Gascoigne was doubtful for this fourth World Cup qualifying match because he'd injured an ankle in one of his insane tackles, committed (and this made the action even more negligent) in a friendly six-a-side tournament in Holland. But Hoddle still seemed convinced that his crusade was working for player and person. 'He has worked extremely hard at the problems he had,' he insisted. 'His form's been very good. He hasn't been in trouble with referees as much. He will always be the cheeky chappie. The main thing for me is his performances, and when he gets out on training grounds he's professional, trains extremely hard and pushes himself.' He then added the all-too-familiar comment: 'Sometimes he pushes himself too far.' After some debate, Gazza joined the squad with his left ankle protected by plaster. Newcastle's Rob Lee was called in as cover.

The walls of mystification the England coach had erected around his selection for that crucial game had begun to crumble when news of Gazza's injury (and his replacement by Le Tissier) leaked to the *Sun* and *The Times*. The usual rumours about the real story behind Gascoigne's omission were stilled only when Hoddle revealed that the player would return to Glasgow for a scan on the ankle, which had reacted after training. Gascoigne said, 'I told Glenn I didn't want to chance being even on the bench.' Perhaps, it could be inconclusively suggested, he had trained too hard after all. He raised the possibility, which must have seemed a dim one at the time, that 'the Italians could be cursing their misfortune the next time they play. Who knows?'

Dim it was. Ince, certainly, thought he knew why England had lost the game: 'A little bit of magic from Gazza could have made the difference.' Gazza's circus tricks, once dismissed as schoolboy indulgence, had come to be recognised as the element of unpredictability England desperately needed in midfield.

So the Gazza complex remained as strong as ever for coach, players and fans. At least until Gascoigne, while his ankle was recovering, was spotted in a stretch limo in Regent Street. He was sighted with his new celebrity pal, Chris Evans, by a Canadian woman who claimed that while she was talking to Evans, Gazza popped up through the sunroof and slapped her in the face (Mel Stein denied the charge on his client's behalf). Gascoigne's wife then revealed that neither she nor her son Regan had seen him for 29 days, and 'we're not expecting to see him either'. Gascoigne then flew to New York in what was seen as an attempt to put the incident behind him, and was seen in a bar, watching the Old Firm game in a Celtic shirt. This was not how Rangers had envisaged him spending the two weeks they'd given him to recuperate from that unnecessary injury. Walter Smith began to lose patience, warning that 'The dreadful pity of it all is that he possesses so much talent as a footballer yet he may well be remembered for his off-the-field activities. He says he won't do it again . . . but he does.'

Smith's statement certainly put Gascoigne's latest apology into harsh relief. In his statement, the player attributed some of his behaviour to frustration: 'I have been injured for some time and it's never easy sitting and watching from the sidelines.' His friend and mentor Chris Waddle concurred with this view, later telling the *Telegraph* that 'When he's fit and playing football he's never really a problem. It's only when he's injured that he runs into trouble, and no manager can control what players do in their own time.'

Gascoigne took Smith's rebuke hard, but in the wrong way, and things began to go downhill. There were more rumours of drinking sessions with Evans, Sheryl filed for divorce and Hoddle weighed in with yet more public advice, telling Gascoigne '[you] can't do certain things when you're 30 that you can get away with when you're 21'. While Hoddle said that every England fan would want to see Gascoigne playing in France 98 like he had in Italia 90, that could only be achievable if the player sorted some things out. 'He has not gone a season without a long-term injury to worry about. His first port of call is to sort that out. If we're going to see Paul back to his best he has to do a lot of thinking and there has to be a lot of prevention work so he doesn't pick up these injuries. We've tried to help him . . . he's started to respond to that. But certain things have to change in his life.' Among those 'certain things' was the player's attitude. 'He's picked up strange things [injuries] on the training ground. He's got to understand that it's a training-ground situation and although I want players to apply themselves, there's a line to be drawn.' Again, Hoddle reiterated that 'Paul is the only one who can change things. There's got to be maturity.'

Graham Taylor was even blunter. 'You have got to look after yourself and you can't continually abuse your body and expect to stay at the very highest level of international sport.' There was, it has to be said, a certain amount of 'I told you so' in all this. Taylor had, after all, identified the 'refuelling' problem some years back and he may well have felt a sense of vindication when he became the latest person to predict, wrongly, that the player's England career was over. But the point was still valid, painful as it was for the player and his fans to admit.

Sports minister Tony Banks also weighed in, but so, more significantly, did Brian Laudrup. The Danish star was never one of Gascoigne's closest mates at Rangers, but his willingness to go on record saying 'he has let a lot of people down' was still surprising. His diagnosis was broadly the same as Hoddle's: Gascoigne's injuries were his body's way of telling him to slow down.

Gazza responded forcefully, if cheaply, by taking a swipe at the easier targets, the rent-a-quote mob led by Tony Banks. 'These people have never played football in their life. I just need to get a few games under my belt.' Nobody could quite foresee, even at this juncture, just how much of a mantra 'getting a few games under my belt' would become in the seasons ahead. He did, encouragingly, say he agreed with everything Hoddle had said. John Gorman then chipped into the debate, mixing up the message somewhat by saying, 'There comes a time when you've got to toe the line and everyone knows that. But you never can afford to lose patience with someone of his ability.'

Despite the nature of this message, Hoddle must have felt that, on balance, a point had been made: shape up, Gazza, or even you will be shipped out.

He sat out the next two games, a friendly against Mexico on 29 March and the home qualifier against Georgia on 30 April, his absence noted, approvingly, by

Kinkladze. It was getting to the point where Gascoigne was getting more credit and recognition when he didn't play for England than when he did. A scrappy 2–0 victory over the Georgians during which England's midfield was all perspiration and no inspiration left Hoddle ruminating again about his need to find a playmaker, but a list which once would have almost stopped and started with Gascoigne now firmly included Beckham, Le Tissier, Merson and Anderton.

Hoddle, who seemed to spend most of his public life answering questions about Gascoigne, spelled out again in May 1997 what the player had to do to earn a recall. And while he threw a few scraps to Gazza's admirers ('If we can get him back to his best, everyone in English football would be delighted – me and the supporters'), there was a noticeable hardening of tone, a sense that (in Hoddle's eyes) the player was about to cross another of those lines. To take Walter Smith's analogy, the percentage support had, understandably, dropped a few points. 'He's got to prove his fitness and he's got to prove to me he wants to put some of the things right again,' said the England manager. 'I don't think there are many players better than Paul when he's at his best; but when was he at his very best? That is the question.' The obvious answer to that question, the press said, was that Gascoigne had not been at his best, consistently at his best, since Italia 90.

Another message delivered, Hoddle picked Gascoigne in his 27-man squad (his mentor Arsène Wenger had advised him to do just that) for the next five England games that early summer, but he had a private chat with the player, some of which he made public: 'The main thing I told him was that he's got to get back to loving the game of football again. Back in his heyday, when he was really at his best, he was in love with football. You can understand the reasons that perhaps that's gone away. It has to come back.'

The players certainly seemed glad to have him back. Robert Lee said, 'On his day, Gazza is the best player England have got.' Waddle also sprang to his old mate's defence: 'I can definitely see him being player of the tournament in France next summer, and my money's on him still being our playmaker in the European Championship two years later.' That's what every England fan wanted to believe in their hearts, but they could also see the logic behind Hoddle's remark that this was almost Gazza's last chance.

In one of those bursts of energy and determination which have marked his many comebacks, Gazza trained like a beast and turned up for the friendly against South Africa at Old Trafford on 24 May looking more like a lean machine than the portly buffoon of recent memory. The match brought him up against the 'South African Gazza', the 29-year-old midfielder Doctor Khumolo, who said he wanted to 'be skilful and entertain. I want to do that against Gazza at Old Trafford.' But South African coach Clive Barker made it clear the comparison wasn't entirely complimentary: 'He's just like your Gazza. He's infectious and he's a pain in the backside for the coach.'

The English Gazza was stretchered off in injury time after the kind of international performance which by this time he could have patented. There were a few perfectly weighted passes, a cunning free-kick which almost crept into the top corner, the occasional shimmy, a couple of flashes of genius, long periods of inactivity and, as he tired, an increasing inability to keep the ball in situations where once his upper body strength would have won the day. Hoddle described him as 'spot on', which, injury notwithstanding, suggested he was a cert to play against Poland a week later. But Clive Barker wondered about Gascoigne's exercise routine. 'I saw him play a few times before he shed the weight and I think he's like a boxer pulling weight before a fight. I think he was a better player when he had a bit more weight and a bit more strength.'

Gascoigne tried to put his performance into some sort of context at Bisham Abbey, saying, 'A lot of footballers do a lot of things outside football but none of them gets a photographer up his backside. None of them has photographers hassling his wife and kids outside the school.' While it was obvious the paparazzi were adding to the pressures he felt, the suggestion they had half-blinded his kid by letting their flash off in the boy's eyes seemed, at worst, like a cheap plea for sympathy, at best, beside the point. He complained:

I was just turning up for games, wanting to get the 90 minutes over. I used to worry about doing this or that, otherwise I'm going to get slaughtered. It's been like that for four years and it's going to continue until I stop playing football. With my first touch on Saturday I nutmegged a guy from five yards. I did all right, but I still got stick. Too fat, too thin. He's not beating players. The same stories again. If I keep on getting hammered, then I'll just play as long as I'm happy. If I then think I've had enough I'll do what is best for me.

There was a certain amount of truth in all this. The press had always been slow to understand Gascoigne and quick to judge him. His early promise had also raised the bar in terms of expectations. What might have seemed a good, solid performance by another player in Gascoigne's case was always portrayed as a disappointment. But if the player was bedevilled by the 'same old stories', whose fault was that? Blaming the press entirely seemed like another evasion of responsibility.

Against Poland, another 2–0 England victory was marred by defeat, of a kind, for Gascoigne: he was stretchered off for the second game in a row, after just sixteen minutes. Hoddle was quick to defend him, saying, 'These injuries have not been because he's not been living correctly, it's what I would call armed combat.' Another cameo role in Le Tournoi against Italy on 4 June – a twelve-minute performance as a substitute – was tainted by an unnecessary booking for yet another reckless challenge. That game belonged to David Beckham, England's new playmaker. Okay, it was only one match, and he didn't display quite the breadth of Gazza at his peak, but then Gazza no longer seemed to be at his peak.

Against France three days later, Gazza played the full 90 minutes and, said Hoddle, probably ran seven miles, at least a mile more than most players. Hoddle was doing his best to give the player a break and to remind the press that Gazza, unlike many wayward midfield geniuses, was prepared to work hard for the team. But it seemed a sad reflection on Gazza's predicament that the focus was on miles run rather than goals scored or made.

Against Brazil on 10 June, Gazza seemed inspired by the opposition. An adroit backheel put Ince through for a shot that Taffarel just turned around the post, and he also hit one of his trademark free-kicks. Hoddle was probably being over-generous when he said 'there were times when I felt he was back to his best', but he had at least looked (and this was a word which could not be applied to many of his post-Euro 96 performances for England) influential. There seemed, certainly, modest cause for hope – which, with Gascoigne, was all most fans needed.

There was little debate about Gascoigne's inclusion in the England squad to play Moldova on 10 September at Wembley. There was even less discussion about the player himself as the nation was still stunned by the recent death of Princess Diana. And, for once, another England player was in the headlines for the wrong reason: West Ham defender Rio Ferdinand was dropped from the squad after being banned for drink-driving. Hoddle was accused of double standards, but he felt that as the player was in court the day before England were due to assemble (and that he had not levelled with Hoddle, the FA or his club about the charge), he had no choice. It's also possible that the general media hysteria and speculation about Diana's death influenced his decision.

Having for a long time blamed the press for his own predicament, Gascoigne took time out in *Match of the Day* magazine to charge them with Diana's murder too. His assertion – 'I do not have respect for any journalist. I hate them, I absolutely hate them, I detest them' – seemed a trifle OTT for a man who had sold exclusive rights to his wedding to *Hello!* magazine and whose smouldering resentment could always be dampened by a large cheque.

Gascoigne is usually at his most convincing when he sticks to the old pro's cliché about doing his talking on the pitch, and he certainly did that night against the Moldovans. Inspired by the emotion of it all, he produced a performance of controlled power and real panache which really did bring back memories of Italia 90. Hoddle was jubilant, saying that Gazza was 'back to his very best. After that performance he can go from strength to strength.' The ease with which he baffled the

Moldovan midfield (scoring one goal and making another in England's 4–0 victory) may not seem that remarkable given the quality of the opposition, but he really did boss the game. His tenth goal for his country came from a run deep into the Moldovan half, a flicked pass to Wright and a run on to the return pass to finish.

Gascoigne dedicated his performance to the memory of Princess Diana, a sincere, if mawkish, tribute. After the match, talking to the press, he wasn't whingeing for once but confident, even slipping into Alan Shearer-speak when he concluded: 'Now we're going to Rome top of the group. We can't afford to sit back. We've got a big job to do and we'll be looking for all three points.'

David Beckham took some of the credit for Gascoigne's renaissance, saying he'd helped keep Gazza out of the papers that summer. More seriously, he talked about how much Gascoigne lifted the other players. 'He talks to me during games and helps me and says things like "just keep going" – not much really, but it is an inspiration to everyone playing around him when you see him doing things like that.'

Perhaps not wanting Gascoigne to take anything for granted, Hoddle mixed praise for the player's new maturity with reminders to focus on fitness and diet. It was all part of Hoddle's regime for managing Gazza. 'Sometimes it's the heavy hammer and sometimes it's a bit of the arm around him to make him feel wanted. You need the manager to take the pressure off you. I've learned that. That pressure was never taken off me.' So Hoddle was giving Gazza the chance Greenwood and Robson had denied him.

Hollywood Central Casting could not have picked a better venue for Gascoigne to confirm his comeback than the Olympic Stadium in Rome, where he had played far too little football in three seasons at Lazio.

Gianluca Vialli's extended pre-match analysis concluded with a fairly accurate assessment of what was at stake for Gascoigne personally: 'We all know he can be an important player for England and, deep down, he may feel it's his last chance of playing in the World Cup finals. There is always the danger that he might get too worked up, too excitable, but he should have enough experience now to read the game and be perfectly tuned in. I have a feeling he's going to play very well.'

As always, Gascoigne was not completely free to focus on the game. There was the vexing business of a threatened writ from an Italian photographer who claimed that Gazza had beaten him up. There were even reports that the Italian authorities wanted to talk to him about his alleged participation in the country's other great national sport, tax evasion. But Hoddle, believing that 'the chats we've had over a period of time have sunk in', urged the player to stay focused and disciplined, and then he could emulate Franco Baresi and be playing in a World Cup when he was 36. He was also relieved that Gascoigne had been relatively injury-free of late. The general air of satisfaction was completed by Mel Stein, who told Harry Harris, 'For a whole year he's been out of trouble because he's realised that football is his livelihood. And he's become very focused, it's as simple as that.'

It would never be that simple with Gazza, especially in the longer term, but he and Ince were the genuine stars of that October night in Rome, a goalless draw that clinched England's place for the 1998 World Cup. 'Paul was magnificent,' said Hoddle afterwards, 'particularly in the first half. They couldn't get near him.' Here was a performance which did indeed suggest, to use the word Hoddle had turned almost into a mantra, maturity. Possession was not given away cheaply; instead, Gazza twisted and passed his way out of trouble, thwarting Dino Baggio and Demetrio Albertini. He even came up with the best gag of the night, comparing the bandaged Ince to a pint of Guinness. Still keyed up, he strode into the post-match press conference to explain the team's game plan.

> Our job here was to pick each player up and catch them on the break. We played them at their own game. The Italians are very good at diving, cheating, trying to waste time. I've been over here. I know what to do. Kick the ball away, let them chase it. It was great to see them running after the ball. They were desperate. We had to concentrate and make sure we didn't get too close to them because they can take dives and pull shirts. I knew I could keep the ball and pass it and try to get everyone involved. And make them work.

And just in case anyone thought he'd turned into a model pro, he did add one caveat: 'Obviously I might misbehave now and again. Maybe that's in Paul Gascoigne, where I come from.'

As was so often the case when he stood up in front of the press, Gazza's remarks resembled a potted autobiography in the manner of Paul Anka's *My Way*. 'I can walk out of here with my chest out, I can be proud. It's been a long time since Italia 90, almost eight years with no World Cup, sad football times. Then we had a good European Championship, we qualified for the World Cup and now let's have a great World Cup. If I make it to the World Cup I can't ask for anything more. My career has been great, I've never had any regrets about it.' But like Anka, Sinatra and Elvis, regrets . . . he did indeed have a few. 'There are regrets about the stupid things I've done, the bad times, the ligaments, the kneecaps. But the good times are right now. I left Italy in 1990 in tears but I was proud to come back with Lazio, and injuries let me down and again I left on a sad note. Now I'm leaving Italy with a smile on my face.' It was possibly the longest public speech of Gascoigne's life. Certainly it was more than eloquent from a player whose most famous public utterances had hitherto been tears, a fart, a burp and an Anglo-Saxon phrase ending in 'off'.

Hoddle, basking in his triumph, contented himself with a gentle reminder that 'even now his fitness levels could be higher. He still lacks high-power games.' But in the immediate aftermath of that night in Rome Gascoigne's comeback seemed complete. It was almost a year since he had admitted (and apologised for) beating his wife. Hoddle, in his eagerness to save Gazza, had virtually become his unpaid counsellor as well as his international manager. But crucially, the player himself seemed to have finally taken responsibility for his own life and career. Whether it was the awful memory of what he'd done to his wife, the shock of approaching 30 and getting a glimpse of his own professional mortality or just the fact that, as friends said, he was better when he had something to aim at and he was able to play football regularly again, to get out on the pitch, the only place where (he had once famously said) he felt free – whatever the reason, or combination of reasons, there was little doubt that he had pulled himself out of the mire and helped give himself and his country a crack at the World Cup.

Gascoigne had been vindicated, Hoddle had been vindicated – hell, even we as fans had been vindicated for putting our faith in him. We had always made excuses for Gascoigne, a mirror image of the way the press seemed to make no excuses for him whatsoever. Now he seemed, at the age of 30, to be one of a handful of players who were bound to be in Hoddle's squad for France 98. A long-awaited sequel to Italia 90 was on the cards, a sequel denied us in 1994 by Gazza's injuries, Taylor's lack of nous and that referee in Rotterdam. In the hype and triumphalism which followed Rome, there was even talk of England going one better than in 1990.

In offices throughout Britain a list was handed around which seemed to prove the point. Taking the 1982 World Cup as the fulcrum, the sequence of World Cup winners going backwards was Italy (1982), Argentina (1978), Germany (1974), Brazil (1970) and England (1966); going forwards from 1982 the sequence ran Italy, Argentina (1986), Germany (1990) and Brazil (1994), which meant England must win in 1998. There were less tangential causes for optimism too: England seemed finally to possess a core of genuinely world-class players, and Hoddle, with his secrecy and kidology before the Rome game, seemed as tough, wily and cynical as any of the continental coaches. And above all there was the prospect of a resurgent Gascoigne.

In November 1997, before a friendly against Cameroon, Phil Neville told the writer Mark Palmer, 'There are only four players you can look at and safely say that only injuries can keep them out of the final squad, and they are David Seaman, Paul Gascoigne, Paul Ince and Alan Shearer.' So there were seven months to go and, it seemed, barring accidents, eighteen places up for grabs.

Unfortunately, you could never rule out accidents, or worse, where Gascoigne was concerned, even if he was hoping to play in the most important tournament of his life. A suspension-cum-hamstring injury kept him out of action in the closing weeks of 1997 until the New Year

Old Firm match where, taunted, he played the flute again, which Hoddle gloomily saw as 'a step backward after his progress in 1997'.

He came back in style in January 1998 against Motherwell, but when he turned up for England's friendly against Chile, Hoddle decided the player 'needed a jolt'. The two talked in private for an hour. In his World Cup diaries, Hoddle noted with a confidence that would subsequently prove to be misplaced, 'I know how to treat him – with a mixture of love and discipline.' Hoddle's worries about Gascoigne were the familiar ones: his mind and his fitness. 'At least 50 per cent of his problems are his own making. He has to learn to shut out private things, but I think he's been almost constantly preoccupied with all the problems surrounding his separation from his wife and son.'

What only Hoddle and Gascoigne know was whether he also told Gascoigne that day that he had a dozen games to get fit, and that if he wasn't fit he might not be in the squad. This was, according to Hoddle's diaries, running through his mind at the time, although such thoughts were carefully concealed from press and public.

At the time, Paul Merson seemed the obvious candidate to replace an unfit Gascoigne, but he was never sure, right up until that controversial stay in La Manga, whether he would be in the final 22. Yet when Mark Palmer, who was given considerable access to the England team and staff when writing his book, *Lost in France*, suggested to Gorman after the Chile game that England still needed Gazza, Hoddle's number two replied, 'Paul Merson can pass the ball better than Gazza with us in many ways.' Gorman didn't elaborate, but it does suggest that Hoddle and his team were already considering their options if the unthinkable happened.

Merson was part of an experimental team which played Switzerland in Berne on 25 March, and he spared Hoddle's blushes with a goal in a 1–1 draw.

Three days before that friendly, Hoddle had discussed Gascoigne's prospects with the press. He'd seemed relatively confident that the player's fitness could be turned around, saying it was more important for Gazza, who hadn't played for nine weeks, to get fully fit than to rush back into action. 'There is a danger zone if he comes back too early and pulls another hamstring or collects another injury. That would put him out for another three weeks and we would then be in that danger area of running out of time. At this moment in time he needs a rehabilitation programme to get him on his way, to know that when he comes back he is going to be at his very best and not likely to break down again.'

This all sounded reassuring, but it did convey how finely balanced the timing might become if Gascoigne was unlucky enough to pick up another injury. But Hoddle did suggest that if Gazza played half a dozen matches for his club, that might be enough, given the pre-tournament friendlies. He did, though, follow this up by saying that while some of the players might be rested in May, 'we might have to work to get him [Gascoigne] ready'.

There were other problems, apart from Gascoigne's domestic life, to preoccupy him, the most obvious being the business of which club he would play for next season. Walter Smith was to retire upstairs at the end of the 1997/98 season, Rangers chairman David Murray had said publicly he had no interest in keeping Gascoigne as a declining asset and Aston Villa, among others, had already made a bid for him. Gazza talked longingly at this time of America, a land where they knew how to treat celebrities and famous for 'great pina coladas', he told one reporter, but he didn't want to move until after the World Cup. He was even willing to take a pay cut to make the move if he felt it was the right one.

Crystal Palace Football Club is not renowned for its pina coladas, but that was the first club Rangers tried to sell Gascoigne to. That stalled, and Middlesbrough came in with £3.5m. He was officially unveiled to the fans the day after the Switzerland friendly. Hoddle seemed relieved, although he was not consulted about the move.

Player and manager were reunited before the friendly against Portugal in April. 'Bryan Robson seemed to have sorted him out,' Hoddle noted. 'His fitness still wasn't right, though. He'd definitely lost the definition in his legs and wasn't fit enough to play against Portugal, which was why I released him early.' A groin and ankle problem had prevented him from training. He'd missed out on his third friendly in a row.

If he looked ordinary when playing for Middlesbrough (in his first three games he was booked twice and was substituted in the third with a bruised foot), there was at least the consolation that he was behaving like an ordinary bloke off it. By his standards, he had been a model citizen. His only front-page appearance since the rumours about what he and Jimmy 'Five Bellies' Gardner might have been up to at Hogmanay came when he was accused of assaulting a fourteen-year-old girl in his desperation to use the telephone box she was in, a charge which soon vanished.

But the player (and the media) made up for lost time in May. Ian Hamilton suggested, in his book, that there was a 'near vendetta' by the media at this time. Paul Merson and Tony Adams, both of whom made it into the final 22 for France despite their own well-publicised personal problems, probably wouldn't agree. Indeed, Merson would later advise Gazza to stop blaming the press and admit his own responsibility. 'Vendetta' is probably too strong a word; the reality was probably more cynical and commercial than that. Gascoigne always sold newspapers, and never more so than in the run-up to a World Cup, and with what the press already knew about his lifestyle it did not take a Pulitzer Prize-winning editorial team to find front-page stories about him. And Gazza, after what had (for him) been a period of almost monastic seclusion, was about to give them the nails with which to crucify him.

The Pharmacy, a swanky new restaurant in Notting Hill, was not the place to go if you wanted a quiet night out. But that's where Gascoigne, Gardner, Chris Evans and Rod Stewart headed three days before the player was due to report for England duty. The front pages were duly plastered with pictures of Gazza looking, well, plastered, although some of his drinking companions insisted that he hadn't drunk that much. Gascoigne then turned up on Evans' breakfast show on Virgin Radio and said, defiantly, 'Tomorrow I'll knuckle down. I've had a seven-day break, so what? I've got nearly a month to get fit. If I'm good, I'm in the squad for the World Cup. It's as simple as that.'

The story got slightly more complicated when Gascoigne was spotted, in the early hours of a Sunday morning, scouring London in search of a kebab with onions. This was no paparazzi plot; the pictures were taken by a student who wanted to use the money the *Mirror* offered to pay off a student loan, go on holiday and pay for a white filling. Some football writers saw the whole thing as a bit of a farce or a set-up, but the public didn't. In one poll, 74 per cent told Hoddle to dump him. The England coach also claimed that 'reliable people' told him of another Soho lunch lasting until late in the afternoon.

Even before Kebabgate, there was the 'revelation' that Gascoigne smoked up to a packet of cigarettes a day (i.e. his daily consumption could be anything from one to twenty). He would not have been the first gifted footballer to smoke – Platini and Cruyff never let the habit interfere with their playing careers. The difference was that Gascoigne's fitness had been a subject of intense national scrutiny almost since 1991. At various times, the very future of the England team seemed to hinge on that over-analysed and injury-prone body. Opinion differed as to whether he'd taken it up again recently or, as Hoddle had said, had acquired the habit at Lazio in the early 1990s. Whenever he'd acquired it, it seemed like just one more thing he didn't need to do if he was serious about battling back to fitness and making it to France.

Hoddle didn't dump him, but he did tell the player 'forcefully' to sort himself out. (Apparently Gascoigne hadn't got the message at first.) 'If he had behaved like that while under my control with England he wouldn't be with us now,' he told the press. 'But I can't control what he does when he's not under my wing.' In his diaries, Hoddle stated that he 'got Gazza into my room and told him in no uncertain terms enough was enough ... Paul Gascoigne left my room knowing exactly where he stood. There were no grey areas ... I told him he couldn't have more alcohol unless I said so. I hoped the message would sink in because I still thought we could train him, play him – and get him 100 per cent fit.'

In the light of what happened next, it's hard to read this without suspecting that a case was being made, an alibi prepared, if you will. The official reason for excluding Gascoigne from the squad would always be fitness, nothing else. Yet it is hard to see how Hoddle, at this point, could not have felt other than betrayed by a player for whom, as he saw it, he'd risked his own neck to try to save. And how was Gazza repaying him?

Although much has been made of Hoddle's faith, his capacity to forgive was not infinite. He was generous to those, like Adams and Merson, who had transgressed and taken it upon themselves to reform, but he could also be unforgiving, as he was, for instance, when Chris Sutton spurned the chance to play in an England B international. His treatment of Le Tissier, once a favourite, also showed how ruthless he could be when he felt it was required, and how easily he could justify such decisions to himself. Le Tissier's 'offences' were on the pitch (to put it bluntly, he was deemed not to work hard enough); on the evidence of his diaries, Hoddle does not seem to have lost much sleep over deciding that the player was surplus to requirements.

Hoddle would not have been human had he not felt, at best, severely disappointed with Gazza, at worst, let down in such a way that all his faith in the player was destroyed. The player's own bravado didn't help. On the training pitch on his first day of England duty, Gascoigne was spotted by Mark Palmer running around in a long-sleeved tracksuit top, his face as red as referee Paul Durkin's hair. It was, Palmer noted, 'the hottest day of the year . . . you could almost see steam rising from the back of his neck'. With members of the football fraternity, he behaved like a schoolboy who knew he'd sinned and was trying to compensate by being over-conscientious. To the press, he was defiant. 'How can you not be fit for eating a kebab?' he challenged them. 'Every England player goes out for a night with his mates, but then perhaps they don't have a camera up their arse. Two nights out don't make a bad footballer. OK, I had a couple of beers with the guys. It was unfortunate it was in the papers. I'll train as well and get myself ready. I can't believe the fuss over one night out, doctors coming on television to talk about it. It really pisses me off.' Asked if he felt old, he replied, 'No. I feel like having a nice kebab with onions on it.'

Somehow the joke wasn't funny any more. Kebabs, beer, cigarettes (including a 'hilarious' appearance on Chris Evans' *TFI* show with a mouth full of ciggies) – was this the way the most important player in the England squad was supposed to prepare for the World Cup? Especially when to most objective observers (i.e. not himself, Evans or Danny Baker) he seemed 20 to 40 per cent below match fitness. As Henry Winter wrote in the *Daily Telegraph*, at this stage before a World Cup 'most of his opposing numbers are studying match videos, chewing broccoli and curling up in bed with a cup of isotonic cocoa'.

Gascoigne's stupendous gifts as a player weren't the only reason he was adored by England fans. Throughout the last decade, through all the injuries, the one thing that nobody could ever accuse Gascoigne of was taking the right to wear the three lions on his shirt for granted. He seemed to exemplify the do-or-die commitment so beloved of fans. Even at his worst, he was, for England, wholehearted, darting around, gasping, chasing, trying to force himself into the game. Now, England was on the eve of its first World Cup for eight years. And (the usual pre-tournament feeling) the suspicion in the back of the nation's mind that our weaknesses were about to be exposed on the world stage had been replaced by a feeling that, this time, more than any other time (as the England 1982 World Cup squad had sung), England were in with a shout.

And the player who should have understood all this, who had always worn the England shirt with immense and obvious pride, seemed to be taking it all for granted, more interested in kebabs, cigarettes and nights out on the town with celebrity hangers-on. His remark, 'If I'm in, I'm in, if I'm out, I'm out', was taken to mean that he was incredibly, cockily, certain that he knew he was in. This might have seemed endearing in the past but now it looked, finally, as if Gazza wasn't taking things seriously, not as seriously as the fans were and not seriously enough to do what he'd done only the summer before: knuckle down and get into shape. Friends of his will protest that this is a tabloid caricature of his life and lifestyle in those weeks, but Hoddle did not carpet him for one kebab with onions and one night out, but for a lack of focus, a lack of a sensible lifestyle and a lack of understanding that even a player with his natural gifts couldn't do the business if he wasn't match fit. Had Kebabgate been accompanied by serious evidence that he was taking on board his manager's warnings about fitness, he might well still have made the final 22.

The mystery remains. Did he simply miscalculate the time it would take for his body to recover? (He had, indeed, told the press that he was not far from match fitness, but that may have been sheer bravado for the consumption of a press he'd always mistrusted.) Was he trying to prove something to the papers, prove to them that they would not control his life, that he could do this and still do his stuff when the whistle blew? Had he relied too much upon Hoddle's talk of forgiveness? Or was he fatally distracted by the knowledge that his soon-to-be ex-wife Sheryl had what in tabloid parlance is termed a 'new friend'?

Against Saudi Arabia in the lead-up to the finals, Gascoigne spent the first half sitting on the bench, occasionally trotting up and down the running track. After half-time the crowd began to chant, 'If you want Gascoigne, stand up . . .' Almost everybody did stand up. After 60 minutes he came on for David Beckham, probably England's best player on the day. One fan shouted, 'Take 'em on, you fat bastard!' But Steve Curry, writing in the *Telegraph*, included one chilling sentence in his match report after this performance: 'There seems little doubt that Paul Gascoigne cannot sustain a 90-minute performance at this level.' Curry's guess-timate at Hoddle's preferred starting line-up for England's opening match against Tunisia on 15 June didn't feature him. Nor, after those 30 minutes against the Saudis, could you honestly describe Gazza as a 'super sub'.

On 25 May, the England party flew to La Manga. There were now two games in the King Hassan II International Cup to play before the squad of 30 was whittled down to 22. Jamie Redknapp was already ruled out by injury, so that left seven spaces on that plane home to be decided. Against Morocco, Gascoigne celebrated his 31st birthday by playing a full 90 minutes for only the fifth time under Hoddle. The performance itself wasn't much to rejoice over, though: in the first half, some of the Moroccan players amused themselves by casually strolling up to him, taking the ball off him and saying what looked like the Moroccan equivalent of 'Ta very much, guv' before passing it to someone in their own team, although after Steve McManaman and Michael Owen had put England ahead, Gascoigne began to get into the game. Afterwards, Mark Palmer remarked to the England doctor, 'Gazza looks a long way from being fit.' The doctor nodded. Even further from being fit was Ian Wright, who had broken down with a hamstring, which left just six players to be disappointed.

Gascoigne, from being one of four players (according to Phil Neville) guaranteed a place in the starting line-up, was increasingly looking like someone who might be brought on to change a game.

There was just one game left for Gascoigne to make an impact, and the odds of making it were continuing to move in his favour. Andy Hinchcliffe had broken down in training the day before the Belgium game and wasn't on an eleven-strong subs bench. He looked doubtful. In all probability just five players to weed out to get to that final 22.

Before the game against Belgium, Hoddle noted the England dressing room was pin-drop quiet, possibly because 'Gazza was out in the middle of the pitch, talking on his mobile phone. Again.' In the manager's eyes, this was his second offence of the day (he'd kept the team bus waiting that morning because he was on the phone). Only the afternoon before, he said, he'd had a 'bit of a heart-to-heart' with the player after realising that 'he'd spent most of the afternoon on the phone to his wife when he should have been resting, and it seemed to have affected him mentally'. Seeing Gazza on his mobile yet again, Hoddle sent Roeder over to have a word. 'Gazza got off the phone pretty sharpish after that and came into the dressing room to prepare for the game,' Hoddle stated, but staring across at Gascoigne in the dressing room, 'I started to seriously doubt he could do a job for us in France. Physically, he wasn't 100 per cent; mentally, he was all over the place.' While Hoddle sat there looking at the player and reflecting on what a massive game this was for him, he didn't see any evidence that Gascoigne understood this. 'I think he was complacent, never dreamed in a million years that his place was on the line. All I said to him was I wanted to see him last 70 minutes.'

However distracted Hoddle thought Gascoigne was, he was significantly more effective against the Belgians, hitting two fine passes, one of which would have led to a goal for Les Ferdinand but for a bad call by the assistant referee. He was bandaged, à la Ince in Rome, after an accidental collision with Enzo Scifo. He was then clattered, and was visibly limping when the half-time whistle blew. And he missed Hoddle's pre-match target, lasting just 50 minutes. 'And it was at that moment, after all I'd seen of him physically and mentally that day, that I knew deep down he'd probably run out of time. Of course, I had to be positive during the press conference, but afterwards at the airport, I just sat and thought, and it kept coming to me that I couldn't take Gazza to France.'

In between those sweetly struck passes, Gazza had, at times, looked like a bloated parody of his old self, although to be fair, the team performance as a whole wasn't up to much. The cruel jibe, first heard before Euro 96, that he had degenerated into a pub player finally seemed to have an awful ring of truth about it. But at the time it was easier to focus on those perfect passes; his right foot seemed to be in good nick even if the rest of his body wasn't. Against that, however, you had to set the fact that, on the evidence of those 50 minutes, one bad tackle was enough to put him out of the game and eliminate any threat that his fine football-ing brain still represented. To his admirers, it would have been (as Woody Allen might say) a travesty of a mockery of a sham if that were to be his last perform-ance in an England shirt; most of us, oblivious to what was running through Hoddle's mind, still expected him to be in the manager's final 22 and still hoped that, somehow, even at the last possible moment, he might yet, in one of those mysterious and miraculous comebacks which had become a trademark of his, turn it all around again.

The 48 hours which followed are among the most controversial in English football history. Jimmy Greaves not making the 1966 World Cup final, in comparison, seems a tempest in a teacup. And yet, there is a surprising amount of agreement about what happened among those parties who have published their accounts of that weekend.

Hoddle, by his own account, slept well that Friday night but spent most of Saturday, 30 May with the Gazza question spinning around in his mind. He tried to clear his mind by playing golf that afternoon. That night, Hoddle had told the players they could have a few beers and enjoy themselves. While most of the squad relaxed in the bar (Adams and Merson, as recovering alcoholics, took little part in the proceedings), Hoddle hosted a coaches meeting with Ray Clemence and Peter Taylor. Gorman was in Frankfurt on a scouting mission and Roeder, the member of the backroom staff who knew Gazza best, was not, according to Hoddle, at the meeting. 'I told them I wasn't sure about him,' Hoddle wrote. 'Apparently I wasn't the only one.' The view, as summed up by Hoddle, was that if any other player had behaved like Gascoigne he wouldn't have been in the squad. He phoned Gorman to ask his opinion. It was decided that Hoddle should sleep on it and call Gorman in the morning if he'd changed his mind. But, the manager said, 'I was pretty certain that I would not be picking up that phone.'

The meeting came to a natural end at about 11 p.m. and the coaches decided to join the players in the bar. Hoddle insisted that all the players were there, 'but Gazza stood out. Gazza was drunk. He wasn't out of order, he was having a good time on the karaoke. Just about everyone had had a few beers but no one had had as many as Gazza.'

Some players stayed drinking until 1 a.m., but Gazza had gone to bed by then. In Hoddle's words, 'he was ushered up to his room by David Seaman'. Seaman agreed that Gazza was drunk, but wrote in his memoirs that 'we all were, Gazza was the only one who got caned for it'. The England goalkeeper went on to admit that, as Hoddle alleged, 'he was certainly not in the best frame of mind, but his stress was coming from home, not from a bottle. For a start, there was a lot of paper talk about his wife allegedly going out with someone else.' So for Seaman, Gazza's drunkenness did not stand out.

Adams and Merson both resented what they regarded as, in Adams' words, 'a contrived attempt to get everybody together'. But they dropped in to be sociable anyway. 'When we walked in, Gazza was on the karaoke machine singing "Wooden Heart". Nobody could get the microphone off him. There was a sadness in me for him because he was obviously worse the wear for drink. He shouted at me, "C'mon, Tone, give us a song, you boring bastard." ' Merson's view was that 'Gazza had had a few beers and gone way beyond that time where you could say anything constructive to him that he might listen to'. While Merson and Adams might be said to be watching Gazza through the hypercritical eyes of reformed addicts, the same could not be said of Teddy Sheringham. In his updated autobiography, he wrote, 'We all had a few beers that night but nobody got silly – with the exception of Gazza. Whether he sensed something from Glenn's attitude to his fitness and was trying to drown his sorrows, I don't know, but whatever the case, he got pretty drunk that night. I wondered that evening, and not for the first time, whether Paul had a bigger problem with alcohol than even he cares to admit.'

Sunday morning dawned. Hoddle didn't make that call to Gorman. He sat having breakfast feeling 'very bubbly', convinced he 'had made the right decision'. At 10 a.m. a notice went up saying that Hoddle would meet the first player, David Seaman, at 4.15 p.m. The other players would be told their fates at five-minute intervals after that; the unlucky six (Hinchcliffe probably suspected he was one of them because of his thigh injury) had to be among the first eleven players to meet Hoddle so that they could be whisked out of the hotel to the airport to catch the private plane home. Gazza's appointment was scheduled for 5.15 p.m.

The tension that day must have been almost unbearable, both for the staff, who knew the outcome, and for the players, who didn't. A handful of them, like Seaman and Shearer, were certain of their places, but even Graeme Le Saux, the only natural left-footed player in the squad, was fretting that Hoddle hadn't made up his mind about him. If he'd already proved himself, he asked a colleague, why had Glenn played him against Belgium? As Merson recalled, 'everyone was a bag of nerves'.

Most of the players tried to distract themselves by going back out on the golf course, as Hoddle did with Gary Neville and Darren Anderton. Gazza was playing in a four with Ian Walker, Phil Neville and David Seaman. There was, Seaman said, a lot of 'nonsense spoken and written' about 'Gazza secretly drinking on the golf course, smuggling bottles of beer out in club bags'.

This was rubbish for a start, because beer was not banned on the golf course. The beer cart was coming round to all the players, courtesy of the management. If you don't want the players to have a beer, don't send the cart round. Some players only had soft drinks, but it was our choice. We [Seaman's foursome] all had a beer; it was hot and thirsty work going round the course. The press had been asked to stay away, but there were cameras everywhere, most of them pointed at Gazza. But we all knew that so we were hardly going to make idiots of ourselves by getting drunk.

The media evidence that Gazza was drunk rested on a piece of film which showed him doing his 'demented spider routine' on his back. In fact, wrote Seaman, he was just laughing his head off at how bad his golf was compared to Seaman's and Walker's. Sheringham, though, remembered that Gazza 'had downed a few beers during our golf game and he'd downed a few more after he'd finished. And I've got to admit he was quite the worse for wear when he went in to see Glenn.'

Rather incongruously, the players met on the hotel terrace for tea and scones at four in the afternoon. Merson thought 'Gazza was drunk, no doubt about it. He had apparently had some cans of beer on the golf course, against all orders. Some of the boys were laughing, but I didn't find it funny. "This is sh*t. I've gone," he was saying. "I can't do it any more." He had played well at the golf, despite the drinking, I was told, but now he had stopped it was all kicking in.' In a desperate bid to liven him up, Merson and Adams took him down to the swimming pool, took off his clothes and threw him in. 'We sat with him by the pool for half an hour, and he was saying, "I won't go, I'm finished."' To cheer him up, Merson insisted that it would be him who was going home, and that if he was, he'd be smashing up his hotel room. 'To this day Gazza blames me for putting the idea in his head,' wrote Merson. At one point, Gazza turned to Adams and said, 'I'm not going to go, am I, Tone? Am I going to go?' As Adams said in his autobiography, 'At this point I still thought he was, but it was becoming easy to see how he might not be.'

The press consensus on the six who were going to be sent home was Les Ferdinand, Rio Ferdinand, Ian Walker, Andy Hinchcliffe and two out of Merson, Phil Neville and Nicky Butt. Phil Neville was stunned to get his bad news, but by this stage, according to Sheringham, 'the odd whisper started to circulate. There was going to be a shock, went the murmurings, and it possibly involved Gazza being sent home.'

In the hotel, Gazza steadied himself to meet Hoddle. Although Adams said that Gorman put an arm around him and forewarned him, the player himself and Hoddle reckoned he read the bad news on Glenn Roeder's face. Gazza later said, 'I took one look at his face and I knew something terrible had happened. He looked upset and couldn't meet my eye. He just said, "The gaffer wants to see you." I didn't need to ask any more.'

Hoddle was waiting for Gazza in the Royal Suite with Kenny G's saxophone muzak providing the soundtrack. The CD was supposed to make the players feel less nervous; with the muzak on they wouldn't be walking into a silent room. But, as Gascoigne entered, the lite music could only have enraged him more. Hoddle, too, must have been tenser than usual because he'd had a call before his first meeting telling him that Gazza was half-cut.

Hoddle looked at Gazza and said something like, 'Paul, I'm sorry, you're not coming to France. You're not fit enough.' He later said that he might have added 'It's nothing to do with anything else.' Gazza started crying, which gave Hoddle a strong sense of *déjà vu*: just a few nights back he'd had a dream in which Gazza was sitting across the table from him in tears. Gazza, according to Hoddle, said something like, 'I don't believe this, gaffer. My career is finished.' While Hoddle was wondering if Gazza was in any state to listen to reason, the player shook his hand and wished him all the best. Hoddle then stood up and gave Gazza an affectionate squeeze on the shoulder, saying, 'Look, we've just run out of time with you.'

Gazza turned to go, but then – and both participants agree on this – he went berserk. He kicked the chair over, turned as if to go again and then let fly a volley of abuse. In between the swear words, he told Hoddle that it had been a crap week, with all the stuff surrounding his wife and now this. He turned again, and seemed to Hoddle like a man possessed. 'This time I had my arm ready . . . I thought he was going to hit me. There was a lamp to his right and he just punched it. The glass shattered all over the room.' Either Roeder or Gorman then came rushing in to steer Gascoigne back to his room.

As Hoddle stared at the broken glass, word that something had 'gone off' between Gazza and the gaffer quickly spread. Seaman, Ince and Merson rushed up to his room. Seaman found Gazza 'in a worse state than I had imagined. I had never seen a man like it. He was crying his eyes out and it was like watching a man totally destroyed.' Merson remembered that 'Dave Seaman and one or two others were telling him not to worry, that he was still a great player. It was stuff he didn't need to hear in my opinion. What he needed was to hear the truth about himself so he could wise up and do something about it before it was too late. He was not in the mood for anything like that though.' Adams, who had sat next to Gascoigne on the plane back after the

Belgium game, said that because 'he felt he had so many things weighing him down – like his relationship with his wife and the worries of whether he would be able to perform again at a World Cup – once he woke up that Sunday morning after a drinking session, he was probably in pain again and needed an anaesthetic. I've been there. The smashing up of his hotel room showed the anger and self-loathing that we can feel. There was no dignity there.'

There wasn't much dignity, either, in the speed with which, via Sheryl Gascoigne and her friend Rebekah Wade, the deputy editor of the *Sun*, a six-figure deal was struck for the player's side of the story (Mark Palmer suggested that Sheryl was keen to keep in with the Murdoch empire to further her ambitions as a cable TV presenter). Whatever the truth of the matter, Gazza's side of the story turned out to be a well-paid suicide note. It did not differ greatly from Hoddle's account and seemed to serve little purpose apart from to boost his bank balance and the *Sun*'s circulation.

Gazza told the *Sun* readers he was '100 per cent convinced I was going. Glenn and the team of coaches had given me no indication that my place was in jeopardy.' That doesn't quite square with the harrowing accounts of Merson or Adams. Sheringham also wondered if, 'looking back, Gazza wasn't half expecting the axe', but the conspiracy theory soon became the basis for the case for Gazza's defence. The idea, if that's not putting it too strongly, was that Hoddle had at the last minute, in some rather underhand way, staged some sort of coup to deprive Gascoigne of his rightful place in the squad. Ian Hamilton put the case most eloquently: 'In every public statement he made during May 1998, Glenn Hoddle allowed us to believe that, come what may, Gazza would almost certainly be in his final squad.' And now this. 'There was no need for this public banishment,' Hamilton argued. The subtext, according to Hamilton's updated biography, was that Hoddle did not want a 'soccer god' in a squad with many young players who had been in their teens at the time of the tears in Turin and knew nothing of Hoddle's achievements as a player. Surely, Hamilton suggested, it couldn't have all been just a question of physical fitness. If that had been the case, why not pick Gazza and keep him on the bench and use him as and when Hoddle felt the occasion demanded?

Hamilton certainly made a better case for Gascoigne than the player's celebrity friends. Danny Baker's oft-quoted remark that 'Gazza is bigger than the game' was a gift for anyone who wanted to convict Gazza in the media through guilt by association. Mel Stein said his client was being treated like a Nazi war criminal, another gift to the Gazza-haters. His father, John Gascoigne, called Hoddle a 'liar', much as Baker had labelled Hoddle's decision 'weasely', but sounded more convincing when he said, 'I don't know how he's [Gazza's] going to cope.' His son's immediate coping strategy – flying off to Florida with Sheryl – at least kept them out of the immediate spotlight while Britain adjusted to the heretical idea of an England World Cup team without Paul Gascoigne.

Hamilton was right to say that Hoddle's 'what's all the fuss about?' air was slightly disingenuous and that fitness, despite what the manager said at the time and since in his diaries, could not have been the only issue. And the idea that Gascoigne was somehow shabbily treated that weekend has been fed by revelations of Hoddle's subsequent limitations as a man-manager. Yet Hoddle might, to some extent, have been protecting the player. Was he really supposed to stand up in public and give chapter and verse on every piece of advice, every coded warning, every last chance the player had ignored? Or was he (and there is some evidence for this) best served by telling the world that Gascoigne was no longer a source of inspiration to his fellow internationals but a cause for division?

Merson, in conversation with the writer Dave Bowler, said, 'I did feel for Gazza. He'd worked so hard, but it all got on top of him at the wrong time. I don't think he was in the right state to go, and now he's got to be honest with himself, I think he'd admit it as well. When you're playing that kind of football you have to be spot on or you can't play.' Adams echoed Merson's view: 'Glenn was making the right decision . . . As far as I'm concerned, Gazza was an ill man and Glenn did not understand properly the illness of addiction, even if he tried to deal with it the best way he knew how.' Sheringham, while shocked by the decision, did not seem to feel it was unfair, speculating, in his book, more on how Gazza's 'colourful past had finally caught up with him'.

David Seaman, Gascoigne's fishing pal, said clearly that he thought it was the wrong decision, and so did many of the other players. There's some evidence that Gary Neville, still grieving after his brother's departure, also agreed with Seaman. Against that, apart from the reactions quoted above, is the story in Mark Palmer's book that Alan Shearer and Robert Lee had been to Kenny Dalglish's villa not far from La Manga to complain about Gazza's attitude. Hoddle, as you would expect, said the players understood why he'd made his decision and generally supported him; the truth, as far as it can be discerned, is that the squad was split, probably more split than the rest of the country, which lined up in significant numbers behind Hoddle. 'Any other decision, based purely on football, would have been ludicrous,' the *Sunday Telegraph*'s Patrick Barclay asserted, although dissenting opinions were never too far away. 'I'd have taken Gazza,' said Terry Butcher. 'I'd have locked him in a padded cell for the tournament. He's a joker, but a big-game player who will get you out of jail.'

But even though many will argue he brought it on himself, it is impossible to read any account of that Sunday without feeling deeply sorry for Paul Gascoigne. Equally, it is impossible to envisage the incoherent, drunken figure who had his clothes taken off and was shoved into a swimming pool so that he could pass himself off as sober enough to meet the team manager and suggest, seriously, that he was in any state to cope with the pressure of the World Cup finals. Gascoigne's fragile personality might, that weekend, have been on the brink of a nervous breakdown (indeed, he would suffer one of a sort a few months later).

Exactly when Hoddle made his decision to exclude Paul Gascoigne is ultimately irrelevant. There is evidence that he had been considering since February what he would do if Gazza couldn't come through, but only he and his staff really know when that plan became a serious proposition. But that decision was probably based on two sensible grounds: a severe lack of match fitness and the player's state of mind, which could, if it persisted, seriously disrupt the squad's morale, just as, Hoddle maintained, all the debate over Kevin Keegan and Trevor Brooking had disrupted England's 1982 World Cup campaign. It was not an easy decision for Hoddle to take, but neither was it a stupid one.

Another World Cup odyssey had ended in tears for Gazza. But this time not in a stadium in Turin, in the semi-final of a World Cup in front of many thousands of adoring fans, but alone in a hotel room in Spain.

8. STARS IN HIS EYES

I've made more money out of tears than Ken Dodd.

Paul Gascoigne

TONIGHT, MATTHEW, I'M GOING TO BE . . . RAY STUBBS

Still got your Paul Gascoigne boxer shorts? Thought not. Bet that Paul Gascoigne doll you bought, for a laugh, is in the garage. Fair enough, have it your way, you never owned one. Nor did you buy a copy of Gazza's number two hit single 'Fog on the Tyne' (made with Lindisfarne). We knew his lawyer had triumphantly declared 'Gazza's in the Beatles league', but wasn't that taking it all a bit too literally? As for the follow-up, 'Geordie Boys (Gazza Rap)', to give it its full technical title, it might have got as high as number 34 and spent two weeks in the charts but it was probably the most disposable slice of vinyl since, well, Ken Dodd's last hit single, 'Hold My Hand' (which got to number 44 in 1981 – that information is, of course, strictly for the anoraks).

For a real piece of Gazza memorabilia, you need to find a shop with a decent stock of videos and ask them if they've got a copy of Paul Gascoigne's *Referee!* (you have to say it in the same tone of exasperation you'd use at the ground on a Saturday afternoon, or the effect just isn't the same). Now, most sporting videos are obviously just another way of extracting hard-earned cash from the terminally loyal fan. Yes, for just over a tenner, you can get the minimum amount of action and film required under the Trade Descriptions Act for whatever you're buying to be officially classified as a video. As for sporting videos hosted by a sports 'personality', well, that noise you hear is the sound of a barrel being very loudly (if profitably) scraped.

All of which makes Paul Gascoigne's *Referee!* such a pleasant surprise. Because it's well worth £9.99 of anybody's money. Even yours. It's not just the footage, although there is stacks of it, on the hoary old theme of the mistakes made by the man in the middle (and, for that matter, the men on either side – they don't get off lightly either). There can be few other football videos which give you the chance to watch the entire board of directors of a Spanish Third Division club chase a referee across the pitch, almost over a high fence and around the back of the terraces. As if that isn't enough, you also get a rare glimpse of Paul John Gascoigne esquire, man about town, wit, raconteur and sports presenter.

It has to be said straight away that our man can be a bit wooden when he's talking straight to a camera, but no more so than Ray Stubbs when he's presenting *Final Score* on BBC1 on Saturday afternoons. The set leaves a little to be desired too. Our hero is shot in front of a moodily lit bar and, while the ambience is supposed to be one of smoky night-club sophistication, it's more Bailey's in Stoke-on-Trent than Las Vegas or Monte Carlo. A small mob has been gathered together, presumably to give Gazza the feeling that he's doing his stuff before a live audience, but they don't seem terribly responsive. If you watch the video the whole way through, your abiding memory of the invited audience will probably be the tall woman in the front row with the frizzy hair.

Mind you, this isn't one of Gazza's better hair days either. He's in his bleached period, but either he's just come back from the wrong hairdresser or he's only a day away from his next appointment, because his hair in this video is disconcertingly soft and fluffy. He hasn't looked this girlish since he did that shoot for *Esquire* magazine when he was slim and trim and the art director put mascara on him. (Not exactly the kind of clipping you want nailed to a wall in the dressing room.)

As for the one-liners . . . some are really quite funny: the Ken Dodd–Tears crack, for instance; the ageing but still amusing line '"We've all made mistakes," as the hedgehog said climbing off a lavatory brush.' But others are so awful you fear they must have been filed in a gagwriter's drawer since being summarily rejected by the stand-ups who 'starred' in *The Comedians* for Granada TV in the 1970s.

In his flick through the worst refereeing decisions of all time it would be impossible for him to leave out the Hand of God. So we see Shilton and Maradona in unequal combat umpteen times (Paul blames the linesman on the far side by the way; he had a clear view and never said a thing), only this time Gazza does the voiceover as if he's Maradona. The two had met, in a friendly between Seville and Lazio, and the great Diego had shaken Gazza's hand after he'd scored a wondrous solo goal against the Spanish side. That said, Gascoigne's attempt to get inside the mind of Maradona (an opportunity too good to resist really; after all, how many managers, fans, journalists etc. have tried to get 'inside the mind of Paul Gascoigne'?) lacks any great psychological insight. In a unique hybrid Argentinian–Geordie accent, Gazza says 'Goalll! This ees the hand I score goalll weeeth. Next time I use two hands.'

If you can stand the script's insistence on using all the obvious puns (Maradona saw the opportunity and, er, grabbed it), the endless parade of 'dodgy decisions' is quite fun. And talking of dodgy decisions – Paul, where did you get that shirt? But it's good to watch because although Gazza could take a few lessons from Des Lynam as a presenter, he seems boyish, naive even, just one of the lads having a bit of a lark, meaning no one any harm and all that. You have to remind yourself that, by this stage in his career, Gazza had been through two leg breaks, three seasons of hell and purgatory in Lazio, been reviled and revered (often simultaneously) for six years and was approaching his 29th birthday. Yet you can still see why most of his team-mates would echo Bobby Robson's famous description of him as 'really a lovely, lovely boy'.

TONIGHT, MATTHEW, I'M GOING TO BE ... GEORGE BEST

While as a boy he wanted to be Georgie Best, as a man he has spent the best part of a decade trying to evade the precedent set by Best. When Henry Winter, football writer for the *Daily Telegraph*, was interviewed for this book about Gascoigne, he said, 'I admired Gazza the footballer but not Gazza the tabloid celebrity.' Unfortunately, for most of the time that Paul Gascoigne has been famous (and he's been a national figure for twelve years now), the two have been inextricably linked like Siamese twins.

This is not to say that Gazza has been a sacrificial victim of the tabloids. The media has not set out to destroy him in the way that he believes, sincerely but wrongly, that it destroyed Princess Diana. (Can it just be coincidence that his best performance in an England shirt for years came on that Candle in the Wind memorial night at Wembley?) Gazza is not purely an innocent victim, a fox torn to pieces by the world's newshounds.

When he signed for Tottenham, he was already contracted to give the story to a national newspaper. Over the years, he has had a column in the *Sun*, has given an (unwise) exclusive to the *News of the World* about his ill-treatment of his then girlfriend Sheryl Kyle, has given another (professionally suicidal) exclusive to the *Sun* on his shock exclusion from the 1998 England World Cup squad, has raised £150,000 from *Hello!* magazine for his wedding pictures, and has even authorised his own agent to invade his own privacy in an authorised biography by telling us that after some engagement where Buckingham Palace officials had warned him not to get touchy-feely with Princess Diana, he burst into tears in his hotel room looking like 'a frightened, tear-stained boy totally unable to cope with the world around him'. He is probably one of the few footballers who has gone to talk to his new bank manager with a TV crew in the car with him (as happened in Rome once).

We're a lot wiser in the ways of celebrity these days, but the unpleasant truth is, as Gascoigne and his advisers were to discover, if you start your career as a footballing celebrity by appearing in a clown's suit in the *Mirror*, it's going to be hard for you later on to argue that what you really really want is artistic credibility.

Like Best, Gascoigne rapidly learned that his every move, real or invented, would be judged by tabloids on behalf of their millions of readers. The relentless public scrutiny wore Best down, and after just a few months of Gazzamania began to eat away at our hero too. The advantages of not being known to the average reader of the *Sun* only become apparent once you've become famous. As Gascoigne complained in 1991 after an incident in a Newcastle night club:

> People call me flash. I like to stand my mates a drink or two even if the bill is over the top. It's not me being flash. It's just that I would

feel embarrassed in case people would think I was a tight bastard. You can't win. I get on a train and sit in second class and people think, 'Tight bastard. Money he's got, and he sits in second class.' So I think 'F*** them' and go in first class, and then they say, 'Look at that f***ing flash bastard in first class.' Where do I win?

Even before that, just after he'd moved to London, he'd moaned to *Time Out* about

girls I wasn't seeing, but they put them in the paper, a girl I was supposed to be having an affair with, which was untrue. Some girls go in the paper and say, 'I've been with Paul Gascoigne.' I mean, it's all right for me, she could be a good-looking girl so the lads are like 'Cor!' even though I don't like it. What must this girl feel like? She must feel like a right tart. They camp out at the end of the drive in cars, like little kids. I mean those people have to go back to their families. Imagine one of them going home and his wife saying, 'How did your day go?' 'Great. I sat outside Gascoigne's house all day and all night waiting for him to come out.' His wife must say, 'What do you want to do that for, you prick?'

And, although he has been known to admit (well, occasionally) that the sporting critics were right to give him a hard time, he has also not been afraid to hit back in outrage. 'I'd like to see some of these guys if their father has an operation, if their uncle has a slit throat, your house gets robbed, they take a helluva lot of stuff, then you come back and they expect you to be happy straight away.' It sounds self-pitying. Heck, it *is* self-pitying, but it is not stupid.

Best, for all his public spats with Gazza, would have known exactly what the player was going through. There is even a suggestion that, as the depth of Gascoigne's personal problems became apparent, he regretted being used by the tabloids as a blunt instrument with which to hit Gazza over the head. Both have seen their lives disappear into a tabloid food mixer and emerge as grotesque two-dimensional cartoon caricatures of their real selves. Both have, for instance, been the subject of national appeals by tabloids concerning their drinking habits.

TONIGHT, MATTHEW, I'M GOING TO BE . . . ELVIS PRESLEY

George Best, for obvious reasons, was always going to be the celebrity Gazza most often got compared to. But it seemed intriguing that, on that night in La Manga before he was exiled by Hoddle, one of the songs he was singing on the karaoke was Elvis Presley's 'Wooden Heart'. Because Gazza is almost the Elvis of English football.

It may sound stupid, but think about it. Both are known by a single name, and only a handful of people have been famous enough in the last 50 years to be known that simply. Both came from unfashionable, poverty-stricken parts of their country (Gateshead in Gazza's case; rural Mississippi in Elvis's). Each is regarded as an *idiot savant*, a person of immense natural gifts without the intelligence to handle them (this doesn't mean this is true, of course, but this is the media perception of the two of them). Both have clung, controversially, to friends from their youth for protection against the outside world (for Five Bellies read Red West and the Memphis Mafia). Both have had long-term relationships with a woman who, ultimately, they married relatively briefly (Sheryl and Priscilla). Both have been marketed relentlessly, down to having their own brand of toothpaste. Both have been the subject of obsessive, intrusive criticism by the media (the difference being that Elvis was dead when Albert Goldman did his stuff; Gazza has been 'Goldmanned' alive). Both have been sneered at for their alleged flashiness and lack of good taste (for Graceland read Gazza's wish to have a trout farm at the bottom of his Roman garden). Both have been famous for their weight problems, and both have been synonymous with fast food (kebabs for Gazza; Elvis became, posthumously, the burger king). Both have had one event which is deemed to have changed their lives and careers for good (Elvis 'died' when he joined the Army; Gazza was never the same player after that tackle). Both have been compared to royalty (Elvis was the king, a title he disliked; Gazza was the clown prince and, in Italy, the 'little king'). Both were originals (Elvis was too big to be confined even by rock 'n' roll; Gazza was too naturally talented to adhere to the squad-drill discipline of the training ground). Both have had pretenders to the throne (Cliff, Ricky Nelson, Bobby Darin; Dazza, Macca, Becks). Both have been famously misunderstood by the critics yet adored by their fans. And in both cases, the fans have sought to shift the blame from the person concerned (Elvis fans blame the Colonel – Tom Parker, his manager; Gazza fans blame Mel Stein and the press).

It is the Gazzas of this world, partly through their own weaknesses, who seem most likely to get torn apart by the 'bastards in news'. No disrespect to David Platt, but if every footballer is going to have to be like him just to keep out of the papers, English football is going to be an infinitely duller place. Comparing Gazza to Platty is a bit like comparing Elvis to Cliff Richard. Given the choice, most fans would take Elvis every time.

Gazza is also, like Elvis, a consummate performer. At the heart of his appeal is a wonderful contradiction. He looks, as his old team-mate Terry Butcher said, just like a punter who happens to be on the pitch. The tantrums, the backchat, the exaggerated gestures seem borrowed from the park on a Sunday morning. Even his shape is not what you'd expect from a world-class footballer (when he was at Lazio the club doctor told him that on the football pitch he'd always look fatter than he really was). On bad days he turns salmon-red and begins gasping for air. All this helps to create the illusion that he is just like you and me. And then, just when you're consoling yourself with this thought, he'll hit a 30-yard pass with the outside of his foot over and through the defence. Gazza is one of us, and yet not one of us at all, rather a member of some select, gifted species which can see passes and do things with a ball that we can only dream of. Even in our dreams, our fantasies, we're making the passes or scoring the goals in the manner of someone else. We're copycats. He is the inventor. Just like Elvis.

And more than most footballers he brings to what can be a kick-and-rush sport the drama of a theatrical performance. As Patrick Barclay said, 'Those tears in Turin, that was an incredibly theatrical moment.' He has cried often since – in the Olympic Stadium after equalising in the Rome derby; on television for Walkers Crisps; in a complex in Spain where his dream of World Cup glory died; and on Stevenage station, where he had what seems close to a nervous breakdown – but without that first set of tears (from which all the sequels sprang) football would not be what it is today. Nor, for that matter, would Gascoigne, as he recognises with his one-liner about Ken Dodd.

But he doesn't have to cry to capture your attention. You can get lost in the simple business of trying to figure out what he's going to do next. There's a tangle with the keeper, they both fall over, Gazza darts up, you tense . . . is he going to have a go? Do something really stupid? Just when you're bracing yourself for the worst, he's brushing the keeper's hair with his hand and giving him a hug. The joke over, Gazza moves on.

Gazza has a performer's grasp of his audience. In his prime, he would sense the fans' attention slacking and do something, something which would just underline that very quality of daft-as-a-brushness or something stunning like that free-kick against Arsenal in 1991. Something so stunning that even the other team are exchanging glazed gazes and saying to each other, 'Did he really do that?'

He has been and always will be accused of playing to the crowd by some of the coaches who stand in professional judgement over him. They have a point. But it also looks very much like unselfconscious show-manship, the natural instincts of a performer who is as original and, at times, as strange as they come.

9. NOT JUST ONE OF THE LADS

When God gave him this enormous talent, he took his brain out at the same time to even things up.

Tony Banks, ex-sports minister

If Tony Banks has done nothing else (and right now it's hard to name any of his other achievements – let's skip over England's 2006 World Cup bid, shall we?) he has succinctly summed up the prevailing view of Paul Gascoigne. The remark, made in an after-dinner speech, is a more insulting echo of Bobby Robson's much-quoted observation that Gazza was as daft as a brush, and of Gazza's own subsequent observation that all his brains were in his feet. George Best put it even more bluntly in one of their public spats when he said that he'd thought 10 was the number on Gazza's shirt and then he realised it was his IQ.

Just for the record, Gazza passed two CSEs, one more than Alan Shearer, who is fortunate enough not to have his intellect questioned by the likes of Tony Banks. Not that paper qualifications are that relevant in this context. With both players it's possible to imagine that they just couldn't be bothered with schoolwork. That, certainly, is the impression you get from Robin McGibbon's account of Gazza's schooldays. Gazza knew what he wanted to do from an early age. When a teacher told him that only one in a thousand youngsters makes it, he replied, 'Yes, I know, and that one will be me, sir!'

While Gazza isn't likely to win the Nobel Prize for Mathematics, people who have met him may think he's daft but they don't refer to him as stupid. 'Thick is not a word I would use,' said Patrick Barclay of the *Sunday Telegraph*. 'Unusual, certainly, lyrical, obsessive, witty.'

Another writer, who has observed him at close hand for several weeks, said of him: 'Stupid is not a word I would use. He's different, but I would say abnormal not sub-normal. There's something different about him, whether it's something to do with his background I don't know, but he can be very sharp, very funny and yet capable of acts of breathtaking immaturity.'

There are stories of Gazza being told, in his early days, to go incognito if he found the attention too much, and him asking, 'Where's cognito?' Again, though, if you weren't there it's hard to say if he was just being dumb or joking. There is certainly evidence of naivety. Brian McClair tells a wonderful story of the day Gazza came down to the Manchester United training ground at the Cliff. 'Bryan Robson was over an hour late for training, which was unlike him. His mobile wasn't working. His wife said he'd left hours ago. Eventually the skipper turned up white as a sheet, his car almost a write-off. He'd been clattered by a lorry. But, being Robbo, he still managed to sell the car, at a profit, to Gazza, who was last seen sitting behind the wheel of it as it was hauled northwards up the motorway.'

The player himself, whether as a means of self-defence or just as a private joke he plays on the outside world, has long since begun to play up to this stereotype. In the Channel 4/Chrysalis documentary *Gazza's Coming Home*, there's an amusing scene in a Sainsbury's car park where Gazza is due to rehearse the next Walkers Crisps TV ad. A senior member of the production crew, possibly the director or the script-writer, is telling Gazza what to do (the script consists of the demanding line 'I've got one of these and it didn't hurt a bit'). Gazza, who'd already shot the famous tear-jerking instalment with Gary Lineker, asks if Gary is going to be there. The scriptwriter, who, Gazza decides, bears an uncanny resemblance to Peter Reid, says no, Gary won't be there. So Gazza asks him again. As the scriptwriter walks back to the crew, Gazza grins at the camera and says, 'Watch me wind him up. I get him every time.' The Reid lookalike runs through the script again with the star. Gazza, after sticking his tongue almost into the bloke's ear, peers at him intently as the bloke is talking. Gazza's face is screwed up in concentrated effort as if the director is actually reading him a chapter of Stephen Hawking's *A Brief History of Time* rather than a one-liner for a crisp commercial. After a few seconds, Gazza can't be bothered to screw up his face any more and lets the gag go with a brief smile to himself.

But then Gazza knows how to play dumb. He has done it ever since Bobby Robson first compared him to a brush back in 1989 (the next day, at England training, Gazza had turned up with a brush down his sock). There was even a book of Gazza jokes called *Daft as a Brush*, which backfired when the FA threatened to charge him with bringing the game into disrepute (the blazers at Lancaster Gate were not amused by the swear words or jibes at referees). All good, slightly unclean fun, but Tony Dorigo, an England team-mate at the time, told one biographer, 'Daft wasn't the impression he wanted people to have of him. He certainly didn't want the boss thinking that way. He made light of it because that's his way, but I know from talking to him that he was angry and annoyed. The thing really got to him and fired him up.'

But he never gave up on the joke. Even when his life had reached some kind of personal and professional nadir, in the King Hassan II International Cup in May 1998, he was spotted playing to the crowd at an England training session, picking up a plastic cone and sticking it on his head, as if to signify that, nine years after that first crack, he was still the dunce. In a way, he's just getting to the punchline first, just as, at school, kids learn to make a joke of physical deficiencies like obesity and short sight to stop the other kids in the class taking the mickey. There's also a sense with Gazza that this cartoon character is his gift to us. That, on the matter of his grey matter, he's living down to our expectations.

In any list of adjectives usually used to describe Paul John Gascoigne, daft wins out. A full list of the most commonly used words says as much about our attitude to the player as it does about the man himself. Here (in no order of importance) is a representative sample: bloated, boorish, bubbly, charismatic, clown, controversial, crying, drunk, father, flawed, funny, genius, heart-of-gold, husband, hyperactive, immature, inspired, jack-the-lad, kid, lad, magnificent, mischievous, misunderstood, overweight, refuelling, string-pulling, strutting, troubled, victim, wife-beating, yob.

Somewhere behind all this is a real person. Because this is a footballing biography, this chapter is not intended to be a journey into the inner recesses of Paul Gascoigne's psyche. Nor is it an attempt, just for the sake of it, to expose the most intimate details of his private life. It is just that with Gazza, even more so than with most other footballers, it is virtually impossible to draw the line between the private person and the professional footballer. His various managers have frequently, over the years, recognised this. Hoddle wanted him to get his 'sensible head' on. Even Venables, the coach who understood him best and got the best out of him (at a price), said of him, 'He's probably got a wider variety of behavioural patterns than other players.' And Smith, when he signed him for the second time, at

Goodison, told the press, 'He's never been long at one club because it is always difficult for someone with his mentality to have continuity in his life.' So what follows is a purely provisional investigation of his personality based upon the considerable, but still ultimately limited, evidence available.

He was born on 27 May 1967 in one of the poorest parts of Gateshead. He was the second of four siblings (he has an elder sister, Anna, and a younger brother and sister, Carl and Lindsay). Every account of Gascoigne's childhood agrees on two things: the family struggled to make ends meet (father John, not having a trade, found it hard to get a job in an area of high unemployment) and Paul Gascoigne loved to play football. He was nine months old when he took his first kick, and by the time he was two he was kicking a ball against the garden wall. In the winter of 1971, his mother confided to a neighbour that it was touch and go whether they could afford to buy Paul the football and boots he wanted for Christmas. They managed somehow, and he spent most of that Christmas Day kicking the ball around the street having, eventually, to be dragged in for lunch by his mum. He had often had to make do with a knackered old tennis ball in the past, although this hadn't stopped him showing off his dribbling skills to his grandfather and shouting, 'Look, grandad, I'm just like Georgie Best.' (At least Gazza was the first one to make the comparison.)

The boy-Gazza sounds very much like the man-Gazza, ammunition for those who maintain that he's never grown up. Certainly until he was 29, the press often referred to him as a lad. As a young lad, he is described as cheeky and naughty (but never nasty), daft about football and not that bothered about his schoolwork, a boy with a sweet tooth. His prodigious gifts as a footballer were, it seems, recognised from a very early age. One of his teachers, Geoff Wilson, talking in 1998, summed it all up in a short paragraph: 'Paul was just a little thing when I first had him, a tiny lad but fantastically skilful. He was like a robot – he could put the ball anywhere you asked. He could also be a right little devil, but he was never nasty, there was no malice in him. You see all these negative things about him in the press, but they're not writing about the person I know.'

So far it sounds like the classic footballer-made-good story torn out of the pages of any footballer's autobiography. But Gazza's childhood wasn't quite that simple. His father didn't always, as Robin McGibbon put it in his book, live with his mother, which must have had some effect on the children. Then, when Paul was eleven, his dad collapsed with a brain haemorrhage. It took a seven-hour operation to save him, but he was warned he should never work again. Like many members of his family, John Gascoigne had suffered from severe migraines for years, only as he got older, his got so intense he would have to sit in a dark room. He'd been told he just had to live with it, something he had grudgingly accepted, until that day when he collapsed.

The family had just made another of their moves (to Dunston) when the attack happened, and Paul's mum, Carol, began working almost around the clock to pay the bills. 'We had to scrape for every penny we had,' said Gazza later. 'I had holes in me shoes, couldn't do PE lessons because I didn't have this and that.' It was the kind of catastrophe that could happen to anybody, except that, according to the psychologist Oliver James, this kind of calamity is more often found in the childhoods of famous people. One in four US presidents, for instance, lost a parent in childhood (the proportion for British prime ministers is estimated to be about the same). Cary Cooper, professor of social psychology at the University of Manchester Institute of Technology, pointed out that the same high incidence of parental loss and childhood trauma can be found in the lives of business leaders. James said that part of what gives these people the drive to be famous 'is the desire to recreate the situations of your childhood, the difference being that this time you're in control. Feelings of parental rejection, no matter how unreasonable they might seem, are a powerful driver for many celebrities.'

This is all a long way from football, Dunston and Gazza, but the point seems relevant. Rationally, Gazza could not blame his dad for 'rejecting him' when he was eleven (although his dad did leave the family home when Gazza was a trainee at Newcastle), but emotions can be unreasonable things. It was at this time that Gazza began to 'adopt' another family, the Spraggons, whose son Keith was thought, locally, to have as much promise as a footballer as Gazza. Keith's dad Harry told McGibbon that he 'would come round for a weekend and stay a fortnight'. This sounds a bit extreme, but certainly Gazza went round to the Spraggon's as often as he could. The Spraggons were the first family Gazza 'adopted' in this way, but they were not to be the last. Later, Chris Waddle's wife would try to persuade Gazza to leave the Waddle household by packing his luggage and putting it in the hallway. Later still, at Rangers, his manager, hearing that he was going to be alone on Christmas Day, invited him round for Christmas lunch. His future 'father figures' would include ex-Newcastle Joe Harvey, who would encourage him in his battles with the club's youth coach, Bobby Robson (they bonded as fellow victims of the media) and Terry Venables.

One of Gazza's great gifts, and somehow he manages to convey this even through the media, is to make people feel responsible for him. Even as worldly-wise a manager as Sir Alex Ferguson was not immune to this. He, of course, had tried to sign him in the summer of 1988; in his memoirs he wrote: 'I still don't know Paul well, but at our meetings I warmed to him. There is something strangely appealing about him. Perhaps it is his vulnerability. You feel you want to be like an older brother or a father to him. You might want to shake him or give him a cuddle, but there is certainly something infectious that gets you involved with him.' This is a remarkable thing for any football manager to say, let alone Sir Alex, but most of Gascoigne's managers would understand what he meant: they've all wanted to shake him or cuddle him at different times. Glenn Hoddle even said the same thing, in slightly different words ('the hammer and the arm around the shoulder') as Gascoigne's England manager.

There was one more childhood trauma to come for Paul Gascoigne, one that, outwardly, affected him much more than his father's attack. In the summer of 1979, when Gazza was twelve, Steven Spraggon, Keith's brother, was run over and killed by a car in front of an ice-cream van near a sweet shop which Gazza and the boys had been in. Paul was probably a helpless bystander as Steven lay in the road with blood coming from his mouth while a friend ran for the boy's mum. Paul was driven home by a friend's dad who remembered, as he dropped the boy off, that he was crying and shaking like a leaf.

Only Gazza really knows what effect that had on him. But some immediate effects were obvious to his friends. Understandably enough, he began to have bad nightmares and to wake up in the middle of the night crying.

(This might be the starting-point of his habit, so annoying to future room-mates, of sleeping with the lights on. When Waddle and he were room-mates at Spurs, before Gazzamania and all that, Waddle recalled being woken by a draught of cold air. 'There was Paul standing at an open window, stark naked, looking down two floors and asking timidly, in a frightened voice, "Is there anybody there?"') He began to spend even more time with the Spraggons, which comforted them at first, although on his visits he would often just lie awake at night thinking about the accident. Later, they came to feel that there was a real danger of his becoming a surrogate brother to Keith, so they quietly discouraged contact. He found other families to tag on to, though; in the words of one friend, 'he would go to other people's homes and cling on'.

His mannerisms began to change: he started stuttering more often, blinking, making funny noises, twitching; later, as a young player at Newcastle, he would acquire a nervous cough and even a habit of barking. (The symptoms came and went. One of the club scouts said to him once, 'You've got rid of the dog then, Paul?') His parents took him to therapy. These habits formed the basis of a repertoire of facial expressions which have led some writers, notably Ian Hamilton, to speculate as to whether Gascoigne suffered from a form of what is known as Tourette's syndrome.

Again, this might sound far-fetched. Just because, to adapt Venables' phrase, he has a wider variety of facial expressions than most footballers, does he have to be suffering from a syndrome? The symptoms listed by Hamilton in his book make intriguing reading though: 'an excess of nervous energy, and a great production of strange motions and notions: tics, jerks, mannerisms, grimaces, noises, curses, involuntary imitations and compulsions of all sorts, with an odd elfin humour and a tendency to antic and outlandish kinds of play'. There is also a 'capacity for inspired improvisation'. Sufferers may also swear or make inappropriate remarks (when Gazza was booked for swearing at a referee once, he complained that he had been swearing but not at the referee – a Tourette's sufferer would know just what he meant). Usually, the syndrome, which is hereditary and most often found in boys, develops before a person is eighteen. Gazza's mannerisms started in his early teens, though they might also have been some sort of post-traumatic stress reaction. But there's no denying there's a lot in that list that sounds like Gazza. You don't have to watch videos of him playing football for too long to see 'strange motions' come over his face. Some of them are deliberate, but some suggest, as his old scout said, that he doesn't know he's doing them.

Take the Everton–Aston Villa game at Goodison Park on 5 November 2000. A sodden Guy Fawkes day, and no fireworks from Gazza either, whose most conspicuous act is to slip when taking a free-kick and injure his thigh. But let's rewind the match to an incident early in the first half when Gascoigne is angry with the referee. The Sky cameras pick up the usual stream of expletives from the player, which neither the commentators or the pundits seem inclined to translate. The eyes are blinking, the head is shaking, and it all just seems oddly exaggerated, as if his reactions are magnified somehow, completely out of proportion to the actual event. It is, after all, a free-kick in a not particularly dangerous area.

This is no isolated incident. Stick *Gazza's Coming Home* in your video and fast-forward to near the end, when he has just scored a hat-trick against Aberdeen to clinch another title for Rangers. He runs into the tunnel, raises the ball in his hand and shouts his son's name, dedicating the hat-trick to him, but shouts it loud enough to raise the Ibrox roof. He is hyped up, obviously – he's just clinched his first League title – but the violence of the shout is still slightly shocking. Then, as the reporter with the mike and the camera crew circle him, you can see him trying to calm down, to look just normally pumped up. He bends over and takes a deep breath. It takes a few seconds for him to revert to a state where he can look sensible on camera. Even then he turns to the other set of cameras, points and says, 'That's the comeback!' It's a glimpse of the cocky, twitching, hyperactive Gazza which so many of his team-mates have described seeing moments before kick-off.

There is abundant evidence of this excessive natural energy. In 1990, after a pre-World Cup finals warm-up game against Cagliari, he partnered Steve Hodge in a three-hour tennis match on the same day (they won 4–6, 6–3, 7–5). There was an even more notorious tennis game before the tie against Belgium. His PA in Italy (when he was at Lazio), Jane Nottage, noted, 'His brain, hands and nervous system were rather like a complicated electrical circuit and there was a danger that the whole thing would blow a fuse.' (It was his manager, Bobby Robson, who blew a fuse that afternoon.) He had an apparent inability to sit still during England team briefings in 1990 and a boredom threshold which was, to use one of Gazza's own sayings, 'lower than a snake's belly'. Waddle, in his autobiography (ghosted by Mel Stein), tells of the trauma of sharing a room with Gazza, of his reluctance to sleep, even with the lights on, the daft pranks used to postpone the dreaded moment when a room-mate might say 'Good-night, Gazza'. For Spurs and England, Venables would often have to tell Gazza to stop training (he was back to the same old routine at Everton, training till 4 p.m. on most days and winning the squad's head tennis contest). As for the improvisations, we've seen enough evidence of those on the pitch over the years.

Even so, Tourette's is a possibility, nothing more. And one needs to be wary when exploring this because it is all too easy to turn Gazza into a circus freak; indeed, the media might already have done so, partly with the player's assistance. And here we're not talking about tabloid exclusives but his appearances on stages like Danny Baker's TV chat show, where he admitted to his fixation with towels. 'All the towels in my home have got to be level [when piled on a rack]. That's terrible, isn't it? I put a towel down and if it's a bit out of shape I tell myself, "Don't worry about it. Go to the pub and forget it." So I would lock the door but still go on about the towel all the time. I'd be 200 yards up the road and think, "No, go back and sort it out." I'd run back, open the door and put the towel straight.' When he bought his first house, he added, he hated bringing friends home in case they moved things. It is, as Hamilton observed, odd stuff from a jester who used to make burgers out of cat poo for his mate and once greased the door handles of some Rangers team-mates' hotel rooms so they couldn't get out of their rooms on Scottish Cup final day.

For further evidence that Gazza is, well, different you need only read Brough Scott's interview with him, done a month after the player's most recent self-inflicted injury. Looking at the marks on the player's recovering left arm, Scott asked the obvious question. 'The plaster cast was due off in the hospital today,' Gazza told him, 'and I was a bit bored last night so I decided to cut it off in the kitchen and spiked myself.' As Scott noted at the time, you couldn't make this stuff up. Again, it's no proof, but people who have Tourette's syndrome are more likely than the rest of the population to suffer from obsessive compulsive disorder. Patrick Barclay remembers meeting him in Lazio for an interview and going to a restaurant with Gascoigne and his party. 'There must have been ten or twelve of us. He got a bit hungry waiting for the meal to arrive and they had put some mozzarella rings on the table. He had one, and then by the time the meal had arrived, he'd eaten all twelve of them.'

Not exactly your average working-class boy made good. Yet the man himself still feels obliged to say, as he did after his ejection from the 1998 England World Cup squad, that 'What people don't understand is that underneath I'm just an ordinary bloke from Newcastle. I'd much prefer to go to a working men's club and have a pint, play dominoes or a game of cards than go to flash parties or film premieres.' Nice try, Gazza, but it's not quite true, is it? Sure you might find film premieres a yawn, but neither are you just one of the lads, if you ever were. Indeed, being 'one of the lads' may just be another of your disguises.

As a teenage boy, after those twin traumas, he seemed to one friend more nervous, 'frightened in a way', while another said that to many who didn't know him he came across as 'an arrogant boy with too much to say for himself and a cocky way of saying it'. But friends saw this assertiveness as masking his own insecurities at coming from such a poor area and having to fight for what he got. He has never lost this cockiness, this arrogance, this (as Hoddle put it) cheeky chappiness. Indeed, it's one of the reasons he became so famous so quickly. As Pete Davies wrote in an article for *FourFourTwo* magazine in March 1995, 'What won over so many was the way the skill was so seamlessly an expression of character, a mix of fearlessness and cheek, as if your favourite naughty kid had been let loose in the toy shop.'

To return to Oliver James's research about celebrities who suffered childhood traumas, he observed that such arrogance is part of what drives them to become famous. 'They have a determination to show the world, to be different. But it isn't the same as having healthy self-confidence. Often these people suffer from terribly low self-esteem which may have to do with the fact that they feel they haven't had the normal amount of parental love as a child. This is why, often, the very people who become famous are the least well equipped to deal with it.'

Certainly Gazza has, at times, seemed lost in his fame. Jane Nottage wrote of the time when Gazza invited her to sit next to him for dinner with his party in a restaurant in Rome. The atmosphere was reasonably tense because the next day he was due for more tests on his knee. As soon as Nottage sat down, Gazza blurted out, 'I don't want it to get like before, with everyone always on at me. I can't take that kind of pressure. I hate it.' She said it was her job to take the pressure off him, and he nodded. 'Don't let it get like before, Jane.' Part of the subtext of Nottage's book is a suggestion that Gazza's lawyer and accountant (Stein and Lazarus) mishandled their client, and this story obviously fits in with that theme, but it sounds authentic enough. The 'before' of which Gazza talked was the heady days of Gazzamania when the footballer and the human being became a product (well, lots of products, actually). And the man at the centre of all this confessed that 'The only time I feel safe is in the middle of a football pitch.' He even admitted that there were times when he felt like 'doing a runner'. Five years later, in a television interview, he would say, 'People ask me how do I cope? I don't honestly know myself.'

In Nottage's view (her book was finished in July 1993) he was too sensitive, fragile even, to cope with it all. Not really one of the lads. There is, as Sir Alex noticed and Smith identified, a loneliness, a vulnerability about him. Often he tries to overcome this by surrounding himself with people, with a recreated family. In Italy, he hoped to 'adopt' Glenn Roeder and his family, but that didn't work out. At Spurs, he took over the Waddle household until Lorna finally told Chris that it was Gazza or her. And when Gazza did move out and proudly invited them to his new house, Waddle saw that his mate had created 'a carbon copy of the Waddle household. It was odd going to visit Paul. For a long time I felt I'd come into the wrong house, it was so much like my own.'

It is not, ultimately, clear why Gazza's so averse to being alone. 'When I'm alone I start thinking, and I don't like to think a lot,' he once said. Again, doubters might say the only reason he doesn't like to think a lot is because it makes his brain hurt. (This view patronises both Gazza in particular and footballers in general: Winston Churchill, another famous heavy-drinking extrovert, hated thinking as well, as Anthony Storr pointed out in his excellent book, *Churchill's Black Dog*. The chapter on Churchill is worth reading for its surprising echoes of Gazza's story.) But in a 1996 television interview, he put it rather differently: 'When I'm alone, I think of things that happened, with friends, accidents and things, and I get scared.' So the death of Steven Spraggon was still playing on his mind, even then. (There have been other accidents too: the sudden and unexplained death of an old friend after a meal, the tragic and accidental death of one of his nephews.)

Is this a plea for cheap sympathy? In the context of the documentary in which the claim is made, it doesn't appear so. The programme graphically conveyed the claustrophobia which surrounded his life at that time, as a Rangers player. With the press camped outside the hotel, his girlfriend and children and step-children still in Hertfordshire, and no Jimmy Five Bellies (on camera at least), the player seemed incredibly isolated, worrying about his form, about his relationships and, as he said, 'letting things get on top of me'. In this context, his admission that he was 'emotionally depressed' for a while in that first season at Rangers (1995/96) seems perfectly understandable.

Fishing seems to be the one solitary pursuit during which Gazza can relax. He said in that interview, 'I could be having problems with Sheryl, with my football, but when I'm going fishing I don't think about any of those things. But when I've stopped doing it, they all come back.' David Seaman took Gazza fishing to calm him down before the quarter-final against Spain during Euro 96. The idea was to stop 'Gazza becoming pumped up'. And it might have worked if the press hadn't hid behind a bush at the trout farm. But Gazza didn't given up on fishing. Years later he told Brough Scott, 'I can go fishing, me, from seven in the morning to eight at night. I caught two trout yesterday. When I was up in Scotland I caught one, eleven pound. I got a badge and I was in the fishing magazine and all that.' As Venables pointed out, the idea of Gazza sitting perfectly still for hours on end with a rod in his hand is a completely different side of him to what most people expect.

Not that Gazza is your archetypal angler. Seaman said, 'If he doesn't get a bite, he always changes his bait. He complains that I catch more than him, but I tell him that's because he spends so much time tying new knots to his lines. One time, we were fishing from a jetty when he saw a fish rise much further out than we were casting. He was in such a hurry to catch it that he put too much force into his cast and his momentum toppled him head first into the water.'

There's no suggestion whatsoever that this incident was a deliberately comic pratfall, a private equivalent to the very public stunts such as the giant plastic breasts and the belch. Such stunts are hardly the work of a latter-day Oscar Wilde, but at his best, Gazza can be genuinely funny. In the Rangers documentary, for instance, when he was being interviewed about his family, he said, 'My dad's never asked for anything . . . apart from a house, a 740BMW, a boat and a decent wage.' On paper it doesn't read like the greatest joke in the world, but on camera the comic timing was perfect. And during the 1990 World Cup, when the Italian press submitted questions to him in writing, they often came back, as Nottage noted, with one-word answers. 'For example, "Do you think England gave a good performance last night?" would be answered "Yes".' Nottage disapproved, saying that this was just making journalists' jobs harder, clearly missing the joke.

Patrick Barclay, who believes Gazza can be genuinely witty, recalled seeing him play for Spurs against Arsenal. 'He'd been tearing around and getting hyped up and it was clear it was only going to be a matter of time before the referee, I think it was Roger Milford, booked him. When he finally got his book out he held up four fingers to Gazza as if to say "That's four fouls now", and Gazza immediately put five fingers up to say to the referee "Five fouls ref, you missed one." ' However, his more famous joke at a referee's expense, the mock booking, backfired when the robotic ref slapped his name straight into the book.

From a very early age he would do almost anything to entertain people, to keep their attention – another way, perhaps, to stave off that loneliness. 'Anything' could mean swapping the boots around in the dressing room before a match, walking around an Italian restaurant with an inflated condom on his head or, as Stuart Pearce recalled, covering himself in toilet paper and throwing himself off the diving board. Some, notably Chris Woods and Brian Laudrup, have found these stunts hard to take. Even Tony Adams, who understood better than most his colleague's restlessness, said, 'Sometimes you just have to say, when he is being a nuisance around the team hotel, "Look, Gazza, just naff off and go fishing." '

Barclay finds the man 'fascinating. He is beautifully natured.' Fragile? Sensitive? Beautifully natured? Are these really the words to describe a self-confessed wife-beater? Or shouldn't we rather, as Richard Littlejohn did in the *Sun* in 1998, think of him as 'a lowlife thug who battered seven sacks out of his wife'?

At different times, Gazza can be both. If you put Littlejohn's description to him and asked if he thought it just, given what he'd done to his wife, he'd probably say yes. Nor, in his public statements, has he ever taken the easy option and blamed it on the booze. 'I'd had a bit to drink,' he admitted, 'but I wasn't drunk.' There is no defence for what he did to his wife and, to be fair, he hasn't attempted to offer any. But that does not necessarily make him incapable of sudden, outstanding acts of generosity. As Walter Smith, no stranger to Gascoigne's 'deeper, darker side', pointed out, 'He can be a lovely, lovely lad. Whenever we were arranging a trip to a children's hospital or the like, he was the first to put his name on the list. He did an enormous amount of charity work in his free time but, typically, refused to allow anyone to publicise the fact.'

Richard Gough, one of his Rangers team-mates, recalled how Gazza would invariably end up giving his tracksuit top away to a kid who had asked for one. Stuart Pearce once asked him for a signed Lazio shirt, and, after Gazza had said it would be no problem, cynically assumed the request would just be forgotten. It wasn't. Again, during England's opening game of the 1990 World Cup, against the Republic of Ireland, it was Steve McMahon's mistake that gifted Ireland the equaliser; the next day it was Gascoigne who went round to cheer him up. As a boy, trying to console his bereaved friend Keith, he used up all his pocket money to buy his mate two records he wanted. It's hard to mention all this without sounding like you're getting ready to nominate him for one of Esther Rantzen's Hearts of Gold, but this is also part of the real Paul Gascoigne, and no appraisal of his life can be complete or fair without it. Similarly, the many acts of personal kindness to children to which those who know him can testify have to be balanced against, for instance, his absence from his wife's hospital bed (on an alcohol-fuelled bonding exercise with Rangers) while she was giving birth to his son, Regan.

The question that is so hard for any outsider to know the truth about is how much influence alcohol has had on his life, behaviour and even his injury problems. Stuart Pearce, in his memoirs, suggested that part of the problem was the different attitude to drink in the north-east. Other players privately admit that the culture of English football hasn't helped players like Gascoigne. For decades, binge-drinking has been an approved, almost institutionalised, part of the game for British club footballers.

But many of his team-mates have also gone on record saying that he isn't the heavy boozer of popular myth. Talk of him downing pint after pint at Newcastle is disputed by his colleague (and mentor) Glenn Roeder, who has insisted, 'The lads would train in the morning, then go down to the snooker hall, and play all afternoon. This was often followed by a Chinese before going back home. The only time they had a drink was on a Saturday night in one of the clubs, and then after three shandies they were all on their backs.' You might think that Roeder was exaggerating for effect, but Ian Durrant, who played alongside Gazza at Rangers, backed this view up: 'This reputation as a boozer bewilders me, because he can't drink. He's very bad at it. Try taking him to TGI Friday's for cocktails and you're on a winner. It's a cheap night.' Lawrie McMenemy, Gascoigne's unofficial England minder when Taylor was manager, observed, 'Paul is the sort of lad who can have a laugh and a good time. He's full of fun and very bubbly and he can do all that without needing a drink. It's the people who surround him who need the drink, and more often than not it is Paul who forks out the readies.'

Gascoigne may well be the type that gets drunk quickly. He would also probably be as conspicuous when he's drunk as he is when he's on a football pitch. He might also have brought the same manic, fizzing energy to his nights out. Venables recalled taking the Spurs squad to his bar, Scribes West, the Monday before that 1991 FA Cup final. Gazza arrived late, saw the wine flowing, and decided to catch up.

He asked Nick, the barman, for a quadruple Drambuie and drank it straight down. He had another – straight down in one – and another, and another. Nick came over and told me Gazza was getting pissed. I did not see how he could be because he had been in the place for less than five minutes, but I told him not to serve Gazza. When

Nick told Gazza, he said, 'Never mind that, get me another drink.' Nick refused. Gazza told him, 'You'll never work in Newcastle.'

The booze was a crutch for him. Even at the 1990 World Cup there was talk of him slipping Bailey's into his coffee in the afternoon, and in Stein's authorised biography there is talk of him persuading the hotel waiters to fizz up his water with a little wine. Nottage's account of his early years at Lazio suggested that he often turned to alcohol when it all (his fitness, form, Sheryl, the press) got too much for him. Graham Taylor was much criticised a few years later for going public with his slightly ambiguous concern about Gazza's lifestyle, but he was not the last manager to make such a warning and he probably deserves some credit for trying to make the player aware of the dangers ahead. At Rangers, Smith once dropped him and didn't speak to him for ten days for violating the club's no-booze-for-48-hours-before-a-match policy.

The best that can be said about Gazza and drink is that at some point after 1990 alcohol began to play such a large part in his existence that by October 1998 he had to check into the Priory to rebuild his life. He had been found, shaking and sobbing, at Stevenage station in Hertfordshire, after coming back from a bender in Dublin. Someone said he looked ready to throw himself under a train. Paul Merson visited him, along with Eric Clapton, who had read of the player's distress. According to Merson's account, 'Eric asked him if he drank on his own. "I like half a bottle of wine in front of the telly," Gazza said, with the alcoholic's understatement. Clapton told him, "You better get used to that, man, because that's all your life will be from now on." ' Both Clapton and Merson rang Gazza's manager at the time, Bryan

Robson, to urge him not to let Gazza talk himself out of the clinic. In the end, Gazza stayed for two weeks. Merson said, 'You could see that his illness wanted him to leave, but the part of his soul that was screaming out for recovery knew he needed to stay.'

Just in case Gascoigne was in any doubt about what was at stake, an alcohol addiction counsellor called Steve Jacobs spelled it out for him: 'The pattern of Gascoigne's life is, as I understand it, terrifying. If his behaviour continues as it is, the boy's life will progress in one of three ways. He will end up in the gutter, in prison or he will die. I have this horrific fear that one of these days I'm going to pick up a paper and read that he's committed suicide. If he doesn't change he will never celebrate his 40th birthday.'

Gazza was 30 when he checked into the Priory, yet Jacobs still referred to him as a boy. The tag just never goes away. An editor of the *Beano* had famously called him 'the naughtiest kid in Britain'. As astute an observer as Barclay called him 'child-like'. Then there is Agnelli's 'dog of war with the face of a child' remark. Franz Beckenbauer saw Gazza and was reminded of a street urchin. No story better illustrates this childishness than when he was a player at Tottenham and he threw a bucket of water over a throng assembled for a press conference – and did it again and again and again. An hour later, he found the club press officer and said, in a little boyish voice, 'Are you still talking to me?'

Tony Adams, in his memoirs, joined Jacobs in fretting over Gazza's future. 'I just hope he finds the right path in life,' he concluded. Pearce, too, worried about the influences on him. His former England team-mate Paul Parker said, 'He was a great person, but when he got an audience he could do silly things. The people who consider themselves to be his close friends should look at themselves and ask what they were doing and why. They mugged him really.' Indeed, Gordon Taylor, head of the Professional Footballers' Association, publicly told Gazza's agents to consider whether they had done the best by their client. But as Stein wrote in his first authorised biography of Gazza, you can't get a true picture of the man without admitting that he is plagued by 'demonic instability'. But Gazza's childish helplessness leaves us all wishing to pin the responsibility for what happened on somebody else.

There was shock when Gascoigne was found, a crying wreck, on Stevenage station, but no great surprise. We had all (but perhaps especially the player himself?) been living with the possibility that he would do a George Best (or a Jimmy Greaves, or a Jim Baxter, or a Garrincha) for most of the decade. Yet for all the talk about his fragility and sensitivity and the sense that something (be it a syndrome, a disorder or a depression) within him is amiss, he refuses to give up. At the time of writing there has been a modest upturn in his life and fortunes at Everton, perhaps because, as one football pundit said, 'even he realises that this really is his last chance'.

He is 33 now. He may indeed have, as Hoddle suggested, another two or three years at the top. If Paul Gascoigne has a plan, it seems to revolve around prolonging his playing career in the United States. Alan 'Smudger' Smith reckoned so. 'He fancies that, doesn't he? The wages aren't that brilliant, but I think he fancies getting away from it all in America.' After that, when he finally hangs up his boots, many people who know him fear for him. 'It's hard to see him doing anything other than playing football – that's what he was born for,' said Bobby Robson. 'It bothers and worries me what will happen to Paul when his playing days are finished. He'll find many of his "friends" will disappear when the light goes out.'

His best hope, outlandish as it seems, is that he may find a niche in football management. Paul Parker hoped so. 'He's certainly got a lot of advice to give. And anyone who can't take advice from him shouldn't be in the game.' Bobby Robson, though, remarked simply, 'I cannot see Gascoigne as a coach or a manager. No chance. He won't have the patience.' There is, anyway, as Pearce warned, the risk that whoever hired him would only be doing it for the publicity. At least Gazza has said that before he accepted any coaching or managerial job 'I'd talk to Terry Venables and Brian Clough first'.

Then again, perhaps not even Gazza has any clear idea of how he'll fill the void once he's no longer playing football. Asked what he'd have done if he hadn't been a footballer, he once said, 'It frightens me to think.' Adams probably best summed up the uncertainty surrounding Gazza's direction in life over the next few years when he said, 'You need to let Paul fly, but there's always a risk he'll crash-land.'

10. SIMPLY THE BEST: ANALYSING A FOOTBALL GENIUS

Quite a character, impressive, but not really terrifying.

Franz Beckenbauer

Ray Clemence used to love watching Paul Gascoigne work out on Spurs' old training ground. Patrick Barclay of the *Sunday Telegraph* said:

> I remember Ray telling me that absolute mastery of the football was boring to Gazza. He could do anything with the ball he wanted to. Volley the ball past the goalkeeper from 30 yards out? Never mind the fact that it was probably an international keeper in the goal, he'd do it. He'd do it so easily that he wouldn't find it interesting after a while. So then he'd say to Ray, 'I know, I'll do it with my eyes closed.' So he'd do it with his eyes closed, and he could do that too. So by now he'd be laughing, he'd be trying to find different ways of miskicking the ball but still getting it in the net. In the end, he'd be trying to get the ball in with his knee or some other part of the body. He really could do anything.

Few footballers are born with such natural gifts. Stories like that make you realise that when Paul Gascoigne said, as he did when he joined Everton, that 'the trouble with me is all my brains are in my feet', he wasn't entirely joking, nor was he being wholly self-deprecating. (He might also have been saying something far truer than he knew, but we'll come to that later.)

Identifying, measuring and trying to explain such a talent usually seems beside the point. It's never going to compare to the thrill of seeing the skills in question in person, or even from the armchair. So why bother? Footballing prowess is not scientifically explicable, nor, on the whole, is it genetically programmed. Thank God. The only possible justification is that you might get a better sense of the talent concerned. But in Gazza's case the effort seems worthwhile because, over the years, the footballing genius has been overshadowed by the celebrity, the human being and the myth.

Even football writers, insisting that, as the fans might say, there's only one Paul Gascoigne, see the footballer through the refracting lens of his personal life. So, after he admitted beating his wife, he could not raise or clench his fists in a game of football (not, after all, that unusual a gesture on a football field) without one of the match-day reporters reminding readers that these were the same fists that had been raised in anger against his estranged wife Sheryl.

This seems fair enough in many ways. The star's off-the-pitch antics – the wife-beating, the dentist's chair, Kebabgate, Kneegate (when his recuperating knee took a turn for the worse in a Newcastle night club) – have seemed to more than justify this approach. But the purpose of this last chapter is, as far as possible, to take a dispassionate view of the footballing career of a player who has undoubtedly been the finest English midfielder of the last 20, 30, 40, 50 years (delete according to your view).

Terry Venables, one of Gascoigne's most consistent admirers, says that when he's judging a young player, he does so on four key characteristics: technical, tactical, personality and pace. So let's forget all the hype (good and bad) about Gascoigne, let's pretend almost that we're compiling a report on him for a coach who has never seen him play and measure him, initially, on each of these characteristics. (If this exercise was for real, Venables would probably give a young player he was evaluating marks out of ten in each category and then add them up to give a total. That sounds too reductive a way to measure a talent as unique as Gascoigne's, so stuff that.)

As Patrick Barclay's anecdote about the good old days on the Spurs training ground suggests, it would be hard to fault Gascoigne's technique. When asked to compare him to other all-time greats, Barclay paused for a moment.

The difficulty with Gascoigne is that normally when you're comparing players, you can trace the influences. But with Gascoigne, he's so unusual that it's hard to compare him to anybody. There really isn't anybody like him. In terms of pure technique, well, it's hard to compare anybody to Maradona because, as everybody but the English are happy to recognise, he was such a great player and, for all his problems in his personal life, which were more horrific in some ways than Gascoigne's, always tremendously popular with his team-mates. But in sheer technical ability, certainly in terms of beating a man, Gascoigne was probably up there with Maradona.

Of the four England managers who have played Gazza, the one who saw him in his prime was Bobby Robson. Which may be why he finds it hard to stop talking about him. 'He has all sorts of tricks,' he said when interviewed about Gazza in 1996. 'He has this trick where he can seem to be going one way and then go the other . . . he's being closely marked, some guy's about to take the ball off him and he can do the Cruyff trick where he opens his legs, flicks the ball between his legs and in half a second he's gone in the opposite direction. And he can erupt out of that, changing pace and changing direction.'

Watching videos of Gascoigne's finest moments, it's intriguing to notice how often he plays the ball through his opponent. He did it at Euro 96 against Germany in the semi-final, in a moment of inspiration which saw him take three German defenders out of the game (one of them being Matthias Sammer, no mug or tyro) and race to the byline to slide in a cross which was frantically cleared by a rattled German defence. At his best, he can turn players, baffle them and dribble through them, but as Robson pointed out, he can do far more than that. 'One of his great strengths is running with the ball. Not dribbling with the ball, like Waddle, he can do that too, but running the ball up the pitch some 30 or 40 yards, and he'll do that in the last minute of the game when most players are just waiting for the final whistle. But then Terry said to me that I'd be surprised by his stamina.'

Even in his wilderness years at Lazio, Gazza could still show enough flashes of inspiration to be adored by fans and more than a few football journalists. Ian Hamilton recalled one game against Torino where, in the first half, 'a high-speed shuffle of the feet had taken him through a ruck of four defenders. It was the shuffle, a kind of feint or jinking quickstep, that captured the Italian imagination.' The press dubbed it 'il passo doppio', a term that owes something to the 'paso doble' dance step. So excited were the Italian press that they enclosed diagrams of the move along with photographs of a Bologna player called Amadeo Bavati who had originated the move in the 1930s. The consensus was that Gascoigne was the first player since Bavati to perform that trick with the speed, daring and elegance of the original.

His ability to beat players is mysterious, because even at his peak, in 1990 and 1991, he was never the fastest player on the park. Alan Hansen, though, reckoned Gazza was fast before that FA Cup final tackle.

Physically he was never the same after that. His loss of pace was obvious. Previously when Gascoigne took the ball past an opponent, he would hold out his arms to keep the player away from him. When he started playing again after that Cup final, he was doing that before he had gone past him. For me, that told its own story, and it became even more pronounced when Gazza returned to the game after the further blow of his broken leg at Lazio. It speaks volumes for his talent, touch and his passing that he was able to do well for England in Euro 96.

Yet the pace was not a simple matter of just sprinting faster to a ball or past a defender, his gift was more elusive than that. At times, when you watch the videos, he seems more deadly when he's surrounded by defenders trying to get the ball off him, when he could invite them in to take part in their own doom. He took players on, one against one. He did just that in his make-or-break performance against the Czechs at Wembley in 1990, suddenly gliding past the last man leaving both defender and commentator at a loss to explain how he'd done it.

Sometimes, in a manner reminiscent of those training-ground exercises where he did ridiculous things just to make life more interesting, he would try to beat one player too many. Venables used to say that he had a weakness for trying to do one more piece of artistry than the game strictly required. This attitude to an opponent bears the arrogance and the cheek of a great school team footballer who doesn't care which local school his team plays because he knows he's good enough. And indeed, a large part of Gascoigne's charm as a player is that, at his best, he plays it with the unselfconscious artistry of a gifted adolescent. It's hard to watch him dribble past (or, as he often seems to do, through) a defender without seeing the ghost of the youth team player who would take the ball up to a first-team player at Newcastle, nutmeg him and shout 'Legs!' as he ran past, laughing loudly.

His dead-ball skills, too, are all you would expect of a player who had to shut his eyes in training from 30 yards out just to make it more interesting. Over the years, quite a few British players have been praised for their 'Brazilian'-style set-pieces. Too often this is a euphemism for 'Well at least it didn't go smack into the wall'. But no British player, not even David Beckham, has matched Gascoigne's combination of variety and ferocity from set-pieces. He could, as he proved against Arsenal in that FA Cup semi-final, bend the ball and hit it very hard at the same time. Many other players regarded in this country as free-kick specialists still find these two qualities mutually exclusive.

The Spurs fans had been given fair warning of how deadly he could be. His prowess from free-kicks had helped pacify the malcontents in his first so-so season at White Hart Lane in 1988/89. And from then on, every so often, he would do the business from a free-kick, even if only (it seemed) to prove to himself that he could still do it. Seven years, three clubs and a few stones later, as a Middlesbrough player, he curled the ball beautifully inside the right post, giving Southampton keeper Paul Jones no chance.

One of the few inspiring moments of the Graham Taylor documentary *Do I Not Like That* involves Gazza in training. England are trying to practise their set-pieces but, despite Taylor's instructions, seem to be doing so in a rather witless fashion. After the usual toing and froing, Gascoigne strides on to the centre stage, shakes his head as if to say 'Look, this is how it's really done', and orchestrates a brilliantly subtle set-piece which ends up in the net. It is a fascinating glimpse of Gascoigne's football brain at work. And just in case the cameras missed it, he does exactly the same thing later for real to give England a goal.

To hit set-pieces so precisely or to strike a perfect 30-yard pass with the outside of your foot while leaning back, you need incredible vision. We'll come back to the almost supernatural aspects of 'vision', the ability to see opportunities and spaces which other players don't see, later in this chapter, but it's intriguing to note here the off-the-pitch mucking about which suggests that he was probably better at judging distance and perspective than the rest of us. In March 1989, he was famously caught throwing bars of Camay at chickens on the farm next to the team hotel near Tirana, Albania. While most accounts of this incident focus on Gazza's cheek, both Tony Cottee and John Barnes (who describe the incident in their autobiographies) agree that he was actually very accurate. The distances involved were not massive (Barnes reckoned the hotel room was about twenty floors up), but they weren't small either. Most people faced with that challenge would probably get nowhere near. Bobby Robson was certainly dubious enough as to whether or not the target could actually be hit, so dubious that he asked Gazza to prove it. Which Gazza duly did.

There is other evidence that there was something unusual about Gazza's 'vision thing'. As an England

Under-21, his eye impressed the squad's trainer, Mike Kelly, who recalled, 'He loved to look for challenges, like throwing things in a bin from a long distance, or throwing peanuts into someone else's glass. He had a good eye for those things.' Fast forward to the 1990 World Cup, and Pete Davies, who hung around with the squad as he wrote his book, notices that Gazza can't find anyone to play table tennis with him. So what does he do? He tries to hit the table-tennis ball into a glass of water and, according to Davies, soon succeeds. Again, just as he did on the Spurs training ground, he decides to make a sport more intriguing by working out a new repertoire of shots, including a double-handed backhand. Too much can be made out of a bar of soap, some chickens, a few peanuts and a glass of water, but all this does seem to reinforce the testimony of one of the boy's schoolteachers, who said of him, 'He was like a robot – he would put the ball anywhere I told him to.'

There is a theory, which sounds too sentimental to be true but has been expressed by at least two old pros bemoaning the state of British football, that playing football in the street is actually better for a young player's technique than simply playing on a pitch. The idea is that, if you're kicking a ball against a pavement or cobblestones, it will come back at you at all sorts of strange angles, and you learn to control the ball even when it's moving unpredictably. Gazza, we know, played football remorselessly in the street from the age of four. When it was raining, he'd often be found playing head tennis in the house with his dad, using the doors as goals. The speed with which Gazza can bring a ball under his control is one of the many skills which marks him out as a player. So maybe the street theory isn't a load of sentimental rubbish after all.

Joe Harvey, the former Newcastle manager who became the club's chief scout, had a simple formula for deciding whether a young player had what it takes. 'He either had a trick or he didn't,' said one of his colleagues. Well, Gazza had more than a trick or two, so many in fact that they almost ended his career before it really began. As a youth player at Newcastle, he was told by the club's youth-team coach, Colin Suggett, that 'if I wanted tricks, I'd get a clown from a circus'. Gascoigne's reluctance to do just what Suggett ordered (run up and down the pitch, lay off the ball to a colleague and track an opponent) almost led to his being released by the club when Jack Charlton took over as manager. And Gazza had enough tricks, certainly, to give many of his managers some heart-stopping moments. Even one of his greatest admirers, Bobby Robson, could say of him, 'He's daft in his attitude. He's got to learn about the game, how to play properly – he's still a kid playing backstreet football. Lots of talent – lots of freshness, there's unbelievable things he'll do, but I'm talking about Argentina or Brazil, about being in the last eight of the world. You have to be utterly reliable.' The same note of caution had been sounded by his PE teacher, John Brabban, in 1981: 'We all felt that his lack of discipline on the field was the only thing that could jeopardise his professional footballing future. He enjoyed entertaining and was always a character to express himself in a very artistic way.'

Reliability, playing percentages, tracking – this isn't really the stuff of which Gascoigne's game is made. For a footballer of his obvious gifts, he has never shown much of a broader interest in the game. As John Barnes put it in his autobiography:

Gazza loved football, but he never thought about it. He simply did it. He was happiest with a ball at his feet, always staying behind after training. I would happily talk about football. Chris [Waddle] and I could always be found deep in debates about tactics, but Gazza is a natural footballer, a doer rather than a thinker, who hated discussion about systems. Whenever I went to his room to talk about football with Chris, he would say, 'Oh, you two are always going on about football.' He would turn the music up loud or stick his fingers in his ears and chant, 'La, la, la, I'm not listening, la, la, la.' Chris and I would look at each other and laugh.

Jane Nottage made a similar point when talking about his first appearance for Newcastle against Arsenal. 'The Newcastle manager was going on about Kenny Sansom – what a great defender he was and how they would have to be aware of his sniping runs from the back. After a few minutes, Gazza, bemused by it all, sighed and turned to a team-mate, asking, "Who is this Kenny Sansom, is he a good player?"'

While the idea that most players are big fans of the game is one of the most enduring myths about football (many, like Gazza and David Batty, find it too stressful watching if they can't play), Gascoigne's ignorance about the Arsenal and England full-back suggests either that he was having a laugh (never a possibility which can easily be ruled out where Gazza is concerned) or was deeply and truly uninterested in the tedious business of who he was playing against. But then nobody scared Gazza. He had the arrogance to feel that he could do anybody, and he proved it often enough, 'doing' even Lothar Matthaus for most of that semi-final in Turin.

But even in the middle of the 1990 World Cup, Robson felt compelled to admonish the most naturally gifted member of his squad in public once more, saying,

'He has to learn you can't be the star of the circus all the time.' There's the circus again. It's almost as if Gascoigne was some kind of low comedian – which, of course, at times he could be. He brought to the game something which admirers called 'joy' but could, on occasion, suggest the garish frivolity of the circus ring.

Dennis Wise, though, thought that too many people were dazzled by Gazza's obvious gifts and forgot his other qualities.

Of his generation of English players he was the best. He had natural ability and that was there for everyone to see. But in England you also need to be strong – and, believe me, Gazza was strong. The way he used his arms was really clever. I know a lot of people accused him of trying to elbow opponents, but that really wasn't the case, and I speak as someone who often was one of his opponents. He would put his arm across you while he was in possession and that would enable him to block your run, help him to keep the ball and make sure that you were always off balance if you needed to make a challenge. I can't think of any other English player who was as strong as Gazza running with the ball.

Tony Adams echoed Wise's appraisal. 'The strength he had when he was on one of those diagonal runs which we tried to get him to do for England was second to none. When he drew defenders to him, two or three at a time, he was creating space for another player and could then release them into space with a little pass.'

Nobody has seriously questioned whether Gazza had the technique to be one of the greats. But, to take the second of Venables' criteria, did he have the tactical nous to go with it? The evidence that he didn't seems fairly damning, especially as it comes from many of the people who have coached him, but it is far from conclusive.

As Barnes and Waddle found out during Italia 90, for Gazza, football was something he just did. Just because he did it very well didn't mean that he really wanted to talk about it all the time or learn about it. This would always trouble his coaches, and he worked with some of the finest in the British game (especially Bobby Robson, Terry Venables and Don Howe). Yet Howe said, rather ruefully, 'He did work with some of the best coaches in the modern game. They've given him some great advice over the years. Whether he listened to them or not is another matter.'

Because he was Paul Gascoigne, he would always do the sort of things which would have coaches chewing their nails and leave fans gasping in admiration, downright suspicious ('Flash git!') or enraged if they went wrong. John Pickering, his first-team coach at Newcastle, talking to Robin McGibbon (whose book *Gazza!* is an invaluable source on Gascoigne's early years), recalled: 'Gazza's main fault at the start of the season was that he wanted to do his own thing. In training, when we were trying to get team work organised, Gazza would fidget and not take any notice of what was being said. Yet he would then go and do exactly what you wanted, although not in the way you wanted.'

This same refusal to conform troubled Dave Sexton, the England Under-21 coach, and perplexed the England Under-21 skipper Tony Dorigo, who recalled: 'He would be told what position he was in but when he was out on the pitch he would do his own thing. But wherever he was, he'd end up doing something brilliant.' In the run-up to Italia 90, this tendency would appal Howe, who was trying to make sure England kept their shape while Gascoigne went right and left, forward and back, seemingly oblivious to any words of advice from his coach or his manager. He has always had games like this, bad games when his chasing and running serves only to remind you why Graham Taylor once referred to him as a 'headless chicken', but, as Dorigo said, he could also defy all the rules and do something brilliant which won the match.

His worst performance as a headless chicken in an England shirt probably came not under Taylor but under Dave Sexton when Gascoigne was playing for the Under-21s. Against West Germany in 1988, he was so bad, reckless even, that Sexton took him off at half-time. The coach had warned Gascoigne not to get wound up, not to exhaust himself just running up and down the pitch, but Gascoigne had done exactly that. Part of the problem, as Barnes suggested, was that at his peak Gascoigne could run for longer than many other players. But after that performance, Sexton took Gascoigne to one side and gave him a lecture. To most young players, Sexton was an awesome figure, made even more so by the fact that, although he obviously knew a hell of a lot about football, few of them actually understood any of his instructions. But he was clear that day, laid Gascoigne's future on the line and left the meeting feeling that a point had been made, that lessons had been learned.

Yet when Gazza came on for his first full England cap against Albania at Wembley in April 1989 (when England were 3–0 up), his performance suggested that Sexton might well have been wasting his time. England boss Bobby Robson told Gascoigne to go out and enjoy himself, but ordered him to 'keep to the right-hand side, keep the shape of the team'. So Gazza went on runs straight across the pitch to the left and started playing with his mate Chris Waddle. This was the point at which Gazza's daft-as-a-brushness was born. This was one of the reasons Robson seemed so reluctant (although he always denies it) to take Gascoigne to the 1990 World Cup. There was always the risk that the kid would play backstreet football in the semi-final. He didn't, of course, and he did learn to moderate some of his excesses, but these always seemed to be tactical concessions rather than a change of heart.

Because if you watch Gascoigne play, you can see that he's never really changed his game for anybody, no matter how wise or influential the mentor, how good the advice. With the possible exception of that unsatisfactory sojourn at Lazio, he has usually awarded himself what pundits today would call a free role.

You can take this two ways: as proof that he has no footballing brain, or, as Rodney Marsh thought, as evidence of his guts. 'It must have been very hard for him as a young player with everyone telling him he ought to play one way when he was doing the other. Most young players are so desperate to succeed that they will try and become a different type of player. But, although every coach was telling him the same thing, he never changed his style of play or his approach. To me, that shows tremendous strength of character.' There's a certain amount of identification going on here. Marsh, after all, suffered at the hands of the drill sergeants who for too many years passed for coaches in England. But even some coaches have admitted that talents like Gascoigne's rose despite the system's best efforts to destroy them, not because the system tried to develop their gifts.

So what about his awareness of the game? To be able to hit those perfect passes you need to be able to see the opportunities, and that ability has always been one of the hallmarks of a truly great player. One of the few criticisms levelled at Bobby Charlton when he played for Manchester United was that, in footballing terms, he didn't have a brain. He would hit 40-yard passes which would have the crowd oohing and aahing, but would not necessarily take his team any further forward. Gazza, at his best, rarely made a pointless pass. The speed with which he mastered the ball and made the judgement about what to do with it is impressive. Watch videos of him and you see what Sir Alex Ferguson meant when he said of Eric Cantona, 'He can see things that no other players can see, he can see things that even I don't see from the bench.'

When Gascoigne's on top of his game, his passing and movement are so quick that it's as if he's not having to bother to think, he's just doing something instinctive. Intriguingly, sports scientists are beginning to wonder if footballers like Gascoigne stand out from the field precisely because they don't need to think.

At this point, a little digression is necessary. Footballers have long been mocked for their inability on camera to explain a piece of poetry on the pitch in intelligible prose. A typical account of a goal will, invariably, run along the lines of 'Well, the ball came over and I could see the goalie had come out so I had a go.' This less than eloquent account will often be delivered in the kind of monotone normally employed by the synthesised voice on electronic switchboards. But tests on Olympic marksmen (it's a stretch from football, but bear with me) show that in the vast majority of cases the best competitors cannot describe afterwards what they have done. Indeed, as a general rule of thumb, the more eloquent a competitor's description, the less effective they were. These initially intriguing results were followed up with tests involving electrodes which measured athletes' brain waves. These showed that at the critical moment before the trigger was squeezed their brain waves changed from beta to alpha rhythm. Dave Collins, head of sport at Edinburgh University, who did these tests, commented, 'This means they literally stopped thinking about what they were doing.' Other tests on other sports seemed to confirm Collins' research.

The sports scientists borrowed a Japanese word, *mushin* (literally translated it means 'no thought'), to describe this state of mind. 'They only reach this state at the critical point in their activity, for instance when they're about to kick the ball,' explained Collins. 'And once that's over they can't think their way back there afterwards.' The tests also showed that before the critical moment, athletes' brains suddenly stopped processing as much visual imagery. This suggested, said Collins, that they experience two stages. The first is *attention*, where the footballer processes ephemeral information (the position of the goal, the positioning of defenders); that is followed by *intention*, where the athlete or footballer focuses on his or her own state of mind.

Collins believes great athletes, a category in which he includes footballers, are great because they can do what they do without thinking it through. 'They can pick up the cues fractionally before anyone else, which may be why it's often said that the mark of a truly great player is that they always seem to have time on the ball. They may even see the action almost as if it's in slow motion so they have time to react.'

Certainly Gazza's Middlesbrough team-mate Juninho was fascinated to watch Gazza's play around the goal. 'Some people become blind when they get close to the goal, but not Gascoigne. Take the goal he scored against Scotland in Euro 96. If you were watching the match from the outside, that seemed obvious, the only thing to do. Things are different when you're in there and that's when you see the outstanding player. Calm and cold-blooded at decisive moments.'

And it's true that when you see a great player thread a pass through the eye of a packed defence it's impossible to imagine how he could have done that if he'd had to think it through. If he had to calculate the speed of the ball, assess the state of the pitch, mentally fast-forward a team-mate's run and a defender's position, do all that and decide which part of the ball to make contact with, how hard that contact should be and at what angle that pass should be struck at . . . if he had to do all that mentally he'd have given the ball away.

Far easier to accept, as many scientists and psychologists are coming to do, that there are many different types of human intelligence (depending on which classifications and theories you accept, the number of different types could run into double figures), and that one of those types or categories is an ability to make the kind of decisions which any sporting contest forces upon a competitor instinctively and, to borrow a bit of computer jargon, in real time. Few British players in the last two decades have seemed as able to make those kind of split-second decisions as Gascoigne, a footballer who can change a game with a touch which reverses the pattern of play. It's not quite having all your brains in your feet, but it's certainly a case of letting some intuitive process take over.

When England did finally make it through to the semi-final in Turin, German coach Franz Beckenbauer had one particular player on his mind, and, despite Gary Lineker's strike rate, it wasn't the man who would become synonymous with Walkers Crisps. He recalled later: 'Of the team that reached the semi-final, only Paul Gascoigne was unpredictable. "Gazza" he was called, a true footballer from the streets, defiant, crafty and intrepid like the leader of a boys' gang. His face, his physique, as if he hadn't yet quite overcome the years of puppy fat. Behind his angular forehead, he would cook up ideas you just didn't expect. Quite a character, impressive, but not really terrifying.' It's classic Beckenbauer really: apparently quite generous and yet, finally, quite patronising.

So Gazza has some kind of gift, but is it placed at the service of the team? To answer that question, all you need to do is drop a video of the 1996 European Championship in your VCR. Fast-forward to the semifinal and fast-forward again to the point where golden-goal time is over and the penalties are about to start. Watch Gascoigne talking to Venables. It's clear from the gestures that he's apologising for checking his run prior to that oh-so-close slide in on goal because he was convinced that the German keeper Bodo Illgner was going to get a hand to the ball. These are not the actions of a selfish genius but of a footballer whose immense natural gifts are put at the service of the team, even if that service must be performed on his terms.

But Gary Lineker used to joke that you never got a pass from Gazza without him expecting a return, and Alan Smith, an occasional England team-mate, reckoned there was some truth in that. 'He was a great one for lending you the ball. You'd get it at about 100 mph at your feet while you had most of the defence on top of you and then he'd be running into space and expecting the return.' Patrick Barclay commented, 'You don't want to go too far down that line of him being a great team player. He could always do something in the wrong part of the pitch. He wasn't as good a player for the team as Maradona, say, but like most of the great players he was popular with his team-mates.' Indeed, the sports psychologist George Sik said, 'One manager told me he'd have him in the squad even if he had his legs amputated just because of the effect he'd have on team spirit.' David Beckham, who was played alongside Gazza and watched him in training for England, observed simply, 'There's something about Gazza, as a person and a player. Once you see him in your team, that makes you fall in love with him.'

The truly great players have not seen the pitch as a stage for a virtuoso solo performance, nor have they, in Venables' well-chosen phrase, wanted to be golfers or tennis players with a football. 'The one thing which all great players have in common is that they're prepared to work hard for the team.' Which may be why, in most people's list of all-time great footballers, there aren't that many strikers. 'In the team context,' Venables insisted, 'Gazza is a giver, not a taker.' Indeed, one of the easiest ways to wind the player up was, he found, to suggest he was no longer one of the boys and in danger of becoming a 'big-time charlie'.

The boys would be required to cover for Gazza to some extent, but when the player you're covering for is scoring a goal every other game in the League, as Gascoigne did for Rangers in his first two seasons, other players don't mind covering. Only once in his career, in the summer of 1998 for England, has Gascoigne been a focus of serious dissent in the team. And, although he's appeared regularly in the press, he's never really been one to slag off his own manager or his own players. Even at Lazio, when he must have feared his footballing career was coming to an anti-climactic end, he railed against the club in general rather than against his coach or his team-mates.

Venables always admired Gascoigne not just for his flair but for his drive. 'There aren't too many players around with his skill and boundless joy for the game. He has a football intelligence and a drive which can change games. His mental drive is incredible. If the other players are losing the game and starting to put their heads down, it is Gazza who will rally round and keep them going. You can't put too high a value on that.' It's intriguing that Pele, who you might expect to value Gazza's obvious technical prowess, drew attention to this side of his game, saying, 'I like Gascoigne. He's a tough guy. He is the sort of player everybody wants to have in their team.'

Let's pop that Euro 96 video on again and fast-forward, this time to Gazza's penalty. (At least he got to take one in this shoot-out.) Gascoigne fires his penalty into the roof of the net and poses pompously for the cameras before the sheer joy of what he's just done bursts out of him in a long, ecstatic 'Yes!' And then, inspired, he goads the crowd, shouting 'Come on!', willing them to pump up the volume and put the pressure on the next German player to take a penalty with the 'I can't hear you' hand-to-ear gesture. The commitment is almost eye-popping. And you feel that this is as much for the lads, for the fans and for the country as it is for him.

That is an example of Gazza when he was constructively pumped up, high on the moment itself. But no appraisal of his footballing personality would be complete without a serious acknowledgement that far too often in his career he's been hyped up to the point of self-destruction. The headlong charge to try to dispossess Gary Charles was probably one of the most unnecessary and disastrous since the Light Brigade went into that Valley of Death. There are various reports, perhaps exaggerated in the light of what happened next, of him bouncing off the dressing-room wall before the match, twitching and breathing in the tunnel as if he was a bull.

The bull was always there. In the difficult years, as the 1990s wore on, he could often be seen trying to do too much and would tire himself out after half an hour. But then he'd done the same as a young player at Newcastle; Willie McFaul, the manager who'd given him his first chance in 1985, said in his second season, 'He's trying to do too much on his own. The sooner he realises that he hasn't got the right to dominate a game the better.' At his worst, Gazza entered what one football writer called his 'Dennis the Menace' phase, where he would run around the pitch for 30 minutes like a demented thug looking for an excuse to start a fight.

Reckless acts of self-destruction (the Charles tackle, the shin break in training at Lazio, the broken arm he sustained trying to elbow George Boateng) seem to punctuate his career, to the frustration of his admirers, like Don Howe. 'He was held back by his own impetuosity and injuries, they were his fault really. The injury in the Cup final stunted his development and he always seemed to get injuries whenever things seemed to be going well. Both on and off the pitch he didn't always know where to stop, it is something inside of him. As he's got older I wonder, is he learning?' Managers also learned how to handle him. Spurs had, after all, given him a shot to knock him out before the 1991 FA Cup semi-final, but that hardly seemed the ideal long-term solution. When Venables took care of Gazza as England manager, he let David Seaman take him out fishing to calm him down.

If he didn't get sent off or injured, Gazza would gradually quieten down and adjust to the pattern of the game. But he's been booked and sent off often enough to suggest that for all Sexton, Howe and Robson tried to drill into him the importance of not retaliating, it was always worth trying to wind him up.

He did once go into hiding, in the way that Glenn Hoddle was prone to do, against Wimbledon in 1988 when Vinny Jones set out to intimidate him out of the game. Jones' unique approach to man-to-man marking employed tactics which ranged from the run of the mill, like shouting 'Don't go away fat boy, I'll be back', to the violent, like grabbing Gascoigne's testicles. It may look like a piece of slapstick physical comedy in the well-publicised photograph, but as Jones proudly recalled later, 'He yelled in pain.' The Newcastle pros were sickened by Jones' antics, and even his coach Don Howe told him afterwards never to do that again. But the performance left Gascoigne in a deep state of shock. As a team-mate said afterwards, 'we lost him for a while', but his form recovered and he would never be scared out of a game again. Quite the reverse. He would later be found on video headbutting an opponent while playing for Rangers. It was however, if you will, more of a crime of passion than a cynical gameplan, and it's hard not to agree, in part, with Gascoigne's own explanation: 'I'm just angry about the way I've been treated and I think I've taken that out on to the pitch with me.'

Ultimately, though, it wasn't his personality on the pitch which would lead him to the darkest days of his career but his personality and lifestyle off it. Gascoigne's approach to diet has been even more idiosyncratic than his approach to the game itself. As a footballer of youthful promise at Newcastle, he was given a shape-up-or-ship-out ultimatum by manager Jack Charlton, who took the unusual step of paying for Gascoigne to have a sensible lunch (in these pre-chicken and beans days, sensible meant steak and salad without chips) at a restaurant near the training ground called the Oven

Door. With his career on the line, he stuck to the diet and put in extra training to turn flab into muscle, but the victory was short-lived.

As he began to break into the first team, he turned once again to junk food, tucking into the fish and chips the women in the club's promotions office had got in for lunch, conspicuously consuming Mars bars (at the rate of three a day) and cakes (while saying, as he ate them, 'I shouldn't be eating these. I've put too much weight on.') and once eating a bag of liquorice chews even though he didn't like them, because he was fed up of being nagged about his weight.

Inevitably he paid for his indulgence, having to run around the training ground in a bin liner on the orders of his coach and manager just to sweat off the extra pounds. Later, according to Jane Nottage, he would learn other tricks to reconcile his diet with his fitness. At Tottenham, she stated, one of his colleagues taught him how to make himself throw up to lose weight on the day of a game. She even said that he would turn to laxatives in an ill-advised attempt to shed some of the bulk, which, according to an unnamed member of his family, might have achieved the desired result but also meant that he 'just sh*ts all the vitamins out of his body'.

Perhaps the most chilling vignette in this vein is Graham Taylor's suggestion, to Nottage, that Gascoigne was trying to lose weight in the sauna before the vital World Cup qualifier against Norway. He might or might not have lost weight that day, but England certainly lost the game (2–0) and Taylor, in frustration, speculated in public about his star's lifestyle. In Gazza's defence, Lineker said this habit probably began quite innocently.

He used to have a sauna before a match because people told him he had a weight problem, which, of course, was the worst thing you can do. I used to take little baths to loosen up: just a few inches of hot water, then I would get out, do a few stretches and within two or three minutes I was off for my warm-up outside. At Maine Road once, I came back after my bath to find Gazza up to his neck in boiling water. At half-time, we were 2–0 down, Terry was giving out a few rollickings when Gazza complained he felt dizzy and blamed me.

Excesses seem often to have been part of his life. As has been said elsewhere, no one really knows how much of a grip alcohol, for instance, has had on Gazza's life, but you can deduce a lot from his admiring remark about Bryan Robson: 'The only player I know who can drink sixteen pints and still play football the next day.' Like Tony Adams, Gazza might have fallen for the myth that you could pay for such excesses just by training harder than anyone else. Even a friend and team-mate like Gary Lineker has admitted that he thought 'Gazza's always had something within him that means he'll self-destruct, because every now and then he'll take it too far. In many ways he's like a schoolboy, and he's very hyped up and emotional, so you always fear for him in that sense.'

The astonishing thing is that for at least the first decade of his footballing career his body really did recover. John Sheridan, his physio at Spurs, was amazed by the speed with which his body healed itself after he'd wrecked his knee tackling Gary Charles. 'It was one of the worst injuries I have had to work on. Some footballers wouldn't have kicked a ball again,' he said. 'The fact that he is playing is down to several things, the most important being his love of football and his determination to get fit and play again.'

For every horrifying image of Gazza trying to sweat off fat in a sauna before an England game, there is a contrasting image of him running up and down a hill in Rome in the afternoon heat trying to get fit. The regularity with which he would arrive overweight for pre-season training is matched only by the regularity with which, for many years, he out-trained most of his fellow professionals, not necessarily because he was working anything off but because he wanted to. Gascoigne is one footballer who knows exactly what Bill Shankly meant when he said, 'Ain't it great to be alive, boys? All you need is green grass and the ball.' Even at his most unfit, most jaded, he has always looked like he cared. And, as Alan Hansen pointed out, he's one of the few professional footballers who, if he's driving past some kids kicking a ball around, is likely to pull up, get out and join in.

As Terry Venables said in a 1996 interview, 'He loves the game, he's crazy about it. He loves it so much you worry what he'll do without it. He comes alive when he plays football.' Venables compared his attitude to that of another 'barrel-chested' Tottenham favourite, Dave Mackay: 'You would have 90 minutes of really gruelling training, with crunching tackles flying in, and at the end you'd feel exhausted and you'd just be grateful it's over. But Dave would go straight back in there and do it all over again with the reserve team. Gazza's just like that. He'll play with the first team and then he'll run over and kick it around with the youth team, and he's not doing it for any other reason than he just feels good about it.'

So while it's easy to be infuriated and repulsed by the major flaws in Gascoigne's character, which have so often let him and his talent down, you also have to be impressed by the other side of him, the part which struggles back against ridiculous odds, ignoring the warnings and the premature obituaries, to give him another shot at the one career he's always dreamed of.

When he was a kid, Gascoigne wanted to be George Best. As a teenager, he just wanted to be the best. Whoever the best was at that time – Keegan, whoever – that's who Gazza was when he was playing in the street or at the boys' club. So how does he compare to the all-time greats? Well, here's Tony Adams' view:

> When you get him focused on his football and just give him the ball, he can be exceptional. I used to deny that Paul was such an exceptional player when he was at Spurs because that was the only way I could deal with the situation. We reckoned we could put a stopper on him and nullify him, like we did with Stewart Robson against Glenn Hoddle. Having said that, in that semi-final of 1991 he did for us pretty comprehensively with that free-kick, then by setting up that third goal. But then he could always get up for one-off Cup games. What about a whole League season? You could never guarantee the number of games he would play, what with injuries. The fact is he has never been able to do his job consistently and that type of player will always find it difficult.

While admitting that Gazza's 'greatness over a few games' made him a natural selection for England, Adams ended his assessment of Gascoigne's playing career with the remarkable conclusion that 'For a League season, I would rather have a consistent performer like Alan Smith.' He went on to say that Smudger would not have scored that goal against Scotland and Colin Hendry, but added that he 'probably contributed to the overall picture more often'.

It's a remarkable assessment, even more remarkable because in some horribly prosaic way you recognise the truth in what Adams is saying. Gazza has never played more than 35 League games in a season. Indeed, he hasn't played more than 30 League games in a season for a whole decade. That all-time tally of goals in English, Italian and Scottish leagues (80) is far smaller than you would expect from a player of his stature.

Mackay, Smudger, Hoddle, Maradona . . . all interesting names for any player to be compared with. Venables threw in another comparison: Tony Currie. 'There was a lot of Tony Currie in Gazza, but there wasn't enough of Gazza in Tony Currie. He just didn't have the same knack of scoring goals going forward.' Steve Curry of the *Sunday Times* hurled another name into the frame: 'He was unique. For comparison, I'd say he was better than Colin Bell, and in terms of making things happen he was as good as anyone.' Paolo Di Canio, in his recently published memoirs, tried to come up with a list of 'genuine world-class talents, people with top-notch technique and vision, flair and creativity' in the British game over the last 40 years. The list he arrived at comprised George Best and Kevin Keegan. But he then added this caveat: 'Maybe Gascoigne, if he hadn't had his problems.'

There really ought to have been no maybes, as tributes from the likes of Pele and Beckenbauer make clear. For his admirers, the frustrating thing is that you can't simply point to the record books for proof. He has never won a League championship single-handed, as Maradona did with Napoli. He has never won a World Cup or a European Championship, a failure which says as much about the teams he played in as it does about him. Yet, as Alex Fynn, co-author of *Heroes and Villains*, the seminal account of Spurs and Arsenal in 1990/91, wrote, 'He has done what no other English player apart from Bobby Charlton has done. He has been a creative influence on the game at its highest level, in a World Cup. And that, and that alone, surpasses anything George Best has done and it certainly surpasses anything David Beckham has done so far.'

Ultimately, though, the awful truth remains, as voiced by Gary Lineker when he mulled over Gazza's career with Dave Bowler: 'We'll never really know how good he might have been.'

11. THE TWILIGHT ZONE: GAZZA 2002–

My big worry is that he's going to drive his car over a cliff or something and the story might end tragically
  Alan Cooke, Gazza's PE teacher at Heathfield Senior School

In February 2004, Plymouth Argyle's manager Paul Sturrock asked the club's fans whether he should sign Paul Gascoigne. Only one fan was in favour and Plymouth soon gave up on the idea.

The Argyle faithful might have seen him, a month earlier, returning to Heathrow after another spell drying out in the Cottonwood Clinic in Arizona. With his shaven head, bloated face and look of a man who had aged faster than he ought, Gascoigne hardly looked like the kind of figure who would bring guile and guts to a team fighting for promotion to Division 1. There were, one journalist noted, no friends waiting for his arrival – just photographers.

It wasn't just Plymouth. Almost every lower league club in England has been given the chance to take a gamble on Gascoigne. For all the constant drip drip of 'Gazza in talks with . . .' stories, there have been no takers. The feeling, as expressed by one lower league manager, is that a club would get a couple of sell-out crowds, then the novelty would wear off, leaving you with a hefty wage packet and a player you wouldn't quite know what to do with. The clinics, the latest confessional TV documentary in which he confessed to eating 30 packets of dried squid a day and rumours about his intake of painkillers have all put managers off. As he approaches his thirty-seventh birthday, he must know that the inevitable cannot be delayed much longer.

Many wonder why about the indignity of it all. Why, they ask, does he go on? The answer is obvious. As he said in the BBC3 documentary *Gazza – One Day At A Time*, 'The next thing is nothing'. To his old PE teacher Alan Cooke, quoted in the *Daily Telegraph*, there seemed only two solutions left: 'If you ask me what he should do next, I can't think of anything better than working with the kids at Newcastle. I can't see any other future for him other than ending up in an alcoholics ward.'

Gascoigne might not disagree. He knows there is, as his friend Gary Lineker noted, 'a lot of life to live after football'. And Gazza, by his own account, must fear that he'll fill those empty Saturday afternoons, the vacant days he's not training, with booze.

This isn't how his career ought to end. If this were Hollywood, there would be a last hurrah where the ageing genius would put his gifts to service one last time and discover, as a result, some kind of inner peace, before settling down, content, to retirement. This is, loosely, the scenario outlined at the end of Barry Levinson's baseball movie *The Natural* starring Robert Redford. Gazza may be a natural but this isn't Hollywood, so the publicly expressed worries of friends, former teachers, and sympathetic journalists like Ian Ridley, are understandable. As is Gazza's reluctance to admit defeat.

Ian Bogie, who used to be his room mate at Newcastle, says: 'He loves the game so much that he'll want to carry on for as far as his legs will take him.' Gascoigne proved as much in the BBC3 documentary when he said: 'I still have something to give in football and I don't give a shit where. I don't care if it's at the end of the world.' This was, Martin Kelner noted in the

Guardian, 'just as well because that is more or less where Gazza had fetched up'.

Even in a career notorious for fluctuating fortunes, the speed of Gazza's professional decline since he left Burnley in May 2002 has been astonishing. He found shelter, of a kind, as a roving pundit on ITV's 2002 World Cup coverage. Keen, obviously terrified (you could almost see Terry Venables holding his hand), often incomprehensible, he seemed ill at ease, even when he was turned into a kind of roving reporter.

His hotel bar bill – £9,869.92 and £281 from his minibar in three weeks – probably stood out more than anything he said. The life and soul of the party at the hotel bar, he had bought £200 bottles of wine all round on several occasions. But he was also, according to a member of staff, 'downing glass after glass of wine and getting pretty drunk'. Hardly the best way to end a season which, like so many recently, hadn't so much ended as petered out.

And Gascoigne began to pay the penalty when he tried, a few weeks later, to seal his long mooted move to the USA. The Major Soccer League was not or as grateful – or as desperate – for talent as the North American Soccer League had been in the 1970s and it soon became clear, when he arrived at DC United in Washington, that things might not work out.

Team coach Ray Hudson had, like Gazza, grown up in Dunston next door to Jimmy Gardner. He was initially impressed: 'He was very, very humble, highly strung and eager to impress.' Hudson recalls that the player was like an 11-year-old kid who couldn't wait for training to start. As soon as training started, Gazza began to illuminate the session. They got talking about practicalities – apartments, cars, etc – and Gascoigne said simply: 'Ray, I just wan the ball man, I just want the ball.'

There was a rumble of protest from local pressure groups, especially about the time he had hit his wife. And Gazza began spending too long, in Hudson's opinion, at a bar called the Capitol Lounge. It wasn't that the player was drunk every night. Some nights he just had a tipple with his team-mates. But, Hudson told Ian Ridley: 'He was here for less than a week and he needed to be pretty much like Snow White.' Hudson broke the inevitable bad news to Gascoigne who went to Cyprus for 10 days to rest.

Over the next few months, he would be linked with an absurd cast of clubs in all parts of the world. Dundee, Partick Thistle, Colchester United, Gillingham, Auckland Kingz (New Zealand), Exeter City, Buckley Town, Total Network Solutions (in the League of Wales), Carshalton . . . the list began to resemble the itinerary for a fading rock star's world tour. His agents changed too – Ian Elliott of First Artists replaced his old confidant Mel Stein (who later sued Gascoigne for £60,000) and Elliott was, in turn, superseded by ex-Newcastle player David McCreery who handed over to Jimmy Five Bellies Gardner. By 2004, he was represented by former Derby midfielder Wes Saunders who felt compelled, in February, to deny that Gazza had quit.

By September 2002, he was reported – in the *Sunday Mirror* – as resting in a Durham hotel 'staying up till 5 a.m. drinking whisky'. At one point, according to a barmaid, he was 'so out of it that he fell asleep on the toilet with his hand on the radiator' and woke up with cuts and blisters all over his hand. A friendly appearance for Berwick against Newcastle in October didn't help his cause but then he had, he told the *Sunday Mirror*, 'necked six brandies before I ran onto the pitch'.

Perhaps sensing the abyss he was about to fall into, he turned to a fitness coach called Steve Black, who was associated with the Newcastle Falcons rugby club. Six weeks of hard work, seven days a week, followed with Black finally concluding that he was fit enough to play professional football again. But no one in the game seemed to agree and 2002 ended on a suitably depressing note with the star admitted to accident and emergency at Queen Elizabeth Hospital in Gateshead saying that the left side of his face had gone completely numb.

Two thousand and three started brightly with the offer of a £10,000-a-week contract with Liaoning Bodao but the director Zhao Ronggang wasn't impressed with the trials. He felt Gascoigne was weak and unimpressive in exhibition matches. It was a long way to go for such a snub but, just as the journey began to look wasted, a second division side, Gansu Tianma, stepped in with a slightly lower offer for him to join as player-coach, an offer funded by the Chinese government. He would be playing, as Kelner put it, at the end of the world. Hanna Beech, who visited Gascoigne for *Time* magazine, says Lanzhou, where Gansu Agricultural Land Reclamation Flying Horses – to give them their official name – are based is 'so dirty when you blow your nose the resulting mess is black'.

From her account – and the subsequent BBC3 documentary – Gazza didn't exactly settle. His arrival was something of a shock to his team-mates, one noting 'Growing up, Gascoigne was my hero – but in person, he looks a lot older than he does on TV'. He had probably lived more football lives than most of the squad put together and couldn't even pronounce his own name in Mandarin ('Jia Si Ke Yin'). He lost his first game and his general manager Zhong Bohong noted: 'He has a good sense of the game but he has shortcomings, like leg strength and physical fitness.' Incredibly, he admitted that Gazza might not ever last a full game but concluded: 'He can steady team morale, we would like him to be our spiritual leader'.

Yet, waiting for his father and Jimmy Gardner to join him, he seemed, to Beech, on the edge. At one point, he told her: 'I thought, shit, I am going to get stuck in this bloody ghost town forever. At that moment, I thought: I have to get out of here or I die.' Beech's account suggested that his solitary nights were eased by San Miguel beer and snooker. He also started eating obsessively – 30 packets of dried squid a day probably isn't part of the recommended footballer's diet even in Lanzhou. This may have been a reaction to, unknowingly, tucking into bat for the first time. 'When they gave it to me I thought it was chicken,' he explained later.

Then his entourage – two humans and six bellies – arrived, to the consternation of the club. In training, another coach began to think that Gascoigne should work harder. Yet in March he scored two goals in three games, drawing an amazing crowd of 20,000 to a 1–1 home draw, a game his side might have won if he hadn't been taken off with a sore rib.

The comeback – if that's what it could have been – was cut short when Gascoigne left for Arizona in April. Gardner said: 'It's depression, it's definitely not alcohol, he wants to play in England, shouldn't have left.' After a month at Cottonwood, he flew back to the UK saying he wanted to return to China and was considering Gansu's offer of the manager's job. By May, the SARS virus had led to the Chinese season being suspended – but Gazza was due back on 10 June to fulfil the rest of his year-long contract. By 21 June, Gansu had issued him an ultimatum and threatened to report him to Fifa for violating his contract.

Gascoigne's agent Wes Saunders claimed his player would not return until a row over outstanding money he said the club owed. He may too have been distracted by his old England team-mate Carlton Palmer, then managing Stockport County, who met him to discuss signing him. He had probably already decided that he would never play in China again – if he could find any British club to hire him. By August, he had signed for Al Jazira, the United Arab Emirates side which had just lost George Weah. Another move abroad seemed a gamble but – with his ex-wife and family with him – Gascoigne seemed better placed to cope. But the Al Jazira move never materialised, for reasons that aren't really clear, and Gascoigne asked another old England team-mate Paul Ince to put in a word with his boss at Wolves, Dave Jones.

Gascoigne's arrival at Molineux in October 2003 was greeted with bemusement and derision but the player seemed committed to the idea of training to keep himself sharp. But after three games with the reserves, Jones said:

'Gazza has decided that he can't cut it at Premier League level. His decision now is whether he wants to drop down a level, or look at other things. But that is up to him. He's worked his socks off while he's been training with us. I would say that he was fit at the moment other than for a slight groin strain. He just feels that he falls short of what is needed and you must commend his honesty.'

And that, despite talk about talks with Sheffield Wednesday, Oldham, and Hartlepool, that is where his footballing career stands. There is talk about him as a potential manager, though cynics find it easier to envisage him managing a pub than a football team. His old Lazio boss Dino Zoff started crying with laughter when the possibility was mentioned to him by a journalist. It's a strange, unsatisfactory, way for such a remarkable career to end. Doors keep closing on him –

in January, he amicably separated from ex-wife Sheryl for what friends claimed was the final time – although, again, that's not the first time friends of the on-off couple have said that.

He will, as DC United coach Ray Hudson says, 'always be in his heart of hearts a little boy with a ball'. With the ball no longer gainfully employed at his feet, it's easy to see Gazza as a tragedy-in-waiting, a fear Bobby Robson articulated as far back as 1996. But he knows, after sundry visits to clinics, what's at stake here. Not his livelihood – his life.

Yet there's something about Gazza that even now, when Italia 90 seems a distant memory, makes him hard to ignore. It won't be much satisfaction to him – interviewed once by Football 365 he asked 'What's a website?' – but he has achieved a curious kind of fame in cyberspace where various chat rooms are dedicated to the kind of behaviour which so irritated his critics. The favourite story is that of him forcing Gary Lineker on a tourist Routemaster bus in Piccadilly Circus and persuading the driver to let him get behind the wheel of the double decker. Opinions vary as to whether Gazza forced Lineker and the passengers to join him in song. Not that it really matters, it's still a cracking story. He might have misspent much of his life but he has, finally, spent much of it enthralling millions.

Spurs fans still sing about that free-kick against Arsenal, Lazio fans still smile at his memory (and laugh about the time he was attacked by a group of Roma-supporting nuns), and as one Rangers fan put it in an online forum recently 'we loved the Geordie maniac'. And one past president of the Danish FA will probably never forget the day the player, pretending he could speak Danish, began talking to him like the Swedish chef on *The Muppets Show*.

Paul Gascoigne gave us moments of greatness, rather than the sustained greatness of a Pele or a Johan Cruyff. But his mastery of the ball, his fizzing energy and, in his prime, his belief in his own talent were such that he was, at his best, an improvisational genius, a real artist of a kind that is still all too rare in English football. It would be, as Woody Allen might put it, a travesty of a mockery of a sham if his strange, oblique, retirement obscured his genuine greatness as a player.

PAUL GASCOIGNE FACTFILE

1967   Paul Gascoigne is born in Gateshead on 27 May

1983   Joined Newcastle United as an apprentice

1985   Made his first team debut for Newcastle on 15 November; member of Newcastle's FA Youth Cup-winning team

1987   Made his debut for England Under-21s

1988   Transferred to Tottenham Hotspur on 18 July for £2m, makes his England debut against Denmark in September; voted PFA Young Player of the Year

1990   Achieved international superstardom through his performances and tears in the World Cup finals in Italy; won the BBC Sports Personality of the Year award

1991   Won an FA Cup winners' medal but incurred a career-threatening cruciate ligament injury after a reckless challenge on Nottingham Forest full-back Gary Charles

1992   Transferred to Lazio on 1 June for £5.5m; made first England appearance for over a year

1995   Transferred to Glasgow Rangers for £4.5m on 10 July

1996   Won his first ever League championship medal and Scottish Cup winners' medal in his first season in Scottish football; voted PFA and Scottish Football Writers Footballer of the Year; played in triumphant European Championship. Helping England to semi-finals and scoring improbable, marvellous, goal against Scotland – arguably the goal of his career.

1997 Won a second ever League championship medal and a League Cup winners' medal with Rangers; played a significant part in England's World Cup qualifying campaign under Glenn Hoddle

1998 Transferred to Middlesbrough on 26 March for £3.45m; left out of final 22 for the World Cup

2000 Transferred to Everton on 17 July on a free transfer

2001 Checked himself into an Arizona clinic to be treated for alcoholism and depression on 21 June

2002 Joined Burnley on loan on 16 March; club did not renew its interest at end of season; projected move to DC United in US fell through

2003 Signed a one-year-deal with Chinese second division side Gansu Tianma in January; season interrupted by scare over SARS virus; planned move to Al Jazira in United Arab Emirates didn't go ahead, instead he joined Wolverhampton Wanderers and played a couple of games in reserves before declaring himself unfit.

LEAGUE RECORD

1984/85	Newcastle	2 apps, 0 goals
1985/86	Newcastle	31 apps, 9 goals
1986/87	Newcastle	24 apps, 5 goals
1987/88	Newcastle	35 apps, 7 goals
1988/89	Tottenham	32 apps, 6 goals
1989/90	Tottenham	34 apps, 6 goals
1990/91	Tottenham	26 apps, 7 goals
1991/92	Tottenham	0 apps, 0 goals
1992/93	Lazio	22 apps, 4 goals
1993/94	Lazio	17 apps, 2 goals
1994/95	Lazio	2 apps, 0 goals
1995/96	Rangers	28 apps, 14 goals

1996/97	Rangers	26 apps, 13 goals
1997/98	Rangers	20 apps, 3 goals
	Middlesbrough	7 apps, 0 goals
1989/99	Middlesbrough	26 apps, 3 goals
1999/2000	Middlesbrough	11 apps, 1 goal
2000/01	Everton	15 apps, 0 goals
2001/02	Everton	23 apps, 1 goal
	Burnley	6 apps, 0 goal
2002/03	Gansu Tianma	4 apps, 2 goals

INTERNATIONAL RECORD

U-21	13 caps
B	4 caps
Full	57 caps, 10 goals, making him the 31st most capped player for England

BIBLIOGRAPHY

BOOKS

Adams, Tony, *Addicted* (Collins Willow, 1998)

Ballard, John and Suff, Paul, *World Soccer: The Dictionary of Football* (Boxtree, 1999)

Barnes, John, *The Autobiography* (Headline, 1999)

Bowler, Dave, *Three Lions on the Shirt* (Orion, 1999)

Davies, Pete, *All Played Out* (Yellow Jersey Press, 1999)

Downing, David, *The Best of Enemies* (Bloomsbury, 2000)

Durrant, Ian, *Blue & White Dynamite* (First Press, 1998)

Edworthy, Niall, *The Most Important Job in the Country* (Virgin, 1999)

Ferguson, Alex, *Managing My Life* (Hodder & Stoughton, 2000)

Galeano, Eduardo, *Football in Sun and Shadow* (Fourth Estate, 1997)

Greaves, Jimmy, *Don't Shoot the Manager* (Boxtree, 1993)

Gregory, John, *The Boss* (Andre Deutsch, 1998)

Hamilton, Ian, *Gazza Agonistes* (Bloomsbury, 1998)

Hansen, Alan, *A Matter of Opinion* (Bantam, 1999)

Harris, Harry, *Hoddle's England* (Collins Willow, 1998)

Hoddle, Glenn, *My 1998 World Cup Story* (Andre Deutsch, 1998)

Hutchinson, Roger, *The Toon* (Mainstream, 1997)

Joannu, Paul, *United: The First 100 Years* (Polar, 1995)

Kelly, Graham, *Sweet FA* (Collins Willow, 1999)

McGibbon, Robin, *Gazza* (Penguin, 1990)

Merson, Paul, *Hero and Villain* (Collins Willow, 1999)

Murray, Bill, *The Old Firm in the New Age* (Mainstream, 1999)

Nottage, Jane, *Gascoigne: The Inside Story* (Collins Willow, 1993)

Palmer, Mark, *Lost in France* (Fourth Estate, 1998)

Pearce, Stuart, *Psycho* (Headline, 2000)

Platt, David, *Achieving the Goal* (Richard Cohen Books, 1995)

Robson, Bobby, *An Englishman Abroad* (Pan Macmillan, 1998)

Scholar, Irving, *Behind Closed Doors* (Andre Deutsch, 1992)

Seaman, David, *Safe Hands* (Orion, 2000)

Sheringham, Teddy, *Teddy* (Warner Books, 1998)

Stein, Mel, *Gazza* (Bantam, 1996)

Storr, Anthony, *Churchill's Black Dog* (1989)

Venables, Terry, *The Best Game in the World* (Century, 1996)

—— *Venables* (Michael Joseph, 1994)

—— *Venables' England* (Boxtree, 1996)

Waddle, Chris, *The Authorised Biography* (Pocket Books, 1997)

Wise, Dennis, *The Autobiography* (Boxtree, 1999)

ARTICLES

Davies, Pete, 'Gazza', *FourFourTwo* magazine, March 1995

VIDEOS

Classic England Encounters: The Nineties (Hot Shots)

Eight at the Double (Pearson)

England's Road to France (Eagle Rock)

Gazza's Coming Home/Waiting for Gascoigne (Chrysalis)

Paul Gascoigne: The Glory Years (ILC)

Referee! (Telstar)

INDEX